D0849960

BYZANTINE AND MEDIEVAL GREECE

Mosaics

The 'Painter's Manual' of Dionysius of Fourna:
(Translation and Commentary)

Byzantium

BYZANTINE AND MEDIEVAL GREECE

Churches, castles, and art of the
mainland and the Peloponnese

Paul Hetherington

Monica

JOHN MURRAY

© Paul Hetherington 1991

First published in 1991
by John Murray (Publishers) Ltd
50 Albemarle Street, London W1X 4BD

The moral right of the author has been asserted

British Library Cataloguing in Publication Data
Hetherington, Paul
   Byzantine and medieval Greece: churches, castles and art
   of the mainland and Peloponnese.
   1. Greece, byzantine architecture
   I. Title
   720.9495

   ISBN 0-7195-4725-3

Photoset by Rowland Phototypesetting Ltd
Bury St Edmunds, Suffolk
Printed and bound in Great Britain
by Biddles Ltd, Guildford and King's Lynn

For
Rachael

Συνοδοιπόρος αρίστος

Contents

Illustrations

Maps

The *Nomoi* or Administrative Districts of Greece

YUGOSLAVIA

BULGARIA

ALBANIA

Aegean Sea

Ionian Sea

Administrative districts

1	Lefkada	14	Drama	27	Etolia-Akarnania
2	Kastoria	15	Kavala	28	Evritania
3	Florina	16	Xanthi	29	Fthiotida
4	Grevena	17	Rodopi	30	Fokida
5	Kozani	18	Evros	31	Viotia
6	Pela	19	Thesprotia	32	Attika
7	Imathia	20	Preveza	33	Evia
8	Pieria	21	Ioannina	34	Akhaia
9	Kilkis	22	Arta	35	Korinthia
10	Thessaloniki	23	Trikala	36	Ilia
11	Khalkidiki	24	Karditsa	37	Arkadia
12	Agio Oros	25	Larissa	38	Argolida
13	Serres	26	Magnisia	39	Messinia
				40	Lakonia

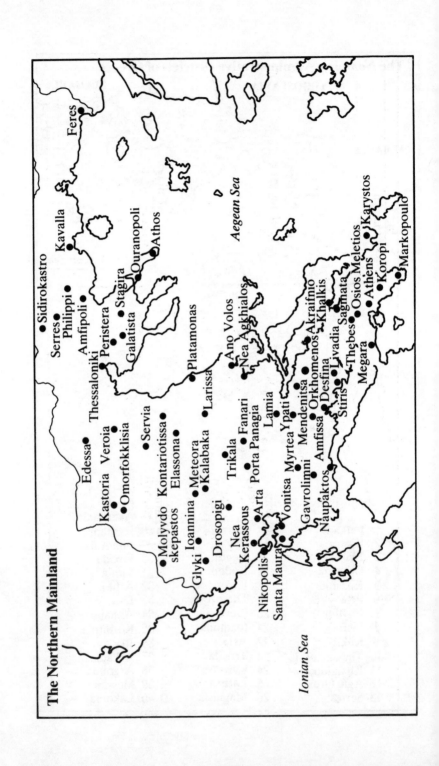

The Northern Mainland

Feres

Sidirokastro
Kavalla
Serres
Philippi
Amfipoli
Peristera
Stagira
Galatista
Ouranopoli
Athos

Aegean Sea

Thessaloniki
Platamonas
Ano Volos
Nea Agkhialos

Akraifnio
Khalkis
Karystos
Markopoulo
Osios Meletios
Athens
Koropi

Edessa
Veroia
Kastoria
Omorfokklisia
Servia
Larissa

Kontariotissa
Elassona
Meteora
Kalabaka
Fanari
Lamia
Ypati
Mendenitsa
Orkhomenos
Desfina
Lividia
Sagmata
Thebes
Megara
Stiris
Amfissa

Molyvdo
skepastos
Glyki Ioannina
Drosopigi
Trikala
Porta Panagia
Myrtea
Gavrolimni
Naupaktos

Nea
Kerassous
Arta
Vonitsa

Nikopolis
Santa Maura

Ionian Sea

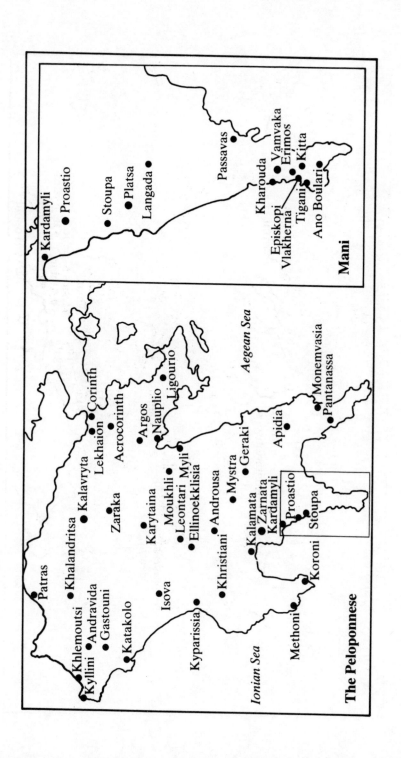

Mani

Kardamyli
Proastio
Stoupa
Platsa
Langada
Passavas
Kharouda
Vamvaka
Erimos
Kitta
Episkopi
Vlakherna
Tigani
Ano Boulari

The Peloponnese

Patras
Khlemoutsi
Kyllini
Andravida
Gastouni
Katakolo
Isova
Kyparissia
Methoni
Koroni
Khalandritsa
Kalavryta
Lekhaion
Zaraka
Karytaina
Moukhli
Leontari Myli
Ellinoekklisia
Khristiani
Androusa
Kalamata
Zarnata
Kardamyli
Proastio
Stoupa
Corinth
Acrocorinth
Argos
Nauplio
Ligourio
Mystra
Geraki
Apidia
Monemvasia
Pantanassa

Aegean Sea

Ionian Sea

Preface

This book is intended to satisfy the curiosity that many visitors to modern Greece have felt when confronted by some feature of the country's medieval past. Its compilation has naturally involved a series of decisions. First came the need to define the period that would be covered, and then to establish within this a basis for selecting from the great mass of material the sites that could be included. The Peace of the Church at the beginning of the fourth century offered itself as an obvious starting-point, and this decision has removed the great majority of classical sites from the text; the most appropriate point for a closing date seemed correspondingly to be the final occupation by the Turks in 1460, following their capture of Constantinople in 1453.

Within this period some further selection was clearly necessary; some may feel that the early Christian sites on which there was no subsequent medieval building have not been treated very generously, while the tendency of later occupiers of Greece (notably the Venetians and the Turks) to modernize – if they did not destroy – many of the medieval buildings they found means that a number of the sites discussed here contain elements that fall outside any strictly medieval limits. The guiding principle here has been related to the book's function as a traveller's *vade mecum* rather than a study in architectural and artistic history: however important a town or site may have been in the medieval period, if there is little or nothing of medieval interest left today within reasonable access, it has been omitted. This means that most of the scores of early Christian sites have been passed over, but this is not intended as a book for specialists; an entry that might only have dealt with the sketchy and disintegrating traces of a controversial ground-plan or some scattered mosaic fragments, however piquant their historical interest, will not usually have been included. It was also felt that, in the interests of space, concentration on the mainland and the Peloponnese, to the exclusion of the islands (except for Evia – Euboea – which is attached to the mainland by a bridge), was justified. To those who will look in vain for some personal favourites, we can only say 'syngnomi!'

A further result of the emphasis of the book on the medieval features of Greece is that it has been assumed that for the most part the reader will have access to another source of maps and street-plans besides those included here.

So what follows is the result of exclusive concentration on surviving creations that were produced on Greek soil during the early Christian, Byzantine and medieval periods. If in presenting them the author makes new converts to the interest waiting in these fields, one aim at least will have been achieved.

The debts incurred during the writing of this book are too varied and numerous for exhaustive listing; from fellow-travellers in Greece, historians of architecture and art, librarians and museum curators, to the innumerable Greeks who have located the keys of locked buildings and had them opened for me – all are owed my thanks. In particular I would like to give the fullest recognition to the unfailing hospitality and kindness of Eufrosyne Doxiadis, at whose house my wife and I were always made welcome, and whose knowledge, charm and expertise could always penetrate the most opaque of Greek language and officialdom.

Practical tips for the traveller

Apart from public buildings like museums, and monuments that have become museums, there are two broad categories of site covered in this book: one concerns buildings which are in some sort of use, or which are sites or ruins that have been, or are being, excavated; the other is of buildings (mostly ruins) which are effectively unenclosed, and so can be visited at any time. (It should be noted that the term 'access' is used in this book to mean arrival at a site, not entry to it.)

The first category is easily the most numerous, and includes the large excavated sites such as Philippi or Nea Agkhialos; these tend to have opening times comparable with museums. Some major castles are also enclosed and these conform to the same kind of opening hours. The majority of the buildings mentioned, however, are Byzantine churches. Here the intending visitor will early on encounter the Greek obsession with locking things up; unlike some other European countries, the normal state in which a chance visitor will find a Greek church is locked. When you have established that this is indeed the case, there are usually three courses that you can take. If you are lucky there will be a chain or string attached to a bell, and if you ring this there is a good chance that someone will appear with the key. Failing this, ask at the nearest dwelling for the key; you may be lent it, or the occupant may come and open up for you, or you may well be directed to the house of the person (perhaps the *papas*) who has it. If neither of these options is available, look for a child and explain your need; most Greek children are not mercenary, but the sight of sweets or money, or the chance of being photo-graphed, can make the difference. It would be unusual for a Greek child not to know where the local key-holder lives, and he or she can usually lead you there. Always be prepared to spend time, and simply hang about; persistence will normally bring a result. This will not apply in centres of outstanding attraction, such as Kastoria or Mystra, where there are paid custodians who act as guides, or in major city churches.

In the case of monasteries and convents, where there are inmates living on the site, different problems arise. Do not normally expect anyone to answer the entry bell between about midday and four, although nuns tend to be more flexible than monks over this. (This does not, of course, apply to the monas-teries on Mount Athos, where the gates are open from dawn until dusk, but all other doors remain firmly locked.) You may well be offered hospitality in the form of coffee and *loukoum*, and it may be expected that you leave a small sum of money in the church box. At major tourist attractions such as Meteora the only advice during the summer is to arrive as early as possible to avoid the crowds; there will certainly be no coffee and you will be charged for entry.

The second, smaller, category is of unenclosed sites. These are mostly castle ruins, but other ruined ecclesiastical buildings (e.g. the basilica at Servia) come into it. The main problem in these buildings can simply be physical danger; the Greeks just do not show the same approach to public safety as can prevail in some other countries, and while entry (at e.g. Rogoi or Katakolo) is no problem, you should not assume that as you have been able to get in your personal safety is assured. *Caveat viator!*

For maps, it is essential to use a large-scale one of not less than 1:300,000; while some medieval towns have grown in size, many have diminished to the point of non-existence on a map with a scale of 1:700,000. As for equipment, it is surprising how useful a modest pair of binoculars can be, both inside and outside medieval buildings. A good torch can also help you to see parts of an interior that daylight does not reach. For visiting any ecclesiastical building men should wear long trousers and women should wear a skirt; keep strong shoes easily accessible, and be sure to maintain a good supply of small change.

Kalo taxidi!

An outline history of medieval Greece

For much of the medieval period the political history of Greece presents a picture that is in some ways profoundly unedifying. All the common human failings are present in abundance: greed, aggression, perfidy, indifference and cruelty emerge again and again. To these are added further failings such as the growing neglect and exploitation of remoter areas by an inward-looking government, and (particularly in later years) implacable fraternal rivalries among its leading representatives. The region also suffered its full share of natural calamities such as plague and other diseases, earthquakes and successive poor harvests. Nor do the wrong-doers appear to have received just punishment for their misdeeds: aggression often paid off precisely because the indigenous population had been so badly treated by the power that should have protected it. Reading of these conditions produces, indeed, a sense of wonder that Greece can still show us the riches that it has among the buildings and art of its medieval past.

The country that the modern world knows as Greece did not exist in this form during the medieval period; the area was just a part of the Byzantine Empire, which was centred on its capital of Constantinople. At its greatest extent in the sixth century it stretched eastwards to the Caucasus and the Caspian Sea, and westwards to Dalmatia, the Adriatic, Italy, North Africa and even part of southern Spain. At an early date the system was adopted of dividing this huge empire into *themes*; these were partly military and partly administrative in function, and would increase with imperial conquests, and merge or diminish as these conquests were lost. During the middle Byzantine period of the tenth and eleventh centuries there were about thirty *themes*. The territory that corresponds to the modern country of Greece was then mainly formed from six *themes*; in some cases their names have survived as those of the modern Greek *nomoi*, although (confusingly) the geographical areas they denote have shifted. So the area now known as Thrace (Thraki) corresponds roughly to the medieval *theme* of Strymon (named after the river still so called), and the *theme* of Hellas, with its capital at Thebes, covered modern Viotia and Attika, and the *theme* of Nikopolis that of Epiros; only the Peloponnese, named as a *theme* after the subjugation of the invading Slavs some time early in the ninth century, has kept its name and identity into modern times, although even this in the twelfth century became united with the *theme* of Hellas. As the centuries passed, and the empire grew steadily weaker and less able to sustain the defence of its more remote regions, so the system of *themes* became gradually obsolete, but it is important to keep in mind the relationship, both geographical and political, that modern Greece bears to the old Byzantine Empire with its capital on the Bosforos.

Travel was slow and hazardous throughout the medieval centuries, and Epiros, Attika and the Peloponnese would always have been regarded as relatively remote from the centres of influence in Constantinople; even Thessaloniki, the second city of the empire, would have been some five or six days' sailing-time at best from the capital. The factor of remoteness would have been felt at either extreme; just as an ambitious cleric in the Peloponnese would probably have been anxious to leave his provincial background to assert himself in the intellectual circles of Constantinople, so an emperor in the capital who wished to consolidate territorial gains in the *theme* of Hellas could not remain there for long and would have had to delegate his authority to officials, or find other ways, such as the erection of impressive public buildings, by which he might assert his influence and power from a distance.

Late antiquity and the early Christian centuries

There is no clear historical division between the world of late antiquity and the period that we now call the Middle Ages. The Edict of Milan, which was issued by the co-emperors Constantine and Licinius in March 313, has often been thought of as such a division, and we have adopted it here as an approximate earlier limit to the period covered by this book. However, while it gave full acknowledgement to the presence of Christianity, and indeed supported religion as a means of bringing some measure of peace to the vast and troubled empire, it does not of itself emerge as a decisive point after which it could be said that nothing was the same again. In their own ways, both the first Church Council, held at Nicaea (the modern Iznik) in 325, or the dedication of Constantinople in 330, could be said to be more decisive historical points, although neither of them, alone, signalled the passing of the world of late antiquity and the arrival of a new era. Rather, it appears that the progressive spread of Christianity through the Hellenistic world, with the new world view that this entailed, was quite a gradual process that continued during much of the fourth and fifth centuries, and that the area of modern Greece was no exception. It would have been only by the early fifth century that all the main towns and many more rural areas would have had places of Christian worship; there is evidence that in the area of Greece by the mid-fifth century basilicas could be numbered in many scores, a few of them being very impressive buildings of great size and magnificence. Even so, it was not until the tenth century that the remote area of the Mani, in the southern Peloponnese, where invading Slav tribes had gathered, was fully converted to Christianity.

In addition, the fifth century saw the start of the conversion of pagan buildings to Christian use. Under a law issued in November 435 by Theodosius II and Valentinian III the great temples of the Athens acropolis, the Parthenon and the Erekhtheion, as well as the mausoleum of Galerius (the Rotunda) in Thessaloniki and other temples elsewhere, were all converted into churches. Even these moves do not seem to have entirely eradicated pagan teaching, however, for in 529 the Emperor Justinian found it was necessary to prohibit the teaching of philosophy and law in Athens, so effectively closing down the Academy; this was over two centuries after the Edict of Milan, and the Academy had survived until then as a centre of pagan teaching. The truth is that there was a lot that Christians could learn from educated, if unbaptized, Greeks, whose company they may well have enjoyed; long before the end of the fifth century the forms of classical rhetoric had been moulded into the Christian sermon. Justinian was not neglectful, however; this famous action should be seen in the context of his expenditure on restoring the city walls of Athens and many forts, as well as the wall across the isthmus of Corinth (called the Hexamilion) which protected Attika from invasion from the Peloponnese.

The long period of relative peace that co-existed with the spread and establishment of Christianity in Greece and sur-rounding areas was halted during the last decades of the sixth century. This was not, initially, through foreign aggression – that was all in the future – but by a succession of natural calamities, which mainly took the form of repeated decimation of popu-lations by plague and other diseases. Athens was just one of the cities so devastated. For about a century after 580 the excava-tions in the Agora show that the life of the city which had been thriving there since pre-Christian times came almost to an end, and the remaining population withdrew to the acropolis; in Corinth the population removed itself completely to the island of Aegina. Only in Thessaloniki did the conditions allow the city to survive in some form, and it is there alone that any major fourth- or fifth-century building in the whole of Greece was still standing by the end of the seventh century.

The invasions from the north: Visigoths, Slavs and Avars

Greece has few natural frontiers other than its coast – this accounts for its shifting boundaries – and so was always open to invasion; indeed, much of the medieval history of Greece is concerned with successive invasions by different foreign peoples. For a short time at the end of the fourth century the Germanic tribe of the Visigoths, under Alaric, had invaded and done considerable damage in central Greece and Corinth before

the Emperor Arcadius showed sufficient resistance to persuade
Alaric that he would do better in Italy. It was towards the end of
the sixth century that, to the natural calamities which had
befallen the people of Greece, was added another man-made
one when two tribes, the Slavs and the Avars, joined forces and
entered northern Greece, attacking Thessaloniki in 597. Their
numbers may have been as many as 100,000, and they were both
invaders and settlers; before the end of the century they had
penetrated to the Peloponnese, which they were to dominate
completely for over two centuries. Slav tribes were still active,
although much more confined in the southern parts of the
peninsula, at the end of the thirteenth century.

   The disintegration of everyday life, particularly in the cities,
which is the main feature of Greek history of the later sixth and
seventh centuries, continued into the ninth century. The scourge
of disease was followed by economic crises affecting the currency, and so the stability, of the whole empire; in addition the
rise of Arab power from the mid-seventh century, although not
directly affecting the *themes* forming modern Greece, had
massive indirect results for the whole Mediterranean world. The
rapid expansion of the Arabs, which included their occupation of
the Greek island of Crete in 823, and possibly even part of the
mainland for a time, was accompanied by the upheavals of the
Iconoclast controversy. Ostensibly a theological debate concerning the existence, validity and function of images, it also
took on political overtones, and endured intermittently from 726
until 843. While having less immediate political effect in the area
of modern Greece than it did in Constantinople, the movement
pervaded many aspects of life, and is to some extent bound up
with the rise of Islam. It is known, for example, that the Greeks
living to the north of the Gulf of Corinth rose in revolt against the
iconoclast decrees of the emperor Leo, and it took a small
military expedition to enforce their subjection. In Greece as a
whole it certainly had a real impact on the appearance of church
interiors, the results of which in a few cases can still be observed
today.

The middle Byzantine centuries and the Norman invasion

This depressed and (where Greece is concerned) poorly recorded period began to change towards the end of the ninth century, when a new dynasty – the Macedonian – became established on the throne in Constantinople. In Greece the effect of this essentially military dynasty was to bring a strengthening of political boundaries, and a return to a level of stability and prosperity that the area had not known for centuries. From the tenth century we can find a renewed sequence of buildings that must be a sure indication of this greater security. The Emperor Basil II, one of the most successful of all Byzantine military rulers, conducted a victorious campaign against the Bulgar power to the north from 1018 to 1019, and on its conclusion he paid a visit to Athens. He must have been the first emperor to do so for centuries, and left many magnificent gifts in the church of the Parthenon – the Theotokos Atheniotissa.

A foretaste of later invasions by Western powers occurred in 1146–7; the Norman King of Sicily, Roger II, invaded Greece, unwisely attacking Monemvasia, from which he was repulsed, and then occupying Corinth and Thebes, and possibly even Athens. He is said to have transported local silk-weavers back to Palermo when he returned; this must have been the only export industry operating in Attika at that time. Although inflicting some damage, Roger II's invasion did not end in permanent occupation, unlike that of the Slavs before, and those of other western powers later.

By good fortune we have an interesting view of life in Athens and Attika in the last years of the twelfth century; what is true of life there could probably be taken to apply to much of Greece at this time, with the exception of the city of Thessaloniki. It can be found in the letters and sermons of an educated Byzantine cleric, Michael Akominatos, who sometime between 1175 and 1180 was appointed to be metropolitan, or archbishop, of Athens. He had received a sound classical education in Constantinople – arguably perhaps the best education then available anywhere in the world. Although he stayed on as bishop of Athens for some thirty years, neither the city nor its inhabitants lived up to his expectations; his studies had taught him of the Athens of Pericles and Plato, but the reality that he found there bore no resemblance to his ideal. Shortly after his arrival he delivered a brilliant inaugural address to the Athenians assembled in the church of the Parthenon; it had doubtless been composed with considerable labour over many days, as he would have wanted to make a good impression, but it appears to have been completely lost on his rustic and unlettered audience. 'The generation that loved science has passed away,' he lamented shortly after, 'and their place has been taken by a generation that is ignorant in mind and poor in body.' It took him three years to learn what he regarded as the barbarian dialect that the Greeks of Attika then spoke. In spite of this he was to stay, labouring hard to improve the lot of his flock, until the Frankish invaders arrived in 1205. Then, preferring exile to living under Western authority, he went into voluntary exile.

The picture of twelfth-century Athens that this bishop painted, amplified by many comments on Attika and Greece as a whole, is indeed a depressing one. He continued to be appalled at the low level of intellectual life that he had found when he arrived, as well as at the meagre existence eked out by the medieval Athenian population; he writes of Attika as a land devoured by caterpillar, locust, larva and plant-rust. Despite his own educated origins he noticeably always took the part of the local peasants against imperial taxation: 'The tax collectors [from Constantinople] survey our barren earth with fractions that are so small that they could measure the footprints of fleas,' he complained, and likened the estate-duty collectors, ship-money collectors, hearth-tax collectors, registerers and surveyors that were sent to Hellas to 'the plague of frogs that God once sent into Egypt'. An account that he gives of the visit of an important official to Athens in 1198, apparently to worship at the shrine of the Virgin in the Parthenon, has a real ring of truth: in order to stop his retinue requisitioning more fish, animals, poultry, wine and even gold, than they needed, he demanded personal gifts, and would not leave until there had been a public collection to finance them; later, on leaving, having requisitioned beasts of burden, he then insisted on selling them back to their owners.

The Fourth Crusade and the Frankish occupation

The image of the part of Greece that Michael Akominatos knew, and which he could present with such eloquence, serves as a telling introduction to the one event that was of overwhelming importance for the whole of Greece in the later medieval period; this was the sack of Constantinople by Western forces in 1204, and the subsequent invasion of Greece and dismemberment of the Byzantine Empire. This disgraceful episode, in which greed and perfidy triumphed over all moral considerations, was actually undertaken in the name of Christendom. What had begun as another crusade by Western powers (later called the Fourth Crusade) to recover the holy places of Palestine from the infidel, was diverted to Constantinople, which it captured and sacked. The catastrophe permanently disrupted the distribution of power and authority throughout the Byzantine Empire, but while the city itself was to be recovered in 1261 for a new Byzantine dynasty, the Palaiologoi, parts of Greece were to remain under foreign control right up to the final conquest of the whole country by the Turks. In this respect the effects of the Fourth Crusade were felt even more profoundly and permanently in the area of modern Greece than they were in Constantinople: for the country it was certainly the pivotal event of the entire medieval period.

The Kingdom of Romania was the name that the Western invaders gave to their newly conquered lands. Only the province of Epiros, with its capital at Arta, had already been seized by one of the ruling Greek dynasty of the Doukas named Michael, and so became the one part of the country that was not occupied early on by Western invaders, although even here Italians, Serbs and Albanians eventually arrived. (This action in Arta should be seen in the context of the similar Greek states being set up in Nicaea and Trebizond.) For the rest of Greece a ceaseless cavalcade of Burgundians, Normans, Angevins, Provençales, Flemings, Florentines, Lombards, Venetians, Genoese, Neapolitans, Sicilians, Catalans, Navarrese, Aragonese and Hospitallers (the polyglot Knights of the Hospital of Saint John of Jerusalem) flows to and fro, with Greeks from time to time succeeding in ousting them from one part or another, until finally all gave way to the relentless pressure of the Turkish forces of Mehmed II, the victor at the walls of Constantinople.

But before beginning an examination of these separate areas of Greece, and how they developed under the new occupation, it is instructive to follow the colourful case history of one of the local Greek lords, or *archons*, called Leo Sgouros. It demonstrates with great clarity why the Western invaders of 1204 had so relatively little trouble in occupying the country. Although he had some hereditary basis to his power, he was in essence a self-seeking, land-based pirate, who shrewdly but ruthlessly exploited the power vacuum that had developed at the beginning of the thirteenth century. His base was at Nauplio, but he clearly saw the whole of Greece as his oyster; neither did the fact that he was himself Greek inhibit him from decimating Greek towns whose inhabitants did not share his view of his own potential. Having (independently of the Western powers) occupied Argos and Corinth early in 1204, he tried to annex Athens as well; the Athenians were not convinced that he embodied the answer to their needs and withdrew to the acropolis, whereupon Sgouros burnt down the lower town which then occupied the area of the Agora. Undeterred, he pressed on to take Thebes, and at Larissa met the defeated Byzantine Emperor Alexius III Angelus, who had come there with his family after the sack of Constantinople. Leo Sgouros was able to convince the emperor that, in order that the local archon might become a legitimate ruler of Greece at this time, he really should be married to a genuine Byzantine princess; as it happened the unmarried daughter of Alexius, called Eudokia, was present and available, so without more ado the wedding took place. It was at the first sign of anything like determined opposition to his plans that Sgouros suddenly became cautious. In September he had occupied the pass at Thermopylae (had he heard of Leonidas?) but there he came face to face with the Frankish cavalry of the first of the Western leaders to arrive in Greece after the taking of Constantinople, Boniface of Montferrat. As we shall see, Boniface had established himself as the 'King of Thessaloniki' by the late summer of 1204, and had no intention of letting a local bravo like Leo Sgouros deprive him of his new territory and title. Just the sight of the small force of Frankish cavalry sent Sgouros scuttling back to Corinth, where he settled in on the rocky heights of the fortress of Acrocorinth. The Frankish siege of Acrocorinth lasted some five years, but in 1208 Leo Sgouros, looking out day after day from the heights of his citadel over the surrounding countryside, and despairing of any help coming to relieve the confined existence of his castle stronghold, committed suicide by galloping on his horse over the precipitous battlements of the south cliff. In its grandly posturing futility the life and death of Sgouros speak eloquently of the state of Greece at the start of the period of almost complete foreign occupation; he must presumably have been one of the best military leaders in all of mainland Greece at that time. We certainly hear of no other archon being able to raise an army.

All historians writing of the centuries that followed the Fourth Crusade have had to find a way of encompassing the many movements that developed, often simultaneously, all over Greece at this time. As this is a book for the use of travellers, a system of broadly geographical divisions has been adopted. The fortunes of each of these regions will be followed through to the point at which it came finally under the yoke of Ottoman Turkish rule, which was to last for almost the next four centuries. In virtually all of Greece this had happened by 1460, and this date has been taken as the later limit of the period covered by this book. Although it will be seen that these geographical areas (listed below) did not remain by any means discrete, they were the basis, with the political forms imposed upon them, of most later medieval Greek history:

Attika: the Duchy of Athens, Thebes and Neopatras
The Peloponnese: the Principality of Akhaia, the Despotate of Mystra and the Venetian coastal sites
Epiros: Arta, Ioannina and the Despotate
The Kingdom of Thessaloniki.

Attika: the Duchy of Athens, Thebes and Neopatras

From the start, the new Latin Empire imported into Greece a feudal system for controlling the balance of power and authority. All the Western knights who wanted a share of the new territories had to take an oath as vassals of the emperor. A deed of partition was drawn up with the main divisions set out.

Boniface, the Marquis of Montferrat, had been the leader of the Crusaders when, in partnership with the Venetians, they had taken Constantinople, and so he was the chief rival to Baldwin of Flanders for the Byzantine Emperor's throne. In addition, his brother had previously held through marriage the title of 'King of Thessaloniki'; he therefore decided to adopt this title for himself (his brother being now dead). The deed of partition also allotted him much more territory, even mentioning the relatively remote area of 'the district of Athens with the territory of Megara'. We shall be following the fortunes of the Kingdom of Thessaloniki later, but for the present we can see that Boniface's most important action after his arrival there was to set off southwards and annex Athens. On his way, besides frightening off Leo Sgouros, he bestowed territories on various of his vassals. The most significant of these was that of Bodonitsa, strategically sited above the pass of Thermopylae and granted to the Lombard Marquis, Guido Pallavicini.

It seems that for the local Greeks of Attika anyone was preferable to the previous regime, as we read (albeit in a possibly biassed account) that when Boniface appeared at their villages they came to meet him 'as someone who is returning home after a long absence'. If even half of what Michael Akominatos wrote about the imperial tax-collectors is true, this is not hard to believe. Certainly, there was nothing in Attika like the resistance that William the Conqueror met on invading England, and no equivalent to the Battle of Hastings.

The prestige of ancient Athens must have been a difficult burden for its inhabitants to carry throughout the Middle Ages; centuries after its temples had been turned into churches they were still expected to be wearing the mantle of greatness passed on to them by forebears such as Pericles, Plato, or Sophocles, while in fact (as we have seen that Michael Akominatos found) Athens was a small and backward township of peasants, either abused or ignored by an increasingly weakened central government. (Indeed, the lower town would itself still have been in ruins after the attentions of Leo Sgouros, and it was the ancient acropolis which Boniface would have had to attack.) Yet it must have been this prestige which made Athens one of the ripest of the many plums in the gift of the new Latin Emperor in Constantinople. What feudal soldier of fortune, anxious to acquire new and respectable antecedents, could have remained indifferent if offered the title of Lord of Athens? (The exact date when the title of Duke was first conferred is not known, but 'Lord of Athens', or Megas Kyr, would have been just as impressive; for ease of reference it is here called a duchy from the start.) From quite early on the Duchy of Athens was formed to include Thebes and (for much of its history) Neopatras (Ypati) as well, and it was immediately granted to the fortunate Burgundian knight, Othon de la Roche; he was an esteemed member of Boniface's entourage, and he held it as a fief from him personally. While Athens itself had the greater fame, the plain of Thebes was (and indeed still is) far more productive, and its inclusion made the duchy one of the most desirable among the new acquisitions. With Othon's investiture in the autumn of 1204 more than a century of Burgundian rule in Attika and Viotia had begun.

The Latinization of Athens and Thebes took several forms. While Othon de la Roche went off almost at once to join in the siege of Leo Sgouros at Acrocorinth, Western clerics moved in on some of the Greek churches. Michael Akominatos, the archbishop, left to take up a voluntary exile on a nearby island. His Latin successor was a Frenchman called Bérard, who had no fewer than eleven suffragan bishops under his authority, while another Latin archbishop took up residence in Thebes. A number of churches and monasteries were taken over by Western clerics with ultimate allegiance to Rome, but for the most part it seems that Greek parochial clergy were left largely at peace. Even when we know that the Latin rites must have been celebrated in a number of Greek churches, there is no evidence of this being the cause of any substantial building alterations. Even at Dafni, where under the Cistercian monks successive dukes of Athens found repose and enjoyment, their building appears to have been limited to adding another porch, so leaving the interior and its mosaics unchanged. There were a small number of specifically Latin monastic foundations, such as those at Isova and Zaraka, but it was overwhelmingly in the field of secular building, and above all with their numerous castles, that the Latins left an indelible mark wherever they went in Greece.

Marriages between the Frankish invaders and the local population seem to have been uncommon. For the most part the Frankish nobles would always have expected to marry daughters of the finest French families: soon after he had arrived in Greece, Othon married a noble French lady from Franche-Comté called Isabelle, who was to bear him two sons. The Franks clearly imported a civilized French way of life, and we know that relatives of Othon, when they heard of his good fortune, soon began to arrive in Greece, expecting a share in *la douce vie* reputed to be found in the duchy. We later hear of the most perfect French being spoken in Thebes, where there was also jousting in the finest traditions of medieval chivalry.

An abduction and an ambush were soon to bring enforced change to the distribution of power in Greece. The abduction was of none less than the new Emperor, Baldwin I, who in 1205 fell into the hands of Kalojan, the ruthless king of the Bulgars and Vlachs, and was to die in captivity. There was to be a damaging hiatus of a year before his brother, Henry of Hainault, could succeed him in August 1206. The ambush was of the next most important figure in Greece – Boniface of Montferrat; he was killed by the Bulgars in 1207 in Thrace. The uncertainty over possession of such a valuable prize as the Kingdom of Thessaloniki brought on a power struggle, and this was only fully resolved after a great meeting – called the Parliament of Ravennika – which took place on the plain below Lamia in May of 1209. This settled the ownership of Thessaloniki and established the new emperor's position in a land now deprived of one of its strongest personalities.

Meanwhile the occupation of Greece was continuing. Othon de la Roche, in partnership with the prince of Akhaia, was besieging Acrocorinth and, after that fell, Argos and Nauplio were taken and given by Geoffrey de Villehardouin to Othon. The Athenians were fortunate in the dynasty that had adopted them; the century of Burgundian rule seems to have been both strong and benevolent, and as individuals the de la Roche appear to have been a thoughtful and perceptive family. After twenty years of rule in Attika, Othon decided to return home to Burgundy with his wife and two sons; he left the region of the duchy, secure and more prosperous than it had been for centuries, to his nephew Guy. Under his rule of almost forty years, the duchy continued to consolidate and increase the security of the local population. His son Jean continued the family traditions of wisdom and firmness, even to the extent of refusing, in 1276, the hand of the daughter of the new Byzantine Emperor, Michael VIII Palaiologos; he pleaded poor health and chronic gout as the reason for what must have been an unexpected response. He must surely have been his own man. When his son Guillaume succeeded in 1280 he brought with him substantial additions to the duchy, acquired as the dowry of his wife, the daughter of John Doukas of Neopatras; besides Gravia and Lamia he was lord of Livadia, as well as possessing the fortresses of Argos and Nauplio in the Peloponnese.

Left to itself the Frankish duchy could have survived for many more decades – quite possibly until the onslaught of the Turks – but in 1311 a purely external factor was introduced which brought about major changes. A band, or 'company', of mercenary Catalan soldiers had been hired by the Byzantines in 1303 originally to fight the Turks in Asia Minor. Their leader, Roger de Flor, had later begun to show signs of unwelcome ambition directed at the Byzantines themselves, and so, in 1305 they had had him murdered. These mercenaries of the 'Catalan Company' were now at war with their employers; they remained encamped for two years at Gallipoli on the Dardanelles, raiding almost to the walls of Constantinople, and then set out westwards on a marauding foray that was to take them through much of Greece. They looted, burnt and pillaged everywhere they reached, including many of the monasteries on Mount Athos. When they arrived at Thebes the reigning duke of Athens, Walter de Brienne, employed them for a short time, but when they had fulfilled their contract with him they refused to leave. All the Frankish states had by now realized this band of Spanish mercenaries was endangering all that they had achieved, and in March 1311 they engaged them in a set battle near Halmyros, called the Battle of Kephissos. They lost disastrously and both Thebes and Athens were taken and sacked by the Company, who were from then on the *de facto* rulers of Attika. They occupied Livadia as well as Thebes and Athens, but could not add Nauplio or Argos to their holdings. They were to stay for some three-quarters of a century.

In contrast to the lawless character of its arrival – it had, after all, acquired its territories by conquest and force of arms – the Catalan Company soon showed that it could organize itself as well as the French had done. They drew up their own constitution and statutes (written in Catalan, and based on those of Catalonia), and their chancellor used the Company's own seal. The various towns of the duchy – Athens, Thebes (the seat of the ruler), Neopatras and Livadia – each had its own civic organization of judges, clerks and so on. It was at Neopatras that the Catalans established the headquarters of their new duchy; geographically this must have made for greater coherence.

It is possible to propose that all that the local Greeks of Attika had ever wanted was a reasonably ordered existence. Certainly it was not by their wish that the quite well organized French duchy was driven out. By the same token, when, in 1330 – twenty years after the Battle of Kephissos – the son and heir of the last of the French dukes, Walter II de Brienne, tried to mount an expedition to recover the duchy for his family, they gave him no help and his enterprise failed. By then they had found that the Catalans could run quite an orderly state which, indeed, was to have thereafter over thirty fairly prosperous years with only minor disturbances.

Although Catholic women in Greece were not allowed to marry Greeks, intermarriage between Catalan men and local Greek women became quite common. In contrast to the French, the Catalans had few nobles among their number. Further evidence of respect for the Greek heritage was to come from one of the last of the Aragonese dukes, Pedro IV; it has been claimed that he wrote the first descriptive passage for over a millennium in which the beauty of the Parthenon is extolled. In ordering a guard for the acropolis, Pedro refers to it in terms such as 'the richest jewel in all the world'. In spite of this clear appreciation of his duchy, it was, once again, to be an external force which brought about the next phase in the history of this province and provide it, in due course, with yet another dynasty of Western rulers.

This is another of the many points at which the destinies of the Peloponnese and of Attika become intertwined, as a major new personality had emerged during these years: the Florentine Nerio Acciaiuoli. During the fourteenth century his family had become one of the major feudal powers in the Morea, and he was himself made Lord of Corinth by his cousin Angelo in 1371. Like others before him, he clearly succumbed to the attractions of Athens, and had already occupied the lower town in 1385, soon beginning a siege of the Catalan garrison on the acropolis. This fell to him in May 1388, and by 1390 both Thebes and Neopatras were in his hands. He was to die in 1394, however, and the dynasty that he founded was to be the last to hold this most venerable of the duchies of Romania.

In his will Nerio made his son, Antonio, Lord of Thebes and Livadia, but by a curious device bequeathed the city of Athens to 'la chiesa di Santa Maria di Athene' – i.e. the Parthenon – and specifically involved the government of Venice, and a Venetian official called Montona, in supervising this odd arrangement. It was clearly a recipe for further strife, and Antonio was not slow to respond. He quickly took the lower town of Athens in 1397 and mounted a long siege of the Venetians on the acropolis which did not end until early in 1403. (The Venetian tenacity can be explained by their standard policy of wanting the control of all sea routes; they were afraid that they would eventually be in danger of losing their possessions in Khalkida.)

The half-century of Florentine rule was not unlike that of the Burgundians, only including a few more colourful and even scandalous personalities. The Acciaiuoli were a less consistently able family than the de la Roche; one, Nerio II, was expelled for a time by a more powerful brother, and actually spent two years of exile in Florence. When he died in Athens in 1451, he left a widow, who was a daughter of the Marquis of Bodonitsa, and a small son, Francesco, who inherited the title. His widow, however, had a Venetian lover, Bartolomeo Contarini, and the two of them effectively ruled the duchy for some five years; Contarini had even murdered his wife in Venice to maintain this position. The Turks were pressing closer all the time, however, and it was a Pasha, Omar, who brought this scandal to an end. In 1456, under orders from the sultan, he occupied the acropolis and Western rule in Attika was, after two and a half centuries, effectively at an end.

The Peloponnese: The Principality of Akhaia, the Despotate of Mystra and the Venetian coastal sites

Two personalities dominate the early years of Frankish occupation in the Peloponnese: they are Geoffrey de Villehardouin and his friend Guillaume de Champlitte. Their exploits demonstrate well what could be achieved both because of, and in spite of, the disordered neglect of the region; and what can be brought about when the necessary vacuum exists, by enterprise, by a capacity to organize, and by aggression and sheer luck. Our knowledge of this whole period suddenly becomes much fuller than for preceding centuries through the existence of written accounts, particularly the *Chronicle of the Morea* (the name of the Morea had previously been used just of Elis to the west, but was applied to the whole of the Peloponnese from this period). This long narrative was probably first written in French, but versions in Greek, Aragonese and Italian (all slightly different) also exist, and it contains a great amount of detailed information on the Frankish conquest and its personalities.

Villehardouin was already in Syria on his way to the Holy Land when he heard, in the late autumn of 1204, of the sack of Constantinople. Not wishing to lose out on the spoils he at once set sail with his force; the chance of winter storms drove him west rather than north, however, and he eventually landed at Methoni on the extreme south-west tip of the Peloponnese. He spent the winter there, and was much struck by the richness of the surrounding land. Early in 1205 he learnt that Boniface of Montferrat was to the north-west, near Nauplio, and decided to postpone a planned conquest (with the local archon) of the immediate territory in Messinia until he had met him. When he reached Nauplio he found that his old comrade-in-arms Guillaume de Champlitte was there too; the two of them decided on a joint enterprise. Their aim was nothing less than the conquest and occupation of as much of the Peloponnese as they could.

Boniface appears to have raised no objections (he had, after all, by then taken possession of much of the mainland to the north) and the two set off that same spring with a mounted force of about five hundred. The land that they were going to conquer they called the Morea. They travelled north to Corinth, where Leo Sgouros was being besieged in Acrocorinth, and then turned west along the coast. Their first major prize was the capture of the town and castle of Patras; this must have annoyed the Venetians as they had specifically been allocated Patras in the treaty of partition, but possession was clearly what counted now. Following the coast, they then captured Andravida, and shortly after the castle of Pondiko on the Katakolo peninsula (later called Beauvoir) fell to them easily.

They continued following the coast until they came to Methoni, where Villehardouin had spent the previous winter. It was while they were here that they had their first real taste of concerted opposition. The local Greeks of Lakedaemonia, Nikli and Veligosti, joined forces with some of the Slav tribes occupying the Taygetos, and they were greatly helped by the Byzantine ruler of Epiros, Michael Doukas; he could see a chance to increase his own territory if he could limit this new threat, and crossed the gulf of Corinth at Naupaktos with his own army. Even this considerable combined force (several times more numerous) was defeated near an olive grove at a place called Koundoura by the invading Franks, who continued on their triumphant way. Koroni was besieged and occupied, as was Kalamata; there must have seemed by then to be a good chance of their dream of complete domination of the Morea coming true.

It is possible to portray Villehardouin as an adventurer who had few ideas about what to do with his new conquests once he had acquired them, but this would not be completely fair. In any case over the next few years a number of factors intervened to limit this runaway success. In 1208 Guillaume de Champlitte learnt that his elder brother at home in Burgundy had died; although he was already being addressed by the Pope with the grand title of 'Prince of all Akhaia', Champlitte returned home to claim his inheritance. In a statesmanlike move Villehardouin, on whom the title now devolved, later that year called a parliament at Andravida (Andreville) where a register had been prepared of all the holdings of the new territories; it was in effect a kind of Domesday Book of the Peloponnese. Twelve great baronies were proposed, and the barons who held them were to form the High Court of Akhaia; organization in this detail of any sort had not been seen in the Peloponnese for centuries. Each barony was worth a certain number of knights' fees, which are a clear indication of its value; following the *Chronicle* they are given here with the original holders (where known) and the number of knights' fees: Arkadia (the modern Kiparissia) and Kalamata (Geoffrey I de Villehardouin, 24), Patras (Guillaume le Alemand, 24), Matagrifon, near the modern Dimitzana (Gautier de Rosières, 24), Karitaina (Hugues de Bruyère, 22), Kalavryta (Othon de Tournai, 12), Vostitza, the modern Aigio (Hugues de Lisle de Charpigny, 8), Geraki (Guy de Nivelet, 6), Nikli (Guillaume de Morlay, 6), Khalandritsa (Robert de la Trémouille, 4), Passavas (Jean de Neuilly, 4) and Veligosti (Matthieu de Valaincourt de Mons, 4). The parliament also decided on the ecclesiastical organization of the Peloponnese, dividing up the country into seven bishoprics, much on the lines of the existing Greek dioceses.

Whatever turbulence might lie ahead (and Villehardouin, now in his mid fifties, would have already been regarded as approaching old age) this must have given a framework within which the principality could develop and respond. There was certainly no shortage of problems. The Slav tribes were still troublesome to the south, and the wily officials of Venice, slighted over Patras, were not slow to claim what they saw as their due. The original deed of partition had allocated them a huge part of the Peloponnese, but what they were really interested in from first to last was maritime power. They were prepared to trade off much of the territory to which they had a claim on paper (and which, with their long experience of the Levant, they knew would be an endless expense) provided they could keep control of sea routes. At an early date they secured Koroni and Methoni in the south-west (they already had Khalkida in Evia), although they had to wait until 1388 before being able to buy Nauplio; but it is a consistent characteristic of the Venetians that although they had only specific and limited aims, once they had obtained them they stuck to them to the bitter end; in Nauplio they hung on until 1500, and were to return again later.

In fact Geoffrey I was to live until 1228, and the dynasty he founded was to continue under his able sons, Geoffrey II, who died in 1246, and Guillaume, who lived until 1278. During these years their new principality matured and prospered; it was external factions and liaisons that were to create the main problems. Guillaume, whose reign of over thirty years had periods of great success, was the most Hellenized of the family; he was born in the castle at Kalamata, and spoke fluent Greek. His previously subordinate position as an able and energetic younger brother may have lain behind the evident ambition of his early campaigns. For two years (1246–8) from his accession he besieged, and finally took, Monemvasia; he was helped in this by the second Duke of Athens, Guy I de la Roche, as well as by the Venetians. Throughout these years the Slav tribes in the south had remained a troublesome factor, and in the winter of 1248 he began to build the castle at Mystra, followed by those of Great Maina and Beaufort, with the aim of containing them; in these local operations he was certainly quite successful. It was to be his more ambitious exploits that were to bring trouble.

In 1258 Guillaume had married as his third wife the daughter of the Byzantine despot of Epiros, Anna Komnena Doukaina; this was to involve him in dealings on a much grander scale where he was really out of his depth, and in particular with the new Byzantine emperor from Nicaea, Michael VIII Palaiologos. The bitter enmity between the Byzantine houses of Epiros and Nicaea was to culminate in open battle in northern Greece, at which Guillaume and his Frankish knights naturally joined the side of the Despotate of Epiros. The site was Pelagonia, in Macedonia, and in the summer of 1259, after a series of late defections, including that of his own father-in-law, Guillaume was completely defeated. The Battle of Pelagonia has emerged as one of the decisive moments in the history of this whole period; nothing afterwards was quite the same. Within two years Michael VIII had retaken Constantinople from the Latins, so restoring Greek rule over what was left of the empire.

More important for the Peloponnese, however, was the fact that Guillaume, the proud prince of Akhaia, along with other barons, had been taken prisoner. He was kept apparently in some style ('en une prison honnerable', according to the *Chronicle*) and at first tried to buy his freedom with money ('raenchon de monnoye'), but Michael was not having any of that; the price of Guillaume's freedom was initially nothing less than the entire principality of Akhaia, for which he would have received some cash indemnity. Guillaume refused, and his imprisonment drew out to over two years, until, in July 1261, Michael was established on the throne in Constantinople. It was then that a compromise was reached; Guillaume need not hand over the entire principality, but only some of his castles. All the Western sources say only three were involved – Mystra, Great Maina and Monemvasia (the Aragonese version of the *Chronicle* adds Acrocorinth to the list, although this must be incorrect) – but the one Greek source that mentions the deal adds a fourth, Geraki; a glance at the map tends to confirm the Greek version: to extract Monemvasia and Mystra but leave the Franks in Geraki does not seem like the action of a man as shrewd as Michael VIII, particularly when he had had two years to think about it.

With the Greeks back in possession of important sites in the Peloponnese, and a new Greek dynasty again on the throne in Constantinople, it is clear that the long run of Frankish success in the south was drawing to an end. The process was accelerated by events in Italy a few years later which involved both the Hohenstaufen and Angevin houses, as well as the Pope. Under new treaties the Principality of Akhaia was pledged to pass on Guillaume's death to the Neapolitan house of Anjou; even if Guillaume was to have a son, only a fifth of it would be his. Charles of Anjou, in return, agreed to help Guillaume recover what he had lost in the Peloponnese. As things turned out, when Guillaume died in 1278 the Principality of Akhaia (both in title and in reality) did indeed pass to Charles of Anjou, although he never seems to have bothered to go there. Instead of tax-collectors who, before 1204, had come from Constantinople, the peasants of the Morea now had tax-collectors from Naples; to them the difference would have been minimal, and they must have longed for the return of direct and present Frankish rule.

Angevin control in the Peloponnese was permanently weakened by the famous episode of the Sicilian Vespers, which took place in 1282; Charles died three years later, but in 1289 Charles II, after four years' rule, restored to Guillaume's daughter Isabella the rights he had signed away in Italy. It was under her, as Princess of Akhaia, and married successively to Florent of Hainault and then Philip of Savoy, that a form of the old Frankish rule returned to the Morea. Years of uncertainty followed Philip's death in 1307, with successive Western leaders unable to assert sufficient control to bring any lasting security to the area. As an indication of the absence of authority that characterized the fourteenth century, in 1376 Joanna I of Naples (who was then claiming rights over the principality) had the idea of leasing the entire principality to the Hospitallers for 4000 ducats a year for five years. This form of temporary privatization could not be made to work for long, and by 1383 there were at least four more claimants to the title. Meanwhile the power vacuum was sucking in dangerous elements from further north – particularly the mercenary soldiers of the Catalan Company (see pp. 14–15). They had competition also from another force of Navarrese mercenary soldiers which had arrived in the Morea. In 1380 it was employed by Jacques de Baux, the current holder of the Princedom of Akhaia, in an unsuccessful attempt to oust the Greeks from the Peloponnese. A further result of the confusion was that the Turks took the opportunity to make plundering forays into the Peloponnese, and yet more fragmentation was to occur later when in 1400 the Hospitallers bought Acrocorinth, remaining there for four years.

During all this time the hill-top castle and city of Mystra, occupied by the Byzantines since 1262, was growing in power and influence. It was at first governed by a general, appointed annually from Constantinople; it was during this period that the inhabitants of Sparta began to move out to the protection of the fortress and build their houses in its shadow. As the population of Mystra grew, so did its importance, with major church foundations already occurring before 1300. By 1348 its significance had grown to such an extent that it was the chief outpost of Byzantine power, and a Despot of the Morea was appointed to reside there. The title of despot was normally reserved for the brother or son of a reigning emperor, and is the clearest indication of the importance of Mystra for the Byzantines. The first three despots were all of the Kantakuzene family, and the third brought his own rule to an early end by attempting to initiate a coup and establish independence for himself. Theodore Palaiologos was sent to crush the revolt, and became himself the first of the Palaiologue despots.

As the Turkish threat to the rest of the empire increased, Mystra must have seemed an increasingly attractive centre from which Byzantine rule could be extended over the whole of the Peloponnese; this was certainly to be the dominant Byzantine policy for the fifteenth century. The Turks, too, realized the danger of a securely-held Byzantine Morea; they twice entered the Peloponnese, first in 1423 and again in 1446, but each time were driven back. Indeed, the years after 1429 were the most successful in this area for the Byzantines since the arrival of the Franks, with the whole of the Morea, except for the Venetian coastal ports of Nauplio, Koroni and Methoni, eventually in their hands. But the fall of Constantinople in 1453, and the gradual spread of Turkish power through the mainland meant that in 1460 Mystra had to be ceded, and by 1461 all Greek rule was over for three and a half centuries.

Epiros: Arta, Ioannina and the despotate

With the disintegration of Byzantine rule in 1204, one of the imperial family, Michael Doukas, decided to seize power in the remote and difficult region of Epiros. The dynasty that he founded there, centred on the city of Arta, was to survive (albeit at considerable price, and with many compromises) for over a century and a half. Initially his rule had no legitimacy (he was himself never a despot, this title only being conferred by a reigning emperor) and he established himself by means of a *realpolitik* consisting partly of simple force of arms and partly of rather crude diplomacy. In the deed of partition of 1204 Epiros had in fact been allocated to Venice, but Michael reached a typical accommodation with them by offering to rule Epiros as their agent. Again, so long as they had their coastal sites (here they were Durazzo and the island of Corfu), the Venetians were happy not to insist on all aspects of an arrangement such as this.

This is a good example of the political balancing act that was the history of Epiros for most of its medieval life. Between Italian adventurers on the nearby islands, Greeks in Thessaly and further east and south, and Albanians and Serbs to the north, independence was hard to maintain. The Epirotes were continually having to pay a price for the support of foreign powers, particularly in Italy, to help them keep their freedom intact from dominance by the Greeks or by other powers. This led to control at one time by the Orsini family and at another by that of a Genoese adventurer, Carlo Tocco. Both had holdings in the nearby Ionian Islands. Epiros was also infiltrated by Albanians and actually invaded by the Serbs; this resulted for a time in a Serbian despot in Ioannina and an Albanian lord in Arta.

Meanwhile, the Venetians soon found that Michael should never have been trusted; he turned out to be a land-based pirate in the mould of Leo Sgouros – only more effective. In an expedition to the east he captured Larissa, only a few miles from the Thermaic Gulf, with other territory, and by 1214 he had taken Durazzo and Corfu from the Venetians. On his death in 1215 his ambitious, unscrupulous and wily half-brother, Theodore, continued this expansionist policy; for a time he must have been regarded as a real pretender to the Byzantine throne, should the Latins ever be ejected from it. In a series of successful campaigns he not only drove all the Western rulers out of Thessaly, but then, in 1224, besieged and captured Thessaloniki itself. With the second city of the empire under his control Theodore had to be taken seriously; in 1227 the archbishop of the neighbouring see of Ochrid crowned him as the 'Emperor of the Romans' (the title of all Byzantine Emperors). This was to produce long-lasting enmity with the supposedly legitimate emperor in Nicaea.

At its height – which had now effectively been reached – the rule of Epiros ran from the Adriatic southwards to Attika, Naupaktos and Corinth and eastwards almost to Adrianople. In 1230 Theodore was actually marching to attack Constantinople when he decided to turn north and invade Bulgaria; in a battle at Klokotnica he was defeated by the Bulgarians, captured and later blinded. The developments in Thessaloniki will be followed later, but for the present this can be seen as the furthest extent of the whole Epirote adventure.

With decreased ambitions came greater legitimacy. Michael II Doukas made peace with the Byzantine Emperor in Nicaea, John III Vatatzes, who granted both him and his son Nikiforos the title of despot; there was also a dynastic bond created by the marriage in 1256 of the Emperor's grand-daughter, Maria, to Nikiforos. A year later, however, the first of several intrusions from Italy into the affairs of Epiros took place, when Manfred of

Hohenstaufen, son of Frederick II of Sicily, invaded Epiros; he captured Corfu and occupied several mainland towns to which Michael II had reason to think his despotate had legitimate title by right of conquest. In a diplomatic ploy used often in the history of medieval Greece, this potential enmity was healed by the betrothal of a desirable bride; Michael offered Manfred his daughter Helena with a dowry of much of the territory that Manfred had already occupied, and Manfred was pleased to accept. A potential enemy was now an ally. The ties between Epiros and Sicily were now much closer than they were with Nicaea, and yet another liaison increased Michael's Western links when he gave his second daughter, Anna, in marriage to Guillaume de Villehardouin, prince of Akhaia.

It is now that we approach the Battle of Pelagonia (in 1259, see p. 20) from the point of view of the despotate of Epiros. Michael II sought, in an alliance between Guillaume, his new son-in-law, and assisted by Manfred, to defeat the forces of the Emperor Michael VIII of Nicaea; had he succeeded he might well have been the new emperor. As we have seen, it was Michael VIII who was the victor (the despot Michael and his son actually took fright and decamped the night before the battle), the Villehardouin prince was taken prisoner, and the balance of forces was never to be the same in Greece again.

After 1261, with a new Greek dynasty on the throne in Constantinople, a less independent figure than the despot Michael would have recognized, if grudgingly, the new realities. This was not his way, however, and it took one mission each year for three years, and the marriage of Nikiforos (his first wife having died) to Anna Palaiologina, the emperor's niece, before formal peace was enforced on his independent spirit. It is from this time that the buildings in Arta show that there was a more consistent presence there by the despots, and this more peaceable way of life has been said to be due to the influence of Anna, which was to be felt for some forty years.

So far it has been possible to consider the history of the region of Epiros with only passing reference to its geography; only Manfred's invasion underlined its closeness to Italy. From the end of the thirteenth century, however, this factor becomes progressively more prominent; the huge spine of the Pindos mountain range, running down the centre of mainland Greece, must have always tended to produce a feeling of independence in the broad area to the west, where, close to the foothills of the Pindos, Ioannina and Arta grew up and developed. For much of the fourteenth and fifteenth centuries Epiros was to be much more affected by its position. The Italian family of the Orsini, as well as that of Tocco, reached positions of power in Epiros through their holdings in the nearby Ionian islands. Unlike the Franks, the Orsini converted to the orthodox faith, which gave them a much greater appeal to the local Greeks. The tenuous hold that Constantinople was able to maintain on this distant state was also to be broken by Balkan powers – by Serbs and then by a long period of infiltration by Albanians. Indeed, it is ironical that it was to gain protection from the Albanians that the Epirotes first asked for help from the Turks.

For much of the fourteenth century two factions existed in the political life of Epiros; one favoured some measure of independence even if it did mean suffering under the heavy-handed rule of Italians from the Ionian islands such as the Orsini, while the other favoured the restoration of Byzantine rule. It was the death of John Orsini in 1336 that produced a period of Byzantine government for about ten years, as the Byzantine Empire had by then gained possession of much of the rest of northern Greece. (Also at just this time the troubled life lived by the barons in the Morea drove them to offer to surrender the principality to the emperor if only to be rid of the Angevins.) Byzantine rule would almost certainly have lasted longer had the city and empire not been so occupied in destroying itself through the bitter civil war which lasted for much of the 1340s.

The powerful Serbian king, Stephen Uroš IV Dušan, saw the chance offered by these distractions; he was the most significant and ambitious Serbian leader of the fourteenth century, and took the opportunity to befriend John Kantakuzene, one of the warring Byzantine emperors. By 1345 Stephen's rapid expansion had annexed large areas of Thessaly and Macedonia; the conquest of Epiros was a natural next step and, with the use of his recent friendship with John Kantakuzene, this had duly been achieved by 1348. This brought about a general Serbian occupation that was to last some further ten years, and would have been more durable still had it not been for the other main force in the region – the Albanians. Many had settled in Epiros and were opposed both to the new Serbian presence and to John's encouragement of them.

Even the abdication of John Kantakuzene in 1354 and the death of Stephen Dušan in 1355 made no difference to the basic dispositions; there were able successors for both of them, and the Byzantine despot, Nikiforos II, was in fact the last to bear this title as a hereditary honour. When he died in 1359 the despotate was in effect divided, with Serbs ruling Ioannina and Albanians in control of Arta; this was to last for over twenty years. In the final decades of the life of the Despotate of Epiros, Italian influence made a return; the families of the Buondelmonti, Spata and particularly that of Tocco, whose writ had run in the islands of Ithaka, Zante, Corfu, Lefkas and Kephalonia, and who had even married into the imperial house of Palaiologue, were the last to hold power there. Carlo Tocco even received his despot's crown from the hands of the Emperor Manuel II himself. But the Italian rulers, however legitimate their title, stood no real chance against the might of the Turks. Although their final occupation was in fact of a newly reunited Epiros, it was achieved with little resistance.

The Kingdom of Thessaloniki

Thessaloniki had always been a city of uniquely high status within the Byzantine Empire. Its position on the Via Egnatia – the highway that ran from Constantinople to Durazzo on the Adriatic – combined with its fine port and its busy commercial life even in the world of antiquity, had always ensured that it would continue to play a significant part in the history of medieval Greece. To a far greater extent than in any other of the Greek cities major building had continued during the Middle Ages; it was also a centre of religious pilgrimage and its walls had been continually maintained and strengthened; this ensured that it was both better protected and a more highly prized conquest throughout the medieval period than any Greek city after Constantinople.

As we have seen, a notional 'Kingdom of Thessaloniki' already existed before 1204, and this was at once claimed by Boniface of Montferrat. He was not slow to assert his ownership, and had already taken possession by September 1204. The early stages of his consolidation were brought to an abrupt end three years later when he was killed by the Bulgars in western Thrace. Boniface's heir to his kingdom was his younger son, Demetrius, but already, with such a rich prize at stake, it was being coveted by others with less claim. The guardian of Demetrius was a Count Hubert of Biandrate, and he organized a coup by setting the half-brother of Demetrius, William of Montferrat, on the throne, supported there by a group of Lombard nobles. This represented a direct affront to the new Latin Emperor of Constantinople, Henry of Hainault, who had no option but to come across from the Bosforos and assert his authority in battle. He succeeded in December 1208, installing the rightful heir, Demetrius, on the throne, and capturing the would-be usurper Hubert. The Lombard barons who were party to the coup still defied him, however, until in May 1209, at the so-called parliament of Ravennika (see p. 13) they saw that he was determined to oust them by force from the castle at Thebes to which they had withdrawn. They capitulated and the Kingdom of Thessaloniki was again secure and legitimately ruled.

The next threat to the kingdom's authority was far more successful. There had been uncertainty from 1217, when the new Latin Emperor of Constantinople, Peter of Courtenay, had been killed when taking the dangerous overland route to his new capital; his widow, Jolanda, ruled as regent until her death in 1219, and was in due course succeeded by her second son, Robert of Courtenay (crowned in 1221). At the same time another widow was ruling in Thessaloniki – Maria, who was regent for her son Demetrios, and whose husband, Boniface, had been the first Latin king. The unfortunate coincidence of the two main cities both simultaneously being under regencies was seen by Theodore Doukas of Epiros, ambitious to expand his territory, as his good luck.

Relentlessly he extended the area under his control eastwards, absorbing Larissa, Neopatras and Lamia; by the end of 1221 he had occupied Serres to the north-east of Thessaloniki, so almost cutting it off from the land route to Constantinople. The siege of Thessaloniki began, with the regent, Maria, fleeing north to Hungary and her son Demetrius going to Italy to rally support. The city finally fell late in 1224 and Theodore became the new

Greek emperor; a Byzantine court was set up there and the new emperor was eventually crowned by the Bishop of Ochrid. (All this was of course a deeply shocking affront to the 'other' Byzantine Emperor in Nicaea, John III Vatatzes, whose claims to be the only emperor legitimately to wear the imperial purple, and to sign his name in red, were certainly high.) But in the second city of the empire Latin rule had lasted only twenty years; in Greece once again Greeks were being ruled by Greeks; the fortunes of Thessaloniki, as well as of Theodore, were now as high as they had ever been.

Had Theodore Doukas been content to consolidate his huge territory, which now stretched across the whole of the Greek mainland from west to east, and south to the gulf of Corinth, he might well have ensured that the Kingdom of Thessaloniki had an even more substantial place in medieval Greek history. However, as we have seen, his sights were set on yet further conquests; he must have always hankered after the richest prize of all – the city of Constantinople itself. In fear of just this, the Latin barons in occupation there bought time by arranging a year's truce with him. For some reason that is not clear, Theodore, after the truce had expired in 1230, began to march towards Constantinople, but as described on p. 24, he instead invaded Bulgaria, was defeated and captured at the Battle of Klokotnica. The Kingdom of Thessaloniki was never to recover its old territory or its power. Although Theodore's brother, Manuel, ruled after him as despot, and even continued to sign imperial documents with the red ink reserved for emperors alone, it was now the Bulgars, under John Asen, who dominated the region.

Theodore Doukas, the ex-king of Thessaloniki, was blinded while in captivity for plotting against his captor, but even that disability did not put a stop on his energy and ambition. On the contrary, he succeeded in persuading John Asen (who had suffered various reverses, including the death of his wife) that he should re-marry, and that his new bride should be Theodore's own daughter, Irene. As the father-in-law of Asen he was on his devious way back to some measure of influence, and he was able to have himself returned in disguise to his old power base of Thessaloniki; there he quickly forced out his brother Manuel and set up his son, John, as a puppet emperor. Several years of ceaseless manipulation and intrigue followed, with alliances being made and broken between the Bulgars, the Greek emperor in Nicaea, the Latin emperor in Constantinople, the Doukas brothers and John, the young puppet emperor in Thessaloniki, with the Latin cause being occasionally abetted by the Pope; in all this bizarre scenario the most powerful and effective personality was the blinded ex-emperor Theodore Doukas.

It was due to his continuing influence that he was invited in 1241 to visit the Byzantine Emperor in Nicaea, John Vatatzes, presumably to discuss yet further plans for the ejection of the Latin emperors from Constantinople. In an uncharacteristically trusting move Theodore went from Thessaloniki to Nicaea and was promptly imprisoned by his host. Next year John Vatatzes marched with his army and his valuable captive to Thessaloniki. It was then the turn of Vatatzes to behave naïvely: he arranged for Theodore to negotiate with his own son, John, for the surrender of the city. By this time all that John wanted was to be allowed to become a monk, but his dynamic father persuaded him to stay on in charge; he just had to acknowledge the supremacy of Nicaea, and to have the title of despot rather than that of emperor. These terms were clearly the absolute minimum Theodore could achieve, and John Vatatzes would certainly have liked to obtain more, but no doubt felt it was the best he could manage in these strange circumstances. The twenty-year life of the independent Byzantine Empire of Thessaloniki was drawing to its close.

John died in 1244, and his blind father replaced him with his spoilt younger brother Dimitrios. Even backed by his father he was no match for the older men around him, and in 1246 a plot to betray both him and the city to John Vatatzes in return for old trading rights and other benefits was successful; Nicaea and Thessaloniki were now under a single imperial ruler.

Among the major changes further east during the next twenty years by far the most important was the final extinction of Latin rule in Constantinople after the Battle of Pelagonia in 1259; it had been a moribund and bankrupt regime for many years, and its end would have come sooner if the Byzantine genius for internal intrigue and conflict had not given it lease after lease of undeserved extra life. Imperial rule in Thessaloniki had been maintained through the presence of high-ranking governors, and with the fortunes of the restored empire reviving, the city was to know several decades of increasing prosperity. The price of peace could, though, be high. The Serbian power was enjoying a period of growth, and in 1297 an attempt was made under an able general, the Protostrator Michael Glavas Tarkhaniotes, to defeat them under their new king, Stephen Uroš II Milutin; the Serb would only fight a guerilla war, however, so Glavas advised the Emperor Andronikos II to switch to peaceful and diplomatic methods. After Eudokia, the emperor's newly widowed sister, refused point blank to be married to the lecherous forty-year-old king, Andronikos brought his own five-year-old daughter Simonis to Thessaloniki in 1299 to be married to Stephen – to the scandal, it must be said, of many. Even in diplomacy a high human price could still be paid.

The city's relative strength and stability may well have been the ultimate cause of the next significant change in its existence. In 1320 a rebellion had taken place in Constantinople against the ageing Emperor Andronikos II Palaiologos; it was led by his grandson who was to become Andronikos III. They had reached an agreement of sorts, but it was a debilitating feud and eventually the governor of Thessaloniki, John Palaiologos, felt that he would have little to lose by seceding from the empire; in 1326, like colonial governors were to do in later centuries, he declared independence. The Serbian leader to the north, Stephen Uroš IV Dušan, was a ready ally, and John at once gave him his daughter in marriage. Things might have developed very differently had not John died the following year; the civil war in the empire to the east was coming to a head with the young Andronikos III in the ascendant, and in 1328 Thessaloniki surrendered to him. Not very important at the time, this brief episode must nevertheless have shown how the city, secure behind its still massive walls, could assert its own freedom if the will was present to do so.

Civil strife broke out again in Constantinople in 1341. In Thessaloniki this was accompanied by a revolt against the aristocratic elements in the city's life, and in 1342 it produced a regime in the city unique throughout all the centuries of Byzantine history: for some seven years Thessaloniki functioned as a commune – some have even called it a republic. The administration of this kind of communal government has always needed a motivated group, in this case a faction known as the Zealots; in the way of middle-class revolutionaries of later ages, they devised and then administered some kind of programme of political reform. Although the Zealots did not leave us a written record of their programme, we know from those who wrote against it what its ingredients were. In general, it was a redistribution of wealth from the rich, the aristocracy and the monasteries, to feed and house the poor, to provide money for parish clergy, to arm soldiers and repair the walls. Although the new era, with its high social aspirations, was to begin with a bout of looting and disorder (here again later parallels can be drawn), once the Zealots had restored control Thessaloniki may have been for a time an agreeably orderly city to live in, provided that you were not rich. It is clear that the public good became a justification for any action directed against wealth.

The civil war that was dividing the rest of the empire continued its disruptive and destructive course, but Thessaloniki stoutly maintained its independence; the Zealot leaders made a point of publicly burning all directives that arrived from Constantinople, and even threatened to revive the old alliance with Serbia, rather than submit to the ruling faction from the capital on the Bosforos. By 1350 the civil war was entering its final phases and it seems that this coincided with a popular mood in Thessaloniki that wished for a return to the old days of imperial rule. Certainly when the Emperor John vi Kantakuzene decided it was time to reassert his authority over the second city of his empire, and arrived with his son-in-law and co-emperor John v Palaiologos, they were welcomed by a populace apparently tired of the excesses and abuses of the Zealots; revolutions do seem to follow a similar pattern. (It should not be forgotten, too, that Greece, like the rest of Europe, was then emerging from the years of the Black Death, with all its attendant horrors.)

As with any other feature of Byzantine political life, the Zealot episode had a theological dimension. The subject of current religious debate was a movement known as *hesychasm*; this was in its essence a method of mystical prayer that centred on taking up particular postures and strictly controlling and regulating the system of breathing. The movement was of particular interest in Thessaloniki as its practitioners were a small group of monks in the monasteries of Mount Athos, nearby.

Although few in number their influence was great; the movement had been the subject of two church councils, and it had surfaced as a feature of the civil war. Among the political ramifications was the abhorrence in which the Hesychasts were held by the Zealots; this was expressed very openly when a new bishop of Thessaloniki was appointed. He was Gregory Palamas, who had been a monk on Athos and was an eloquent defender of *hesychasm*; when he came to take up his residence in the city the Zealot leaders would not let him in. It was only with the arrival of John Kantakuzene and John Palaiologue in 1350 that he could enter the city and assert episcopal authority in his see. We even have the text of the sermon that he preached in the church of Ag Dimitrios three days after his arrival, in which he inveighs against the abuses of the Zealot leadership; even allowing for his inevitable exaggerations, his references to their excesses of pillage, expropriation, insult and murder of innocent people make it easier to understand why the populace gave such a warm welcome to the return of imperial authority. There were to be no more communes in Byzantine history, and in 1368 Gregory Palamas was made a saint of the orthodox church.

Possibly with some misgivings John vi Kantakuzene, the older emperor, left the young John v Palaiologos in charge in Thessaloniki and returned to Constantinople. Almost at once that *éminence grise* Stephen Dušan (see p. 26), the immensely powerful Serbian king, was on the scene, but the walls of the second city, like those of the capital, were to defeat him. Although his territories were then far greater than those of the Byzantine Empire, of which he clearly saw himself as a possible future ruler, his dreams were ended by his sudden death in 1355.

With the return of internal peace in the empire Thessaloniki knew a period of relative stability. In the 1380s the Palaiologue dynasty ruled, with John v on the throne in Constantinople, his son Theodore as despot in Mystra and his other son Manuel reigning as emperor in Thessaloniki for five years, to 1387. The major external threat was now not the Serbs but the Turks, and various treaties and agreements were continually being made to placate them; a daughter of John vi, Theodora, had even been married to a sultan's son. But it was becoming clear that whatever was done and whatever defences were made against it, Ottoman power was inexorable and would eventually reign supreme. This state of mind must have been generally pervasive, as in 1387 Manuel decided that he did not wish to continue to rule and defend Thessaloniki; he must have felt that he was giving way to the inevitable when he left the city by boat with a small group of followers. Three days later the city gates were opened by the inhabitants to allow Turkish soldiers to march in: it was a surrender. They could not have been welcome, but if they were to enter at all, it was preferable that they should do so without bloodshed; also, the Sultan Bayezid was in general tolerant of Christianity. We know from the sermons of the bishop at the time, Isidore Glabas, that churches were allowed to function normally, some even being granted special privileges. Some aspects of the city's life continued to be administered by Greek officials. Life could have been worse.

This episode really opens the last chapter in the history of medieval Thessaloniki as a Byzantine city. There was to be just one further period during which it returned to Greek rule, and this was the result of what must have been a masterly feat of diplomacy. The Ottoman Turks had been severely defeated in battle in 1402 outside Ankara by Timur and the Mongols; they were still in a demoralized state, when, early in 1403, they were present at a lengthy summit conference which took place at Gallipoli. They were represented there by a new and much more peaceable and self-indulgent sultan, Suleiman; and besides the Greeks, under John VII, there were representatives of the Serbs, Venetians and Genoese. The terms of the agreement that emerged from the three months of parleying were astoundingly favourable to the Greeks, who must have worked brilliantly on the insecurity of the Ottomans. Not only was all tribute to the Turks to cease, but the city of Thessaloniki and its surrounding territory (with various islands) were to be returned to Byzantine rule. Rejoicing must have been widespread, with the only sad face being that of the emperor's niece, who was later given as a bride to Suleiman to seal the new *rapprochement* between the two peoples; life in even an impoverished Byzantine court would have been more interesting than in the *harem*.

The final occupation by the Turks was to come about sooner in Thessaloniki than in the other Greek cities; the factors of geography and commercial importance that had contributed so greatly to its medieval prosperity had continued to make it the most desirable prize after Constantinople. All that was needed was a less complaisant sultan than Suleiman, and he was soon to arrive in the person of Murad II. There had been various plans of Turkish and Greek factions to find some way of establishing a *modus vivendi* for both powers, but once Murad had taken control as sultan they were doomed. In 1422 land blockades of both Constantinople and Thessaloniki were begun, and a determined attempt was made to mount a siege of the capital. In both cities these blockades were initially unsuccessful; once again it was shown how valuable was the legacy from earlier centuries of their massive defensive walls.

The leadership in the two cities was very different, however. In the capital the wily emperor Manuel II, an old hand (in every way) at the power politics of the Levant, was able to play off one Turkish faction against another and so buy (albeit at great expense) a few more years' peace, but in Thessaloniki the defence was in the hands of a young and rather pathetic figure – the twenty-three-year-old despot, Andronikos Palaiologos. He was crippled with the humiliating affliction of elephantiasis, and lacked the experience and ability to handle such an extreme situation. His solution was a desparate one: it was simply to give the city to Venice. All the arrangements were worked out, dealing through the Venetian presence at Khalkida, and carefully keeping all parties informed. There must have been some among the more cautious Venetian senators who felt that it was a present that might cost them dearly later ('beware of Greeks bearing gifts!') but they were outnumbered by those who saw a chance to further the maritime interests of the Serenissima; in September 1423 Venetian ships duly arrived in the harbour to take possession, bringing with them food for the starving populace. Flags with the lion of Saint Mark now fluttered from the ramparts of what had been the second city of the Byzantine Empire, and which the Venetians now claimed would become a second Venice.

Alas, it was not to be. Although it endured for seven years, the experiment was in the end a failure. Their inexperience in the defence of major fortified cities had led the Venetians to accept quite unrealistic estimates of this cost. In order to save on this they agreed in 1427 to pay a yearly tribute to the sultan in exchange for peace; in 1428 he doubled the amount – Murad was

not a man to underplay a strong hand, and he knew that
Venetian interests were overwhelmingly commercial. The
Greeks in the city, too, were losing heart. The young despot,
Andronikos, had left at once and was soon to enter a monastery
in the Peloponnese; within four years he was dead. Their general
resolve had been kept alive by a remarkable bishop, Symeon,
but he died late in 1429, and with him the will of Thessaloniki to
remain a Christian city began to die too. Early in 1430 the Sultan
Murad arrived to besiege the city, and it was finally taken,
although only after great bloodshed and a gallant defence, on 29
March.

The architecture and art of medieval Greece

Byzantine church building

Leaving aside the sparse but picturesque remains of strictly
Western church building in medieval Greece, as at *Isova* or
Zaraka (names in italics refer to sites discussed in the Entries),
we are left with the two principal building forms of the Byzantine
world. The earliest and the simplest is the type known as a
basilica, where a rectangular central hall or nave, usually separated from side aisles by rows of columns, and with clerestory
windows and a wooden roof, has a projecting apse at the

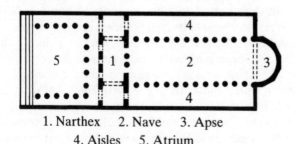

1. Narthex   2. Nave   3. Apse
4. Aisles   5. Atrium

A Basilica

opposite end from that of the entrance; it was normally approached through a colonnaded atrium, or open courtyard. Originating in pagan antiquity as an assembly hall, this is the basic form of early Christian basilica, and from its adoption for Christian worship in the fourth century it became standard practice to give it an east-west orientation.

In size it could vary greatly, and the largest, a few of which still survive (e.g. the *church of the Akheiropoietos, Thessaloniki*), were of great grandeur, many of them embellished with spectacular mosaics. By the later seventh century there were scores of buildings of this type on the Greek mainland, although only a few are still visible, and even fewer standing. In succeeding centuries the basilica design, when used for larger churches, seems to have been reserved mainly for those which were the seat of a bishop, and it was associated with this use (as in the original building of the *Mitropolis, Mystra*) into the later Byzantine period. It has been suggested that the conversion of the *Parthenon* in *Athens* to a church provided a model for this association.

Early variations on the basilica form, besides the addition of further side aisles, could involve the insertion of a transverse aisle, or transept, close to the east end, and a porch, or narthex, across the west end. During the sixth and seventh centuries the grandest basilicas began to have a central cupola, as in the *Basilica B, Philippi*. In the middle and later Byzantine periods it was not common to build large new basilicas – those at *Serres*, *Veroia* and of *the Koimisis, Kalabaka* (which in any case probably replaced an early Christian building of the same design), are unusual in their size. The great majority of basilicas built after the ninth century tend to be quite modest in size, and the absence of a cupola may be due for the most part to a simple shortage of funds; the large number to be found at *Kastoria* or *Veroia* are mostly small or very small and must constitute a local exception, while those of *Ag Khristoforos, Mystra* and *Ag Ioannis Khrysostomos, Geraki*, are more typical.

While the basilica form had links with antiquity, the second of the two Byzantine building forms was developed exclusively in the service of Christian architecture. Byzantine church building after the seventh century becomes overwhelmingly an architecture that exploits the dome. The basilica form was progressively superseded from the sixth century by a variety of designs which have in common a structure that is sufficiently strong to support a drum and cupola over an open, square space. The main centres for experimentation in these new designs would most probably have been in Asia Minor and in Constantinople itself, and there is still discussion as to where certain features originated. (The supreme dome of the entire Byzantine period was always that of Ag Sofia, Constantinople, which was built between 532 and 537, but the architects of this building are known to have come from Asia Minor.) The drum could be supported either on the four wall sections abutting on to the crossing, on free-standing masonry piers, on columns, or (very commonly) on a combination of one or other system. In all cases the weight of the octagonal or circular drum, with the cupola above it, had to be transferred down to the four supporting members, and this was usually achieved by means of pendentives; in their finest form these are a sophisticated piece of engineering in which a concave section of a sphere receives the weight of a quarter of the drum on its upper section and passes it down to the single member (pier, column or wall section) out of which it is built.

The most common solution to this problem throughout all of

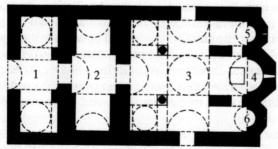

An 'inscribed-cross' Byzantine church; the dome here is supported on two columns and two sections of wall.

1. Exonarthex   4. Main apse (conch above)
2. Narthex   5. Prothesis
3. Dome over square space   6. Diaconicon

Greece became the so-called 'inscribed cross' or 'cross-in-square' plan, and this was in common use by the eleventh century. It involved the dome over the central square space of the naos being supported either on four columns or, very commonly, on two columns and the two wall sections either side of the main apse; to north, south and west there were usually barrel vaults, with often a fourth one to the east adjoining the apse. On the plan the dome and its adjacent vaults thus appear as 'inscribed' within an approximately square outer space. There are many possible variations on this; these include greater or smaller depth of lateral barrel vaults, the insertion of buttressing semi-domes on eastern and western sides of the drum, extending the western bay to enlarge the space of the naos, inserting galleries in the crossing and thus adding a second storey, and so on, but the one constant factor remained the emphasis on the central dome.

At an early stage further spaces were added, such as the two subsidiary apsed chambers built either side of the main apse; these became standard in most churches, and are called the prothesis and diaconicon; only the smallest churches might not have them. Almost invariably the inscribed cross design incorporated a narthex to the west, with sometimes a second, or exonarthex, as well, and larger churches often had a gallery above this. Further domes could also be added – either one over the bema, or over narthex and gallery, or four more over each of the four corner bays. Indeed, either the multiplication of domes, or the expansion of the central dome to exceptional diameter or height, became the chief ways in which builders or patrons could express the importance of a new church; such expression was otherwise left to lavishness of patterns in exterior brickwork, richness of interior decoration in the carving on capitals and templa, and to colourful frescos or mosaics on the upper surfaces of the building.

In some, less usual, cases there was experimentation with the use of further apsidal forms (or absidioles) to north and south, and even to the west as well; examples of this are the churches of *Ag Apostoloi*, *Athens* (*Agora*), the original form of *Ag Andreas*, *Peristera* and the katholikon of the monastery at *Molyvdoske-pastos*. Such apsidal forms provided a more varied exterior profile, with inside a more fluid and varied spatial quality. Far more common, as a way of imparting individuality to the exterior of churches, was the use of brick ornament; this could be quite restrained, as in the ubiquitous form of string courses of bricks set with projecting corners to produce the 'dog-tooth' effect, or more lavish and varied as at *Elassona* or *Gastouni*, or they could be set in blind arcades or niches. This ornament is never found inside, as interiors were completely covered by carefully developed didactic programmes of decoration in fresco or mosaic, as we shall now see.

Byzantine artistic practice

Over the centuries the Byzantines developed an approach to imagery markedly different from that prevailing in western Europe. Mainly codified before and during the period of Iconoclasm (726–843), it involved the concept of an image, when created in the correct way, being a receptacle for the spirit of the person or subject it portrayed. For the Byzantine beholder, an image, or *icon*, was not just a *likeness* of a saint, but contained the essence of the prototype, and so actually *was* the subject portrayed. Other factors followed from this. If by reason of the life he or she had led while in the world, a saint was worthy of veneration, so the image of the saint was equally worthy; one of the church fathers had already written in the fourth century: 'Honour paid to the icon passes on to the prototype'. To pay honour and respect to a person must involve some form of communication, and so the iconic image is invariably shown in a frontal pose (or nearly so) and with the eyes open. To portray a figure in a way in which the beholder could not communicate with it would have been pointless as it could not have been 'understood'.

The Byzantines had a strongly hieratic view of the universe, and this too was clearly expressed in their art. Just as the most sacred subjects, such as the feasts of the Dodecaorton, are of greater sanctity than lesser episodes of Christ's life, so images of these feasts are also more venerable. A hierarchy of sanctity grew up as a product of this outlook, and the most complete expression of the Byzantine view of the Christian universe became the extended sequence of images that can be found in a

Byzantine church. The image of the most venerable of all subjects, Christ Pantocrator, can usually be found in the highest part of the church building – the summit of the cupola; below this are often found adoring archangels. The dome of the church becomes identified in this way with the dome of heaven. The second most sacred part of the church, the main apse, houses the next most holy of images – that of the Mother of God. Either some of the feasts of the Dodecaorton, or else the four evangelists, can then be found in the four pendentives supporting the cupola; below these, in the soffits of the arches and in wall niches and subsidiary vaults, are usually images of single saints from the service books of the orthodox church. The image which displays the church's dedication can often be found on the north wall adjacent to the templon. On the lowest wall areas there was either a cladding of marble sheets, often decoratively cut to form symmetrical patterns (as at *Osios Loukas*), or more commonly, plaster painted to imitate marble; this was ultimately a continuation of an antique Roman practice.

It should be emphasized that complete uniformity can never have been intended; no two church interiors are ever identical, but there are enough features in common to demonstrate the existence of a general approach. It has even been suggested that the marriage of the architecture with the imagery that it housed became so intimate that it is difficult to visualize one without the other; certainly some form of close collaboration between builders and painters or mosaicists must have existed for such a perfectly integrated concept to have become established. It was also within this context that the use of portable icons was established from earliest times. Today icons will be found in large numbers on later decorative wooden iconostases, but the custom of displaying in some special way icons of particular significance, some perhaps relating to the dedication of the church, is probably quite an early one. The practice of kissing icons, which is still universally observed, also certainly has early origins.

The modern visitor to a Byzantine church should be aware that the forms of the building in which he finds himself were developed in partnership not just with the imagery that they contain; they would also have grown up in answer to liturgical needs, and can to this extent be assessed on purely functional grounds. The orthodox liturgy, although subject to modification and adaptation, from early days took on certain formal needs which remained fairly constant. In later centuries new demands also arose which needed to be accommodated; the rite of baptism for example, had been very important in the early church, thus necessitating a baptistry building (as at *Amfissa*). This sacrament was given less emphasis as the centuries passed, and separate baptistries were not built, but it was revived towards the end of the Byzantine period, and started again to have its own accommodation, usually in part of the narthex. In later Byzantine times we begin to find large tombs being constructed for patrons and benefactors; the narthex was also most often used for these and this area began to be given greater emphasis. A visitor to Greece is also aware of the many bell-towers which form a feature of church exteriors; these seem to have been scarce before the later twelfth century, but became very popular after that. So it is above all in the way that the response to liturgical demands was integrated with the expression of universal Christian values in both architectural and visual form that the genius of Byzantine architecture lies.

Castle building

This entire field has only received a fraction of the attention that has been given to churches, but some general points can still be made. The few examples of Byzantine military building in Greece which can still be assessed show a surprising range of priorities, and display attitudes which contrast fundamentally with those of the invading Western builders. While the fortified walls of the city of Thessaloniki were for the most part an effective barrier to would-be invaders (and were clearly inspired by that defensive wall-system *par excellence*, the Theodosian walls of Constantinople), the Byzantines must have built their castles and fortresses with quite different intentions. Those at *Patras* and on the *Katakolo* peninsula, for example, would always have been hard to defend – indeed impossible to do so for long if attacked by a determined and well-equipped force.

There are exceptions to this, but they tend to be the great sites such as *Acrocorinth* and *Monemvasia* where there were pre-

Byzantine fortifications. In Epiros the two most successful forts of *Arta* and *Rogoi* were not Byzantine structures *ab initio*, but absorbed pre-existing classical building. The siting of *Fanari*, and even *Kavala*, is stronger but not unassailable. It is interesting that while *Fanari* is one of the best preserved of Byzantine forts, of the numerous ones that Prokopios tells us were restored by Justinian in the sixth century, hardly any now exist. It seems that most Byzantine military buildings, erected simply where they were needed, often close to the sea, and with relatively thin curtain walls and irregular towers, could never have been intended to withstand anything like a prolonged and determined siege. The walls could be as little as a metre thick (as at *Androusa*), and it may be that we oversimplify or misunderstand the intended function of buildings such as this by thinking of them only as castles with the same priorities as those in the rest of Europe.

Nor do the Byzantines seem to have learnt from the Western invaders; the site of *Moukhli*, built late in the thirteenth century, is in a weak defensive position, and its water supply was very exposed. In military terms this must have been a disaster from the start. It was mainly where sites had been chosen by previous builders, as at *Mystra*, where the choice was made by Villehardouin, or in the admittedly unique case of *Monemvasia*, that Byzantine defenders had any success. *Platamonas* appears to have been one of the more effective Byzantine castles, but the function of its tall keep may have been partly a signalling station; although its design certainly is not matched by any other such building, its site is far from impregnable, and it never seems to have caused much trouble to its attackers, whoever was defending it.

By contrast, the great majority of the castles built by the Western invaders were on carefully chosen sites, with at least one approach guarded by a major natural feature; spectacular cliffs and ravines form an integral part of the defences of, for example, *Karitaina*, *Passavas*, *Geraki*, *Kyparissia*, *Mystra* and the castle above *Tempe*, while at *Livadia* the Catalans clearly learnt from the Franks and *Great Maina* could only be approached with any ease from the sea. Exceptions such as *Thebes* and *Kalamata* had defences taken over from earlier periods, and their locations would in any case have been dictated by considerations other than those of defence. It would have been interesting to know the full range of considerations which prompted the Catalans to instal their headquarters at Neopatras (*Ypati*) rather than Thebes; the new site certainly had much better natural defences. When a site could be freely chosen, a prime consideration seems always to have been to select a precipitous cliff, and then to build above it.

Given these priorities, it is difficult to generalize about the design of the Frankish castles – even when later modifications by Venetians or Turks might allow it; the terrain invariably imposed different solutions in each case. It seems to have been normal to have a keep in the form of a tower (or *donjon*) on the highest part of the site, and then curtain walls formed an enceinte, usually with a sentry-walk, which was strengthened by towers at corners and other points; in some cases the keep adjoined the curtain. Most sites still retain their cisterns, and this must have been an important feature; at *Argos* the channels for feeding rainwater into the cistern can still be seen.

More standardization can be detected in the techniques of construction adopted by the Western medieval builders. Local stone was always used, undressed, and with a mortar mix that was filled out with quite plentiful ceramic slip fragments. Occasionally, when masonry from earlier building was available, this could be reused with this mortar (as at *Amfissa*), but usually the much larger cut stones of earlier centuries were left in place and simply extended upwards by the medieval builders. Refinements were few; the Catalans at *Livadia* took a greater pride in the carefully cut ashlar of their doorways than most of the Frankish remains suggest was usual. Functional strength was the overriding priority.

The majority of the Western castle-builders in Greece would probably have had only slight experience of the crusader castles of Syria and Palestine and other areas of the Levant, which would in any case by then have begun to appear old-fashioned. They would mostly have been drawing on knowledge gained in western Europe. In this context it is interesting that the most spectacular exception to any supposed norm in this field is the huge castle of *Khlemoutsi*, which relates most closely to a group of castles centred round Boulogne; built between 1218 and 1223, one can suppose that among Villehardouin's priorities was the intention that the expropriated ecclesiastical revenues which paid for it should be converted into a form that made their recovery impossible. While its site is more similar to the kind that the Greeks would have chosen, its design seems to run counter to all the usual considerations, with the finely cut ashlar of its vaults unlike anything else in the secular buildings of Greece. After Thessaloniki and Nikopolis, it remains the most prominent example of conspicuous military consumption in the whole country.

Towers

The main exception to the broad categories discussed above is provided by the phenomenon of the many isolated medieval towers of which the visitor soon becomes aware in the Greek landscape. They are predominantly, though not exclusively, a rural feature and can be seen most readily in parts of central Greece, some (as at Aliartos, near *Thebes*) only a few yards from the road. There are still over thirty in the parts of Attika and Viotia covered by the Duchy of Athens, and there used to be over forty more on Evia; they also appear, although less frequently, in northern Greece, as at Ierissos, and in the Peloponnese, as in the middle of the village of *Khalandritsa*. Further substantial groups exist on or close to Mount Athos, and (although mostly late) are a famous feature of the landscape of the Mani, but both of these have their own special characteristics and their defensive function is quite clear.

There is so far no final agreement on when the towers of central Greece were built, by whom, or what needs they were intended to fulfil. Some kind of defensive purpose must be assumed in a number of cases, while in others it is easier to explain their existence as part of an observation and signalling system; when neither of these seems an adequate reason, 'agricultural purposes' and storage are sometimes proposed. Only one (at *Markopoulo*, on *Cape Sounion*) still retained until recently some of the castellation that can be assumed to have been present on others and that would have had some military function, but paradoxically this is the only one with an original ground-level entrance. The norm is for the entrance to be a few metres off the ground. Almost all are now to some extent ruined. Although built of local stone and without any distinguishing features to help in dating them, it is most probable that the great majority of the towers of central Greece date from the thirteenth and fourteenth centuries, and were the creation not of the indigenous Greeks, but of various Western invaders.

Although these towers are certainly medieval and have a picturesque value, their interest is too specialized for them to merit individual entries in this book. As Byzantine towers are so much rarer, they usually have a brief but unstarred entry.

Entries

How the entries work

Headings

All entries are in alphabetical sequence by location except for the individual monasteries on Mount *Athos* and at *Meteora*, and the groups of entries for the *Mani* and Cape *Sounion*.

Location names at the start of the heading for each entry are in bold type, in capitals. Individual churches, castles, etc., within each location are in bold. Cross-references to other entries are in italic.

The headings give the location's name in modern Greek characters, so as to help in reading signposts and maps. Immediately after that comes the name of the modern Greek administrative district (*Nomos*) in which the location is found. By referring to the map on p. xi, which shows these district boundaries, the approximate position of a location within Greece can be found and then pinpointed on the map either of the Mainland (p. xii) or of the Peloponnese (p. xiii). Where appropriate, the headings also give the medieval name(s) for the location.

Greek names in English

The following transliteration of Greek letters has normally been adopted for place names; exceptions are those for which accepted English versions exist, i.e. Athens, Corinth (with derivative of Acrocorinth), Sparta and Thebes.

B, β appears as V, v   ΜΠ, μπ appears as B, b
H, η appears I, i   U, υ appears as Y, y
K, χ appears as K, k   Φ, φ appears as F, f
            X, χ appears as Kh, kh

Where alternative Greek spellings of place names exist, the version that is used on modern maps or on road signs is usually the one that has been adopted.

Abbreviations

To avoid writing a few of the more frequently used words in full each time they occur, the following abbreviations have been used:

Ag for Agios, Agia, Agioi
Byz for Byzantine
c for century
cap, caps for capital, capitals
CP for Constantinople
EC for early Christian
med for medieval
N, S, E, W for north, south, east and west
The sign / (e.g. 4th/5th c) indicates the decades where one century ends and the next begins.

Star rating

The features of medieval and Byzantine interest in each location are usually indicated at the beginning of its entry; accompanying each item is a simple star rating, indicating on this scale the level of relative interest which can be expected:

***   of outstanding interest
**   of considerable interest
*   worth making a detour

This indication appears in the heading when there is only one site at a given location, or when there are so few separate sites that the question of choice would not arise (e.g. *Philippi*). In the case of locations with many sites, where some choice may well have to be made (e.g. *Athens* or *Thessaloniki*), the indication accompanies each individual site entry.

Unstarred entries are usually included for information when a starred item is in the vicinity, or if they are near to a route from which they can be visited with little trouble; they can be regarded either as objectives for the specialist or the very enthusiastic, or merely as a reason for choosing one route rather than another.

ACROCORINTH Ακροκόρινθος Korinthia
Site and castle ruins ***. Access by car almost to entrance, then by foot on rough tracks. Allow at least 2 hours.

Acrocorinth was always one of the superb natural fortresses of Europe; any power with ambitions to dominate the Peloponnese had to hold it, and it is one of the oldest citadels in Greece which has been virtually continuously occupied. Fortified since pre-Christian times, its known medieval history opens in 805 when it was held by a Byz force; it was captured in 1147 by the Norman King of Sicily, Roger II. In 1204, prior to the Frankish invasion, Leo Sgouros, the Greek *archon* of Nauplio, seeing that it was the best position in the area for him to defend, had occupied it and strengthened its defences. It was left to Boniface of Montferrat to besiege him there, which he did for five years (1205–10); in 1208 Leo Sgouros finally despaired of relief ever coming and committed suicide, galloping on his horse over the cliffs on the s side. During this siege the small **fort of Pendeskoufi** (med *Mont Escovée*) was built, visible on a hill-top to the sw. The fortifications were increased by Geoffrey de Villehardouin during the second quarter of the century, and the mint of Corinth under the Frankish principality, operating until 1250, is more likely to have been here than in Corinth itself.

Its position meant that it was an outpost of the Franks when the Catalans held Attika; in 1324 it was refortified by John of Gravina, the Angevin prince of Akhaia, and in 1358 passed from Angevin to Florentine control, under Niccolo Acciaiuoli. It later formed part of his daughter's dowry when in 1394 she married the despot of Mystra, Theodore Palaiologos, and in 1400 it was occupied for a short time by the Hospitallers. The fortress finally succumbed in 1458 after three months' siege to Mehmed II only when he brought up his artillery. The site was later occupied by both Venetians and Turks, and was still inhabited this century.

The site is a huge one, being, with that of *Monemvasia*, the largest in Greece; it occupies over 60 acres, and the outer enceinte is over 5 km. All its many occupiers have left some trace of their presence, although as usual it is not always possible to distinguish with certainty what parts have been left in their original state, or are of material reused by later occupants. At the main s and sw approaches there are three defensive walls, and you will enter the inner area through a sequence of three massive gates. The first gate is of 14th-c fabric, possibly reused by the Turks, and the second gate is Frankish. Close to this you will see 16th/17th c artillery emplacements facing n and w; the flat, paved areas where the cannon were manipulated provide, with some others higher up the hill and to the ne, some of the few level areas in the whole site.

The two towers flanking the third gate span the pre-Frankish history of the site: that on the right is largely 4th c bc with later (probably Byz) additions, while that on the left is 12th c Byz. You can see how the lintels of the gateway itself are formed by reused marble columns, and that there are also the channels for a portcullis, indicating Frankish work. Most of the enceinte that you see both on the approach and from higher up inside is either Byz, or Frankish 13th c. Inside the third gate you will see some marble fragments with Byz ecclesiastical carving; these must come from what is now the shell of a Byz church just below the third gate. This is most probably 12th c; two of its three apses are still standing, as well as the narthex, although its three doors are blocked up. (The fine brick Byz cisterns cannot now be visited.)

The whole steeply craggy area is dominated by the keep, which again must be Frankish (at 575 m, this is the highest point of the entire site). Elsewhere, Venetian additions are modest, proof again that they never had ambitions to dominate the Peloponnesian hinterland, being content with their fortified ports. The Hospitallers installed the further fortifications to the n in 1400; you will also see the mosque and minaret base left by the Turks, who built the further artillery emplacements in the ne. A broken cannon dated 1680, is presumably Venetian. Near the sw enceinte is Hellenistic housing for a spring, with Roman concrete roofing. A careful visit will reveal how almost the whole history of the Peloponnese can be found, written and signed in the masonry of this magnificent stronghold.

AKRAIFNIO   Ακραίφνιο   Viotia. Formerly Karditsa
Church with classical spolia *. Easy access by car.

You can distinguish the **church of Ag Giorgios** above the village by
its unusual round bell-tower. It is a standard domed, inscribed
cross, four-column plan with later narthex and exonarthex; its
exterior is more interesting than the interior, where there is now no
trace of the Frankish wall-tomb of 1311 of Antoine le Flamenc
reported earlier this century, where the frescos have been heavily
varnished, and where the classical Ionic caps are covered in modern
enamel paint. Outside, however, you will find some fine classical
spolia reused on both N and s sides, and large fragments of the 4th-c
Edictum Diocletianum forming the jamb of the N door and a NE
cornerstone. The attractive enclosure has ancient walling to the NE.

AMFIPOLIS   Αμφίπολι   Serres
Ruins of five EC basilicas *. Easy access by car.

This is a rather scattered site, with three distinct areas. Two are
pre-Christian, and include two quite impressive domestic rooms
with fresco painting in the so-called First Pompeian style, and
another Roman house with some attractive floor mosaics. By far the
most extensive part of the site (still under excavation) is occupied by
the remains of **five EC churches**; there is far less remaining here than
at *Philippi* or *Nea Agkhialos*, but the ground-plans are clearly
evident; there are some attractive floor mosaics with representa-
tions of birds, animals and an octopus, and some fine 5th-c caps.
The basilica with the clearest layout (no dedications are known) is
the furthest from the road, and you can here see areas of marble
flooring still *in situ* and some fragments of a marble templon. The
site, in open country on the E bank of the Strymon and above the
modern village, is an attractive one and well repays the small detour
from the road to Serres or Drama.

AMFISSA   Αμφισσα   Fokis. Med Salona, La Sole, La Sola
Mosaic floor of EC baptistry, church and ruined castle **. Easy
access by car to all sites.

The town had substantial classical origins, but declined greatly in
the med period. Its castle was rebuilt in the 13th c by the family of
Stromoncourt, from Picardy; they were feudatories of the kings of
Thessaloniki, and the med name of Salona is said to derive from

this. It became one of the most important of the baronies, in due course even minting its own coinage. In 1311 the new Catalan leader Roger Deslaur was given the castle here, and took the title of Count of Salona, which passed in 1335 to Alfonso Frederic of Aragon. Due partly to its relatively exposed position open to the coast, but also to violent and colourful internal feuds, it fell into Turkish hands as early as 1394, so becoming the first stronghold on the Greek mainland to have a Turkish governor. In 1404 the Hospitallers occupied the castle, having traded it for *Acrocorinth*, where they had been for four years, but could not long survive the combined hostility of the local Greeks and the occupying Turkish forces.

On the N side of the modern cathedral in the centre of the town is an almost complete **mosaic floor** of geometric design; it is from a 4th/5th-C **baptistry** and is circular in plan. It has low walls still standing, and the two doorways show where the catechumens would enter from the W and then leave after baptism by the S door and so enter the cathedral. It is an interesting indication of the continuing importance of the town in the EC period, and of baptism still being given the prominence of a separate building.

On an isolated and peaceful site above the town (about 1 km up to the left off the Odos tou Frouriou as it levels off before reaching the castle) you will find the beautiful 12th-C **church of the Saviour** (Ekklisia tou Sotiros) – an inscribed cross, triple-apse design with its original narthex. Its two columns have fine Corinthian caps reused from an EC source and the cloisonné is of exceptional precision, but its most memorable features are the exterior brick ornamentation, the crosses formed from large stones embedded in the N wall and two sundials carved in the S wall by the door.

The **castle** was built by Thomas de Stromoncourt (or d'Autre-mencourt) partly on the ancient acropolis; it is a fine site, with precipitous cliffs to N and E. (You can reach it easily by car up the winding Odos tou Frouriou.) At all points you will see massive earlier masonry, both polygonal and rectangular. You enter the first of the three gates in the SW corner, and will see here both types, topped by the Frankish builders, who reused some of the large blocks as quoins. The plan involves two baileys, and the second gate is formed from massive blocks set in a partly 4th/5th-C wall. The SW wall of the inner bailey is formed largely of reset rectangular blocks, with Frankish bonding incorporating tile fragments. The highest point is occupied by a round keep, partly still standing; you will find a modest cistern, but (although there are massive other ruins here) there are no evident signs of the church, dedicated to St Anthony, that 19th-c travellers such as Dodwell described as being within the castle area, nor of the Roman building excavated in 1973.

The long history of Amfissa which can be traced in its monuments – each in their own way memorable and reflecting in their variety all aspects of its med past – makes this a particularly interesting town to visit.

ANDRAVIDA Ανδραβίδα Ilia. Med Andreville
Ruins of Frankish cathedral *. Easy access; effectively unenclosed.

It is hard to imagine now how this dull little town (according to the *Chronicle of the Morea*) so impressed Guillaume de Villehardouin '. . . le meillor ville de le Morée, et gist en plain sans murs et sans nulle fortresse. . . .' that he made it the capital of his new principality of Frankish Akhaia. Here in 1208 the important parliament met to decide on the twelve baronies of the principality and, besides being the seat of a Western bishop, it was thus also the site of the creation of the Frankish equivalent of the Domesday Book, and as late as 1427 housed the court of the principality. Now only part of the **Dominican cathedral church of Ag Sofia** (excavated by Americans in 1983–4) survives of the three churches built here by Guillaume II de Villehardouin: nothing remains of the Templars' church of St James, which housed the tombs of the Villehardouin princes, or of the Franciscan church of St Stephen.

Ag Sofia was probably built *c*. 1250, although there is now no trace of the abbey buildings that must have adjoined it; their foundations may well lie under the adjacent modern school. Of the original basilical building, which was over 53 m long, only the E end is now standing, but the main chancel bay with two shorter side chapels to N and S have retained their Gothic vaulted roofing; with the vaulting at *Isova* and *Zaraka* no longer extant, this particular Western technique can now only otherwise be seen in the Peloponnese at *Khalandritsa*. The rather austere leaf forms on the caps are typical of monastic building in France of somewhat earlier date, as is the simple trefoil molding round the wall-niche in the S chapel. The only internal clue to this building being in Greece rather than France may be the two pieces of marble let into the W face of the chancel at the height of the springing of the arch, which show finely carved Byz ornament, and must have been reused from an earlier local building. The partial bricking up of the large pointed E window is the result of this part of the building being used for a time as a mosque. The w end must now lie under the modern road cutting across the site; the moss growing thickly on the N side and the generally undistinguished surroundings make this a somewhat forlorn – if interesting – relic of the courtly capital of the feudal princes of Akhaia.

For the nearby former **Franciscan monastery of Vlackhernae**, see **Kyllini**.

ANDROUSA Ανδρούσα   Messinia. 24 km NW of Kalmata. Med Druses

Castle ruins and church *. Easy access by car.

This pleasant, sleepy little town – hardly more than a village – was once, surprisingly, one of the main centres of med Greece, at times knowing real importance. It had not been one of the original twelve baronies, but later, perhaps partly due to its geographical position, the Navarrese made it their headquarters, and later in the 14th c it was for a time the capital of the principality. John Palaiologos captured Androusa for the Byzantines, and when he returned to CP his younger brother Thomas (with the historian and diplomat Frantzes) was sent there to hold it.

The site of the **castle** is not very spectacular, with large sections of it merging into the town on almost the same level. It is clear that it must have covered a substantial area, however; the chief surviving remains are some 50 m of the E and SE wall of the enceinte, with towers at corners and at intervals on its length. There is a further corner tower surviving to the NW, now isolated and used to house farm machinery, but no signs of a keep, and the other walls are much reduced.

Two features about the building can be mentioned: you will see that the entire length of the wall that survives is built with an arcade of engaged arches, slightly pointed, on the inner side, and with quite regular use of tile courses; this system of construction reduces the thickness of the wall inside the arches to little more than a metre. The second is the very clear difference in the kinds of tower construction; one is of rectangular section, one has four facets forming a section like the prow of a ship, and a third is rounded, and there is no clear difference in the masonry technique of any of them. This particular feature can be found in Byz castles as e.g. at *Arta* and in many parts of the empire, including Asia Minor, and so it may indicate that at least some of the construction, and so presumably the siting, of this castle at Androusa was due to Byz presence here before the arrival of Western forces. It is usually said to have been constructed by Western builders in the 13th c, but its relatively weak defensive position, combined with its siting and construction, is more characteristic of Byz castle building.

A fine view of the E wall of the castle can be had from the modest 12th-c **church of Ag Giorgios**, now used as a cemetery chapel. It is a single nave, single apse hall church, and its interior is innocent of any decoration. Externally, however, attractive use has been made of brick patterns, particularly in the area of the apse.

ANO VOLOS   Ανω Βόλος   Magnisia
Church and spolia *. Easy access by car/bus; entry up path from car park on right of the road from Lower Volos.

The main med interest here is the quantity of Byz spolia built into the exterior of the **church of Ag Ioachim**. The church itself is of medium size, and is a wooden-roofed basilica with a single faceted apse; the masonry of the apse is cloisonné with dressed local tufa, and the double arcade of the window, now partly blocked up, suggests that the E part at least could date from the 12th c. The later repairs will no doubt have been to rectify earthquake damage. The spolia (which include classical fragments) are thickest here and on the N wall, where a Byz monogram carved in marble has been set upside down. There is a late fresco of the Last Judgement on the exterior of the S wall, much disfigured by graffiti; the view from the terrace is magnificent.

APIDIA   Απιδιά   Lakonia
Church and sculpture *. Easy access from a side road at the N edge of village.

The **church of the Koimisis tis Theotokou** has an unexciting exterior, with white cement rendering and a modern roof, but has retained inside quite an interesting range of earlier sculpture. In form it is a three-aisled basilica with a wide narthex; it may indeed be originally an EC foundation, although the basis of the present structure is probably 10th/11th c. The templon contains some good quality marble and limestone carving from this period, and there are four quite good caps, ranging from 4th to 9th c which must be reused from an earlier structure; a fifth column is embedded in a later pier. There is a late wooden iconostasis, and no wall paintings.

AREIA Αρεία Argolida
Conventual church *. Approx. 2 km to s of road from Nauplio to Epidauros; signed (approx. 4 km from Nauplio). In country, but easy access by car.

The **convent of Agia Moni**, also known as the **Panagia tis Zoodokhos Pigis**, was founded in 1143/4 by Leo, bishop of Argos and Nauplio (1143–57); its typikon still survives. The katholikon is of medium size, and is of inscribed cross, domed plan with the octagonal drum of the cupola supported on four columns. The exterior is impressive, with the fine quality cloisonné masonry set off by massive stone cross forms and rich use of brick round windows and apses, and still retaining some of its colourful ceramic bowls; you will immediately feel that this is a building reflecting metropolitan, rather than provincial, standards.

The arcaded window forms have a raised central light, and the drum has a large window in each facet – all confirming the mid-12th-c date. Time has treated the building well, and there are virtually no alterations – just a closing of large openings to N and S of the narthex, and the addition of a later belfry. The interior lacks the distinction of the outside, with no original painted decoration surviving, but the four columns have unusually fine classical acanthus caps. (See also *Khonikas*.)

ARGOS Αργος Argolida
Castle *. Outside town; easy access by car.

The med history of Argos is unimportant before the Frankish invasion. Then, stiffened by Leo Sgouros, the archon from Nauplio, at that point being besieged in Acrocorinth before his foray to Thermopylae, the town was able to hold out against the Frankish invaders until 1212. Thereafter it was granted as a fief by Geoffrey I de Villehardouin to Othon de la Roche, lord of Athens. The town escaped Catalan rule, but was taken by the Venetians in 1388, who defended it against the Turkish invasion of 1395. The Venetian presence was due to the fortunes of Argos being bound up with those of Nauplio, which was so important to the maritime interests of the Republic; it remained under Venetian control until 1460, never reverting to Byz rule.

The **Kastro** here dominates the town, on a high, though not precipitous, acropolis. It was originally a Byz construction on ancient foundations, but enlarged by the Franks of the Enghien family. It is easy to find the ancient 4th/5th-c polygonal blocks of masonry (as in the E wall of the inner redoubt and w wall of the enceinte) but almost impossible to separate the Byz from the later Frankish building – due possibly to local masons being used by both powers. The form is of a double enceinte with quite a large polygonal keep. The curtain walls are supported by towers – some rounded, others square or octagonal; the inner bailey contains an abnormally long, narrow cistern, lined with mortar (as was usual) and with a well-head still surviving at each end of it; its size may have made possible the long resistance until 1212. In the NE corner of the inner bailey are the walls of a small chapel constructed largely from ancient spolia, with, inside, thin brick and stone courses; the apse still has a layer of plaster, but no paintings. Of all the construction, this would seem to be the most certainly Byz, while the artillery emplacement in the N outer wall is clearly Turkish.

You will not find that this castle is a strenuous one to visit, and the outlook over Argos and the Argive plain is spectacular.

ARKADIA
See **Kyparissia**

ARTA Αρτα Arta/Epiros
Castle and eight churches ***.

For the most part the country round Arta is undistinguished, and it is now only some of the buildings in the city and its immediate neighbourhood which still speak of the uniquely important and interesting role that it had in the history of Byz Greece. Ruled mainly by a succession of despots, the district of Epiros, contained on the E by the huge Pindos range, was the most remote area of mainland Greece; neither the rulers in CP nor the centres of government set up by the invaders of 1204 were ever able to exercise any real control, and the independence that this provided is reflected in the monuments you will see here. Its position so close to the Adriatic meant that, when external influences did impinge, they tended to be associated with Albania and Serbia, and the maritime Italian states such as Genoa. (For a sketch of the complex history of the despotate, see pp. 23–27.)

Nowhere can the independence and individuality of Arta's rulers be seen more clearly expressed than in the **church of the Panagia Parigoritissa** ('Virgin of Consolation'). It was built between 1283 and 1296, and must surely be the most bizarre major church building in Greece. It was always the leading church of the city, and for centuries was the katholikon of a monastery; excavations on the N have revealed foundations of an earlier church. The refectory now forms a small museum and a row of monks' cells lines the E boundary wall. The building has museum status and opening times, and the local tourist office is housed in its s aisle.

As you approach the w façade you could be forgiven for mistaking it for a rather massive *palazzo* of the kind seen in central Italy, with the upper two storeys pierced by rows of regular double-arcaded windows; only the sight of some of its six domes against the skyline will reassure you that you are not in Tuscany. Its scale increases this effect, with both height and ground area larger than anything to be seen in the other despotate of Mystra. In fact, this first impression will begin to diminish as you approach and see that much of the masonry is fine Byz cloisonné with patterned courses; the raw stone of the ground storey would have been marble-clad. Going round to the E side the faceted apses (five in all, of varying heights) are even more securely Byz in character.

Entering the narthex is again reassuring, with its high vaulting making it similar to other large Byz churches; the exterior has not prepared you for this, and there are broad aisles adjoining to N and s. Even less do you expect the towering interior space, where the dome is carried high up on three superimposed storeys of columns. It should be said at once that the rough walls would have been clad with sheet marble – now only left on the w wall below the gallery and in mouldings where the w piers meet the floor. This must be remembered when you see the apparently crude engineering by which the supports of the columns are carried, on pairs of horizontal columns embedded in the masonry; these would surely have been concealed to some extent. Where the underside of the columns in the third storey are exposed they have decorative carving, and it seems unlikely that this degree of attention to the decoration of the furthest elements was not matched by at least the same care lower down. Above all, the presence of the mosaics in the cupola – the powerful Pantocrator still largely survives, and there are figures of prophets and cherubim in the drum that are harder to see – is a sign of a serious intention to create a grandly impressive ruler's church, on which expense had not been spared. Thessaloniki and CP itself were the only other Greek centres where mosaics were installed after the 12th C, with even Mystra having to make do with fresco.

Some points to note: the splendour of the interior in its original state should be emphasized, as besides the mosaics in the upper zones and frescos lower down (a few of these still survive in poor condition), there was also much decorative carving; only one of the small free-standing arches straddling the space below the squinches now survives, but there would have been others originally. These areas of carving, which include motifs such as pairs of fighting horses and other animals, and must have been specially cut, were plentiful, and contrast with the caps of the lower columns which are in many cases reused earlier pieces. The supporting structure of the central dome, combined with its height, conceals its massive scale – its 16 windows make it unusually large. The relief of the double-headed eagle in the floor, as at Mystra, doubtless commemorates an event such as a coronation. The emphasis given to the decoration round the w balcony by such features as the double-knotted colonettes suggests this may have been used by the despot's family, in emulation of imperial custom in the gallery of Ag Sofia, CP.

In fact the plan of the Parigoritissa is not uncommon in the late 13th C; it is that of a Greek cross over which an octagon was built supporting a large cupola (it can be seen in *Ag Sofia, Monemvasia* and in *Ag Theodoroi, Mystra*) and was clearly a building form that was called on for larger-scale and expensive churches at this period. It is the marriage of this plan with three Italianate palace façades, combined with the great internal height, that has produced this most individual of churches – 'a church which is half a palace'. After the Battle of Pelagonia in 1259, and long before he became despot, Nikiforos I (1267–96) had gone to Italy, returning with some Italian soldiers; one may speculate if he also brought back with him the memory of some *palazzo* that he had admired there.

The **castle (Frourion)** on the N side of the town occupies a bend in the river and may be the first older building that you see. It was probably mainly built by the despot Michael II (1246–67), but you can see from the road passing the N walls how the undressed local stone that he was using was in places being laid on top of fine rectangular limestone blocks surviving from the classical period.

From the main entrance gate it is possible to see how some of the 18 towers are of successively square, round and triangular section (comparable with *Androusa*); as there was no sustained Frankish penetration here, this is clear indication that this is a feature of Byz construction. The best way to obtain an idea of the extent and character of the castle is to start from the main gate and use the sentry-walk along the battlements to make a tour of the entire enceinte (about 20 min). This is now virtually the only feature left from the original construction, since a modern concrete hotel occupies the area of the keep, but what remains is mostly fairly authentic; the Turks do not seem to have introduced any major alterations. The wall follows the curve of the river to the NE and forms an irregular rectangle to the s and w; from the NE sector you can look across the river to the church of *Vlakherna*.

It must be admitted that the castle here is not spectacularly sited, although it was, for instance, able to withstand the siege mounted in 1340 by the Emperor Andronikos III in person, when Andronikos Basilitzes had proclaimed independence; far more impressive are the massive overgrown ruins of *Rogoi*, 14 km to the w.

Of the two churches in the immediate vicinity sw of the Frourion, the nearest is that of **St Basil (Ag Vasilios)**. It is a simple, wooden-roofed basilica of quite modest size, and was built in the second half of the 13th c; it is not in normal use and remains locked, but its exterior is its chief attraction. With all the care and invention that has been lavished on the churches of Epiros, this must take its place as the most colourful. The simplicity of its design (the lower aisles are in fact a later addition) emphasizes the rich polychrome colours on glazed terracotta tiles of green, white and red that form a broad band right round the upper storey; this is supported below by brick courses set in herring-bone and meander pattern, and the whole reaching a minor crescendo in the gable of the E end where two terracotta reliefs – in effect, icons, still with traces of pigment – of the crucifixion and three bishops flank the upper window. There is no precise parallel anywhere in Greece, and the nearest comparison is with small carved antique spolia, such as the stelae at *Merbaka*.

A short distance further to the sw up a slight rise you will find the **church of Ag Theodora**. The dedication is due to the wife of the despot Michael II (1246–67), Theodora of the family of Petraliphas, whose tomb is located here; she was the only member of the ruling dynasties of Epiros who was known for the sanctity of her life, and the qualities of piety and virtue that she brought to the court of Arta

are reflected in the spate of church building that marked this period.
She is still revered in the locality. Of quite modest size, the church
was built on a triple-apse basilica plan, and dates from the late 11th
c; the frescos are now sooty, but the nave caps are impressive –
reused, double-zone 5th-c pieces, and two have been partially recut
with small standing figures. The simplicity of the wooden-roofed
nave is offset by a fine domed narthex, of which the exterior w wall
bears spectacular brick patterns.

But it is Theodora's tomb, on your left as you enter by the s door,
which is of the greatest interest. It was her burial here which brought
about both the building of the narthex (in the late 13th/14th c) and
the present dedication, and she is the central figure in the relief
which is carved on its w face. The second of her six children is shown
in smaller scale beside her, his regalia indicating that he must be the
despot Nikiforos I (1267–96); the pair can be seen standing under an
arch of double-knotted colonettes fitted with unexpectedly
flamboyant caps. This tomb dates from the last quarter of the 13th c,
and is the only one to survive undamaged of the many that must
have existed in and around Arta.

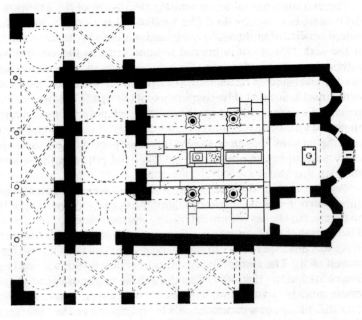

Ag Theodora

Before leaving take a look at the unusual brick-built Byz arch
some 20 m away from the s door of the church; its original function
can only be guessed at, but such secular survivals are rare.

Of the remaining five churches in the immediate vicinity of Arta that
will be mentioned here, two are clearly of unusual local importance.
The most interesting is the **church of the Panagia tou Vlakherna**; it is
now the village church of Vlakherna due NE of Arta, but it was
previously the katholikon of a monastery, and you can see it from
the walls of the castle as you look across the river. Originally a
12th-C three-aisled basilica, in the mid-13th C the despot Michael II
had a large cupola added over the central nave and smaller ones
over both the N and s aisles, giving it in effect the rare form of a
triple-domed basilica; it was probably at the same time that the later
narthex was built. Entry is now through doors in both ends of the
narthex, and each has a carved marble surround incorporating
carved templon elements of great refinement. Before entering you
can see further sculpture in the form of a fine relief of the archangel
Michael on the s wall, and a view of the apses shows that all three are
different in design and have some finely inventive brick patterns.
Entering the naos you will find that the added cupola is rather
uncomfortably supported by a combination of the two thick
columns that formed the E bay of the nave, another lighter pair to
the w and the walls that divide the apses: the result is inventive,
rather than aesthetic. In both of the w corners of the church are
marble tombs, the s one having quite substantial remains of carved
ornament. It is this that is most probably that of Michael II, and it is
possible that the s aisle had the function of a funerary parekklision;
there is an unusual oblique window opening from beside the tomb
into the narthex. For the rest, you will find that two of the caps are
early, and have been recut and reused, and there are some frescos of
the 13th C and later.

Try to take your time over this historic site, where the peace and
calm contrast with the city churches of the despots in Arta itself.

For the other substantial foundation in the vicinity, the **Moni tis
Kato Panagia**, take the small road beside the E bank of the Arakh-
thos signed to Kommeno; the convent is 2 km down this road on
your left, and the nuns will open the gate at the usual times. As so
often, all the conventual buildings are late, but the 13th-C katholikon still stands; you can see the brick inscription of the *ktitor*, the
despot Michael II, in the s wall, close to the cage of some magnificent

live peacocks. The late fresco of the Last Judgement on the exterior
of the w wall was once inside an exonarthex, now destroyed.

On entering the naos the form of a basilica with a broad central
nave and a high transverse crossing becomes clear; the narthex is
hardly more than a further w bay. The four nave bays are formed by
six columns, all with caps from different periods, of which one is
quite a fine 5th-c example. The frescos are again all late, but the
absence of a cupola has given the painter of the cross vault
the opportunity to paint three versions of Christ – Emmanuel,
Pantocrator and the Ancient of Days.

Two more smaller churches are in the country to the immediate N of
Arta, and both are reached by leaving the city on the road going to
Grammenitsa. About 5 km off the road signed to Kostakio, just
outside Plisii, you will find the rurally sited **church of Ag Dimitrios
Katsouris** (key in the nearby house of the papas). Dating originally
to the 10th/11th C, this is one of the earliest foundations in the
region; the high circular drum of its dome is immediately striking,
but after seeing some of the later churches the absence of any
attempt to relieve the rather severe exterior here may strike you as
somewhat unimaginative. Before the 13th-c narthex was built it was
almost centrally planned, with three rounded apses and the dome
carried on four piers; the cupola is unusual in having ribs showing
internally. Two pairs of columns extend the naos to E and W, and of
these three have classical caps reused, and an 11th-c marble relief is
let into the templon. The frescos in the apse are the most interesting; they are of two periods, and must reflect the early history of the
building, corresponding to the period of its initial foundation, and
to the 13th C, when it was enlarged.

The other, and smaller, of these two churches off the Grammenitsa
road is that of **Ag Nikolaos tis Rodias**; you will see it in a field beside
the road on the edge of the village of Kizates. Its name derives from
its dependence on a monastery of the Virgin named Rodia which no
longer survives, and it may have been a private chapel. It is a 13th-c,
inscribed cross building, with only one apse and it has only two
internal columns to support the cupola. Its most evident external
feature is the impressively broad band of meander pattern, set in
thin bricks, that runs right round the whole building. Inside, the
main interest is provided by its 13th/14th-c frescos, although their
condition is poor; the w bays have the uncommon subjects of the
Seven Sleepers of Ephesus and the Three Hebrews in the Furnace.

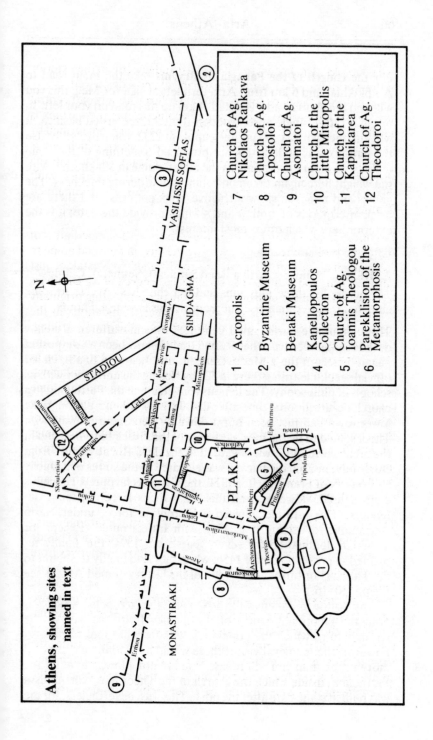

Athens, showing sites
named in text

1   Acropolis
2   Byzantine Museum
3   Benaki Museum
4   Kanellopoulos
    Collection
5   Church of Ag.
    Ioannis Theologou
6   Parekklision of the
    Metamorphosis
7   Church of Ag.
    Nikolaos Rankava
8   Church of Ag.
    Apostoloi
9   Church of Ag.
    Asomatoi
10 Church of the
    Little Mitropolis
11 Church of the
    Kapnikarea
12 Church of Ag.
    Theodoroi

For the **church of the Panagia tis Bryonis** take the main road to
Amfilokhia, and 6 km from Arta turn left at sign for Megathi; you
will find the church, now isolated, 1 km up this road on your left. In
origin a 12th-c single apse, wooden-roofed three-aisled basilica, it
was enlarged with a crossing and cupola in 1232, when probably also
the narthex was added; this has produced something of the same
feelings of slight uncertainty as the added dome in Vlakherna, with
the weight here again taken on columns of differing thickness. The
gables and E façade show attractive brick patterns, and there are
brick inscriptions on both N and S which provide the date; it is the
exterior here which offers most interest.

ATHENS Aθήνα Attika. Med Satine(s), Setine(s), Cetines
The acropolis, three museums and ten churches. Access to some
churches is easier than elsewhere; museums have usual hours.

Throughout the earlier med centuries Athens suffered a steady
decline in significance. The city had traditionally been an outpost of
pagan beliefs in the E Mediterranean, and Justinian finally ended
official secular learning there in 529 by closing the university with its
schools of philosophy. The famous conversion of the Parthenon to a
church occurred some time after this. In 1204 Athens, although the
lower town had just been burnt down by Leo Sgouros, was, with
Thebes, held to be the most desirable of the Greek baronies, and in
the great share-out it was awarded to the de la Roche family, from
Burgundy; in 1260 the barony was elevated to the status of a Duchy
by Louis IX of France. After 1311, the Catalans favoured Thebes as
a stronghold, however, and this left Athens largely without defenders. This attitude allowed a Florentine force, under Nerio
Acciaiuoli, to occupy it in 1385 with little trouble. Except for
Venetian domination for seven years from 1394, this family remained in possession until 1456, when they had finally to submit to
the Turks. (For further discussion of the history of med Athens see
the pp. 10–16.)

Any visitor to Athens will wish to visit the **Acropolis**, which was
both the emotional centre of the medieval city, as well as the
stronghold to which the population withdrew in times of danger;
however, the medieval visitor there would have found a great deal
more to see than you will today. You are not allowed to enter the
Parthenon, inside which the church of the Theotokos Atheniotissa
was built at some date after the 6th c. This was, nevertheless, for the

Byz period the cathedral of Athens, where, for example, the emperor Basil II came in 1018 to celebrate his military victories in northern Greece. The wide flight of steps cut in the rock to the w of the Parthenon, as well as three small steps cut in the marble plinth itself, are part of the approach to the med cathedral, and (besides the many smaller signs at floor level and so invisible from outside) you can see a doorway in the s wall has recently been filled in. With binoculars you can also readily see two rather sad survivals of its decoration, both painted directly onto the marble of the w face inside the portico: a scene of the Annunciation to the s of the entrance side and a sketchy painting of the Lamb of God with a Gothic black-letter inscription to the N.

Your imagination has to supply the palace built by Nerio Acciaiuoli in the propylaeum, which so impressed the 15th-c antiquarian Cyriacus of Ancona, with its many marble columns and a coffered marble ceiling. Only a few rows of beam holes in the N and s wings of the propylaeum are left to guide you. The tower, almost 30 m high, that was probably built by him to the s from reused marble taken from the nearby classical buildings, and usually later known as the 'Venetian tower', lasted longest, only being demolished in 1874 by the combined efforts of the Greek Archaeological Society and Heinrich Schliemann (excavator of Troy and Mycenae) in a typical act of 19th-c 'medieval vandalism' (you can date early drawings and photographs of the acropolis by whether or not it can be seen). Earlier 19th-c travellers could also see the vaulted remains of a chapel of St Bartholomew which, if not Florentine, may have been the only contribution of the Catalans to the medieval buildings of the city. In spite of the continuous Western rule by Frenchmen, Catalans, Aragonese, Florentines and Venetians for over 250 years, the remains of medieval Athens that you will see today are almost exclusively Greek.

Byzantine Museum Βυζαντινό Μουσείο Leoforos Vasilissis Sofias
Icons, sculpture, textiles, works in precious metal, bronze and wood, jewellery, coins etc. ***.

This is the only national museum in the world devoted solely to Byz art and artefacts, and while there are few major masterpieces in the collection, the general level of the material and its presentation is high.

The choice of a mid-19th-C aristocrat's town house for this museum was a happy one, and sensitive use has been made of its possibilities. Visit first the main building at the further end of the entrance court, going to the first room on the right. This has been laid out as a small EC basilica using partly original marble fragments, with others (such as the ambo) made from cast plaster; note the synthronon and the low, open templon in front of the altar, which came from *Nea Agkhialos*. The room adjoining this has an interesting collection of Byz sculpture; some is unexceptional, but note the very unusual 10th-C marble icon with the standing figures of three saints incised in it and painted on wax, the fine marble reliefs of the Virgin Hodegetria from Thessaloniki and the Virgin of the Zöodokhos Pigi – in the original in CP water spouted from tubes projecting from her hands. There are also some fragments of Franco-Byz sculpture.

The next room that you will enter has been adapted to the form of a middle Byz church interior; again plaster casts have been used to complete it, but the general effect is convincing, with the templon higher and more dense, and there are also many sculptural fragments. The final room in this sequence takes the form of a late Byz church with a decorated wooden iconostasis; these rooms demonstrate well the way in which the bema of a Byz church has been steadily enclosed over the centuries, with now very little visible from the naos.

On the first floor (above these rooms) there is a substantial collection of smaller objects: Coptic textiles and later embroidery, steatite reliefs, gold jewellery, coins, EC ampullae, bread stamps, etc. The outstanding pieces here include an entire MS chrysobull of 1301 signed in red by the Emperor Andronikos II Palaiologos and with a headpiece illustration of Christ handing the emperor a scroll, a large mosaic icon on wood of the Virgin Glykophilousa, a fine icon of the crucifixion from the church of *Christ Elkomenos*, *Monemvasia*, and a unique assemblage of five large double-sided icons.

The rooms in the wing on the left as you enter the courtyard are at present closed – unfortunately, as they contain one of the real masterpieces of the Museum, the Thessaloniki epitaphios. On the right is housed the Loverdos Collection. This is an assemblage of Byz sculpture of all kinds, mainly decorative fragments; while something of a specialist interest, there are only a few other places (e.g. the museum garden at *Thebes*) where you can see such a range.

Benaki Museum Μουσείο Μπενάκη Leoforos Vasilissis Sofias / Odos Koumbari

Icons, textiles, works in precious metal and bronze, jewellery, coins, some MSS, etc. and later costume ***.

Unlike the Byzantine Museum, this is a private foundation endowed by Antoine Benaki (d. 1955). Room 3 contains the major portion of the Byz elements in the collection; among the outstanding items are a 10th-c silver processional cross from Adrianople and a 14th-c icon of the Hospitality of Abraham; of considerable interest are a small collection of Byz gold jewellery, an *argyrobullon* (i.e. 'with a silver seal') signed in large red script by Dimitrios Palaiologos, despot of Mystra in 1456, a 13th-c psalter open at two full-page illustrations, a collection of rare Byz weights in bronze and glass, and some 10th- to 15th-c pottery. In Room 8 there is a display of later work in precious metal, including some spectacular book-covers, and some fine later icons, some by known artists such as Emanuel Tzanes and Theodore Poulakis; among the Byz textiles are two unusually rich epitaphia, one dated 1599. The collection also holds two icons by El Greco (Adoration of the Magi and St Luke painting the Virgin) although you may find these disappointing. An entertaining late (*c.* 1800) icon of the Zöodokhos Pigi, with much picturesque detail, was acquired in 1988. (There are also substantial displays of ancient Greek art and quite substantial collections of Islamic material and of ethnic Greek costume.)

Kanellopoulos Museum Μουσείο Κανελλοπούλου*

This museum occupies what was a private 19th-c house just under the N slope of the acropolis. It contains works from many periods of Greek art, but the Byz interest is concentrated on the ground floor and the two floors below. You will find a number of icons of 14th- to 15th-c date and later; in the first room there are interesting 15th-c examples with the subjects of three church fathers and of the Archangel Michael controlling the river at Khonae. While the considerable collection of bronze items is mostly unexceptional, there is a 10th-c bronze processional cross, rare for having a blue enamel medallion, and quite a good cast bronze censer. There are also a number of Byz pottery bowls placed quite high up, and small amounts of Byz gold jewellery, enamel, reliefs in steatite and brass and wood bread stamps.

There follow here entries on ten churches or monasteries in Athens,

all of which have substantial elements surviving from the Byz
period; they are all attractive buildings, some particularly so, and
between them they provide a representative range of small to
medium-sized Byz church building from the 11th to 13th c. With a
few exceptions, they speak for the generally provincial character
of Athens in the med period, contrasting in this respect with
Thessaloniki. (*Dafni* has a separate entry.) Unless specified otherwise, the level of interest in their interiors is mostly not very high,
with decorative carving being usually the most attractive feature.

Three of them form a geographical group within a small area in
the network of streets on the N slope below the acropolis, and they
are mentioned first here; the rest offer no logical geographical basis
and so follow in alphabetical sequence. You will need a map to find
some of them.

The **church of Ag Ioannis Theologou** *, on a rather cramped site at
the corner of Odos Erotokritou and Odos Erekhtheou, is one of the
smallest in Athens. It is a 13th/14th-c domed church on an inscribed
cross design, with simple cloisonné masonry, and unlike most
churches in Athens it has not been subsequently altered. Funds may
have been in short supply, as the most unusual feature of it (which
can be seen from the street) is provided by the two interior columns
supporting the dome: not only are they reused classical pieces, but
the builder needed to place two reused classical caps on each of
them, one on top of the other, to get sufficient height. Its orientation
is almost N-S, presumably due to the fall of the land at this point.

The **parekklision of the Metamorphosis tou Sotiros** * (sometimes
called **Ag Sotir**), on Odos Theorias, is only just larger, but is more
attractively sited and part of it can be seen from a more comfortable
distance. It has been dated to the late 11th/early 12th c and to the
14th; it was built on a more spacious plan than Ag Ioannis, with four
disengaged columns and no separate narthex, and there is a small
chapel opening to the s. At first sight the masonry looks cruder, but
you will find that much of what is visible is later than the original
core of the building. The w bay has been enlarged, the three small
apses and the SE corner are of later masonry, and an opening in the s
wall has been blocked up; it could be that the original construction
of the chapel and its cupola date from the early 12th c, but that
various alterations or repairs were carried out in the 14th. You can
just see traces of the original cloisonné masonry; with remains of
dog-tooth brick decoration in some parts, most consistently in and

around the drum of the dome, although the window openings here are quite modern.

Of these three churches, that of **Ag Nikolaos Rankava ***, on the corner of Odos Prytaneiou, would always have been the most impressive. Originally quite a tall but compact inscribed cross, single dome church, it dates from the late 11th c; like Ag Ioannis above, it is oriented almost N–S. Some quite massive spolia were used in the lower parts of the E wall, and there are quite elaborate brick patterns round the windows. At an early stage a parekklision was built on to the W side, almost doubling the width of the naos; then substantially later a two-storey structure was built on at the N end and this is now incorporated into the church, giving a gallery that extends over the parekklision. You can see all this in the external masonry. The interior was remodelled at a late period, and the ceiling is now formed by a late painting on flat canvas, blocking off the cupola.

The **church of Ag Apostoloi ****, in the SE corner of the Agora, is architecturally the most interesting and distinguished in Athens, and its design is not repeated precisely anywhere else in Greece. (It was restored in 1954–7 to its original 11th-c form.) In its own way it is a small masterpiece, and we are very fortunate that it survived the burning of the lower town by Leo Sgouros in 1204. Here the builders devised a method of sustaining a large cupola with four columns, but ingeniously expanding the space surrounding it; the exterior gives a hint of how this is achieved, with the faceted forms of the N, E and S sides in fine cloisonné relieved with courses of restrained dog-tooth ornament. But it is the interior that benefits most from this ingenuity; it is exceptionally spacious and light, and offers (for only a medium-sized church) a very varied range of spatial experience. This was achieved by integrating four equal apse forms with four small curved absidioles; these eight curved spaces provide not only a strong enough wall system, but a more interesting and varied spatial

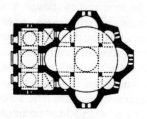

Ag Apostoloi

effect than the far more usual inscribed cross plan. The narthex, too, has a more interesting form than the usual transverse hall, as at either end the space merges with that of the corner chambers adjacent to the two w absidioles. The design, and the cloisonné masonry in which it is carried out, all indicate a date early in the 11th c, perhaps even *c.* 1000.

The four caps are reused, as is *de rigueur* in Athens, and fragments of the original templon are built into the modern reconstruction. Most of the fresco decoration has gone, and what is there is 15th/16th c, but the two w absidioles retain the unusual subjects of the Angel of the Great Counsel and the Ancient of Days.

In a rather run-down area off Odos Ermou the small **church of Ag Asomatoi** is certainly of 11th/12th-c Byz foundation, but has been substantially rebuilt, albeit with sensitivity and care. It has retained its original ground-plan of an inscribed cross with three apses and a dome supported on four columns; it is protected by a good space around it, and this allows you to see the original features retained in the structure – in particular, attractive masonry with large crosses set in three walls. The interior lacks any decorative interest, but its exterior makes it worth a visit if you are in the vicinity.

Up-staging its dour and over-sized metropolitan neighbour, the engaging **church of the Little Mitropolis** * is dedicated to the Panaghia Gorgoepiköos and Ag Eleutherios. It is a later 12th-c inscribed cross, four-column church, and no doubt its modest scale would have fitted well into the low buildings of the large village that formed med Athens. Unremarkable inside, where only the carving over the doorways is of interest, the chief impact of the building is provided by the unique collection of carved spolia which decorate much of its exterior walls; as in other cases these seem to have been a source of pride to the med builders. The most interesting are perhaps those on the w façade, which are representative of the whole, being both ancient and medieval. You can see here the Byz lintel with lions either side of a cross, a classical relief of winged sphinxes and Byz reliefs of birds and other animals, with the largest element a 4th-c BC frieze with a calendar theme; at the corners are richly cut classical caps. The s side shows mainly architectural fragments, including decorated metopes and triglyphs, and a 12th-c Byz relief of an eagle with a hare. The E end has inscriptions and classical stelae sanctified with added recut crosses, and further Byz animal reliefs. The N side has more antique stelae with vases and shields and some relief figures. No other church in Greece can offer you anything approaching such quantity or variety of spolia.

The **church of the Kapnikarea** * (central in Odos Ermou), probably named after its founder, had two phases of building. The core is a simple inscribed cross, four-column, triple-apse church, and must date from the later 11th C, probably 1060–70; the proportions are not completely normal, the bema being longer than the bay to the W of the cupola, and having a second short barrel vault. To this was added (probably in the 12th C, or even slightly later) a substantial exonarthex, with three pitched roofs, and a parekklision dedicated to St Barbara adjoining it to the N, with its own cupola built up against the N gable. The E exterior clearly shows the two periods, with masonry and windows all contrasting. Inside the caps are as usual reused, but the modern marble templon and carved flanking icon frames are good modern reproductions of med originals such as those at the *Porta Panagia*. Most of the paintings are by the modern artist Kontoglou, whose signature, with the date of 1955, you can see in the N gable. The proportions of the bema area emphasize the unusual depth and height of the sanctuary.

The construction of the present **church of Ag Theodoroi** * (corner of Plateia Klathmonos) has been dated to c. 1070 by a metrical inscription which you can see built into its W exterior gable. It is built on a three-aisled single dome, triple-apse plan with quite a large narthex, and the only alteration is probably the belfry extending the S gable upwards. Note how under the Athens grime the severity of the exterior walls is relieved by courses of dog-tooth brick ornament

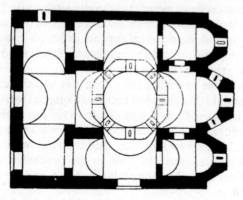

Ag Theodoroi

and other brick patterns round the arcaded windows, as well as by
decorated terracotta bricks with moulded designs. The dome has a
tall drum, also decoratively treated; in open country this would be
an unusually attractive exterior. Inside, the 19th-c paintings are
grimy, but the space under the dome is retained under the N and S
vaults by their height, and the entrance from the narthex is also wide
and high; this may have been a solution reached through supporting
the cupola on wall sections and piers rather than columns. As often
in the Byz churches of modern cities it is the exterior which offers
most of interest here.

Somehow the urban sprawl of N Athens has, so far, been prevented
from engulfing the charming small 11th-c church dedicated to St
George, but now called **Omorphokklisia** * ('Beautiful church').
Originally in open country, and still unencumbered, it now faces the
twin hills of Tourkovounia (not far from the new Olympic Stadium)
across a dual carriageway avenue. (It is disused and normally
locked.) The building began as an inscribed cross, single apse
church with the dome supported by four piers; it is built in cloisonné
masonry with restrained dog-tooth brick courses round windows,
and with small carved marble fragments in the E end. Its main
architectural interest lies in the chapel that was at some point built
on to the S side; this gave it a second apse. From its external masonry
one would think that this was not later than the 12th c, but its
internal construction makes use of two rib vaults – said to be the
only example in Attika, and (with buildings such as those at
Andravida and *Khalkida*) among the very few surviving in Greece;
this has been taken to mean that the chapel must be 13th c, due to
the builder's apparent knowledge of Western systems, but a recent
opinion is that all the masonry appears to be too homogeneous for
this. Only the narthex, which is probably 16th c, is now thought to
be later than the mid-12th c.
    If you are able to obtain entry, you will find the interior is in a
rather poor state of repair, but there is an original masonry templon
and some frescoes; these are mostly from the late 13th/early 14th c
and although not in good condition show some lively scenes which
include the Entry into Jerusalem and the Annunciation to Anna,
with the Koimisis on the W wall; in the parekklision there is an
unusual fresco of the Mission of the Apostles, and the Last Supper.

Be sure to make time to visit the **Monastery of Kaiseriani** **
(museum opening hours), on the E fringe of modern Athens below

Mount Hymettos; it is usually (and with reason, if *Dafni* is excepted) taken to be the most attractive and picturesque ecclesiastical ensemble in Athens. Of the monastic buildings, which include the trapeza, kitchen and bath, the katholikon is certainly the oldest.

You enter the courtyard by the w doorway, and immediately on your left is the kitchen, opening to the N into the trapeza, which runs right across the width of the courtyard. There is evidence of alterations inside, particularly in the window openings and blind wall-arches; their slightly pointed profile has been used to date the present interior to the 13th c on the basis of Frankish influence; this could be true, although it could well be later than this. A feature of Kaiseriani is the frequent use of classical spolia, such as the fine carved marble lintel here.

The katholikon was founded in the later 11th c, and dedicated to the Entry of the Virgin [into the Temple]. It is a centrally planned, domed, triple-apse, four-column design, with quite a narrow dome and broad lateral barrel vaults to N and S, and with the less common feature of two openings leading from the main apse area to the lateral apses, which are almost as broad; its construction is good but not exceptional for the period, with the cloisonné most in evidence in the faceted apses. The domed narthex is later, probably 15th c; the barrel-vaulted parekklision on the N side, dedicated to St Anthony, for no evident reason is usually given a date in the Frankish period. There seems to be no need to involve the Franks, and it is probably later than the narthex. The impressive sculpture enclosed in the templon comes from an earlier building (see below); the frescos are all quite late, those in the narthex being of the late 17th c, and those in naos and apse of the 18th.

One of the delights of Kaiseriani is the range of domestic buildings along the s side of the enclosure; Greece can offer little else of this period and authenticity. Nearest to the katholikon is what seems to have been the domed structure of a rare monastic bath, with a hypocaust now exposed, and nearby a mill for olive oil. Above and to the w are cells for monks, some with the same slightly pointed profile to their arches as found in the trapeza. Whatever their date, they are certainly earlier than what you can now see at e.g. *Megara* or *Osios Meletios*.

Finally, do not leave this site without taking the five-minute walk due w from outside the entrance. The path leads to the unenclosed and substantial ruins of quite a large three-aisled basilica, probably of the 10th c; excavations in 1958 showed that it replaced a 6th-c basilica. It must have been from this that the templon sculpture was

taken down to the 11th-c katholikon when it was built and enclosed
for greater protection. You can see considerable classical spolia
embedded in its walls. The barrel-vaulted parekklision built to the N
and dedicated to St Mark is hard to explain (Western monks are said
to have been responsible), but it could be 13th c; the hall-chapel to
the SE is 19th c. You may feel that this interesting and peaceful
corner could be a logical starting-point for visiting the main monastery below.

ATHOS, 'THE HOLY MOUNTAIN' Αθως, Αγιο Οϱος   Agio Oros / Khalkidiki

Monasteries; architecture and art ***. Restricted entry; stay at least
4 days, and if possible longer.

The autonomous community of monasteries which still flourishes on
this beautiful peninsula has been the subject of countless books and
other studies; its importance and interest lie in its unique status as a
historic stronghold of the Orthodox monastic tradition, particularly
since the fall of Greece to the Turks. As it is well known that travel
on the peninsula is prohibited to all women, and to any male visitor
not equipped with a permit, what follows here will only attempt to
summarize some of the main features of Byz and med interest on
Athos. Those intending to make a serious visit will no doubt follow
their own line of reading.
    The med history of Athos can be said to open in 963 when the
monastery now known as the Great Lavra was founded by the
Emperor Nikiforos Focas. Its first abbot was Athanasios, a monk
who came from Trebizond, and who was known to the emperor; he
assembled in this monastery a number of hermits and anchorites
who already lived on Athos, and imposed monastic rule there.
Successive emperors continued the tradition of benefactions, maintaining a direct interest in the affairs of what came to be called 'The
Holy Mountain', and its monasteries and influence multiplied. The
invasions following the Fourth Crusade did not do great harm until
the early 14th c, when, after the murder of Roger de Flor, the
Catalan Company invaded the peninsula and plundered most of the
monasteries. As part of the process of restoration and reconstruction that followed this invasion of 1307–9, the Emperor Andronikos
II (who throughout his long reign was a fervent protector of the
community) issued a chrysobull in 1312 in which he transferred to
the Ecumenical Patriarch all authority for the whole community of

what was now an important group of monasteries. This remains the most important feature in the history of Athos, surviving to this day as a central aspect of its government. Even after the Turkish conquest the community retained its independence, managing to keep on good terms with the sultans; successive later treaties and agreements have all respected and retained this feature.

There are now 20 monasteries, almost all of which maintain subsidiary dependencies, mostly called *skitis*; of the 20 one is Russian (Russikon), one is Serbian (Khilandari), one is Bulgarian (Zografou) and the rest are Greek. Although there is now a rough road across the peninsula, and some monasteries have a telephone and a few even electricity, there are aspects of Mount Athos and the life lived there which must have changed less in the millennium of its existence than virtually any other inhabited area in Europe.

Normally arrival is by sea at the port of Dafni, from which a bus runs to Karyes, where registration takes place. Thereafter there is no particular route or sequence of monasteries to follow; travel between all the monasteries is on foot by tracks and footpaths (except from Karyes to Iviron, which can be reached by the bus) or occasionally by boat. The monasteries selected for mention here include all those which contain surviving features of Byz or med interest, but the visitor expecting an undeveloped medieval monastic setting will be disappointed by the lateness of most of the buildings and art that he will see; the frequency of fires, and the great expansion in numbers in later centuries (the 1862 census gives 7432 monks in residence) are the chief reasons for this, as both prompted new building. The sequence of monasteries on which entries are given here is that of the order of precedence established in the 16th c, and which is embodied in the Greek Constitution of 1927.

In **Karyes** (Καρυές), the capital of the peninsula in that it is where the governing Council sits, the earliest building is in fact the substantial defensive tower; although it is now largely engulfed by the 19th-c buildings of the governing Council, and possibly slightly reduced in height, it is still a good example of this type. The chief church, known as the **Protaton**, is the only, but major, artistic attraction. While the first building here would have been 10th c, what you see today is 14th c, and results from the rebuilding after the Catalan raids of 1307–9. Its form is a simple but impressive basilica with a high central nave, two broad and lower side aisles, three external apses (the central one very large) and a wide narthex;

there is a chapel attached to the N side. (The use of a basilical plan, without a dome, for what is, in effect, a metropolitan church clearly follows the form of comparable churches at e.g. *Serres* and *Kalabaka*.) Much of its fresco decoration is, with the exception of some 12th-c fragments in Vatopedi, the earliest on Athos, and although without any date or inscription, these paintings are attributed to the legendary painter Panselinos and his school; his name (meaning 'brighter than the moon') does not occur before the 18th c, but a body of opinion now accepts him as the author of these, and the paintings here must in any case be the work of a leading artist of the Palaiologue period.

The paintings can be dated to the early 14th c, are mostly in good condition and are mercifully free of later overpainting; their style is quite close to that of the frescos in the *parekklision of Ag Euthymios in Ag Dimitrios, Thessaloniki*. The church is well lit, with two tiers of windows in the side aisles, and a third tier in the top storey of the nave. The frescos include most of the scenes of the Dodecaorton, with further subjects from the life of the Virgin; note particularly the lively scenes of her birth, and of her presentation in the temple, with a full and rich painting of the Koimisis on the w wall. There are fine standing figures of bishops in the apse and of warrior saints towards the w end of the nave. Although the energy and vivacity of this style is largely a new feature in Byzantine art of this period, as are also the extended figural proportions, the basic iconography of most of the subjects is not significantly changed.

You may not be able to see the few 12th- to 14th-c icons, usually kept in the apse, but you should note the finely carved marble icon frames fixed to the piers either side of the later templon, which are comparable to those in the *Mitropolis, Mystra*.

The **monastery of the Great Lavra** takes the first position among the monasteries of Athos, (*lavra* means cell or cloister) in that its foundation in *c.* 963 and completion in 1004 makes it the earliest, and it houses the tomb of the first abbot and *protos*, St Athanasios. Due largely to the fact that it is the only monastery not to have had a major fire, both its architecture and some of its painting are also outstanding among the Athonite monasteries. The layout of the monastic buildings here is quite characteristic of the plan that was adopted in other monasteries, and is not unlike (although on a larger scale than) mainland monasteries such as *Sagmata* and *Osios Meletios*; only the fortifications are more prominent, with a fine tower possibly dating from the late 10th-c foundation.

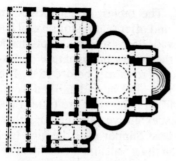

Great Lavra: Katholikon

The centre of the whole complex is formed by the katholikon; as this was the earliest such building on Athos it became the model for many later ones. The form is quite austere on the exterior, with a central core of a basic cross-in-square, but with the N and S arms extended by apses; the central dome, supported by four piers, is prominent, and has eight quite large windows. The liturgical needs of the katholikon were served by a particular interior layout with the W arm of the central cross broadened and extended to form a reasonably large open area. It was from this that the major later additions to the core of the naos are entered: two chapels built to N and S, both on an inscribed cross plan, with single dome and apse. These detract to some extent from the otherwise quite simple design; the W façades are joined by a long and rather tasteless 19th-C exonarthex.

An inscription here means that we know that the frescos of the katholikon were completed by the famous painter Theophanes of Crete in 1535 (he had earlier been at work in the *monastery of Ag Nikolaos Anapavsas, Meteora*). The style is a powerful one, with strong highlights and a dramatic sense of movement, and shows knowledge of the engravings of the Italian Marcantonio Raimondi; the distribution of subjects is quite conventional for an interior of this date.

The fountain immediately outside this typically incorporates some fine 10th/11th-C Byz carved reliefs, but is a 17th-C creation, with paintings of that date.

The trapeza (its entrance here, as usual, opposite the katholikon) is also particularly impressive; it is both the earliest and the largest on Athos and became the model for others. It is cruciform in plan, with the abbot occupying the high table in the extended apsidal W end; it has a pitched wooden roof with exposed beams, and was repaired in 1512. The tables are all formed from single shaped sheets of marble, and offer seating for several hundred monks. The paintings on the walls here are also exceptional for their extent and good condition; they carry no signature and were once dated to 1512, but now usually to shortly before 1535. They are attributed to Theophanes of Crete after he had finished painting in *Meteora* and before the katholikon here; they are (after those of the *Protaton*) some of the earliest extensive paintings on Athos. Note particularly the scene of the Last Supper over the high table, the spectacular Last Judgement on the E wall and the death of St Athanasios on the N wall. These are good examples of the so-called Cretan style which painters from that island brought to a number of monasteries in the 16th c.

As in almost all other Athonite monasteries, the only pre-conquest Byz art takes the form of portable objects – chiefly icons, reliquaries and manuscripts. In the monastery's small museum is a rare and fine miniature mosaic icon of St John Theologos of the late 13th to early 14th c, set in a particularly rich silver-gilt filigree frame with ten Byz enamel roundels; a silver-gilt reliquary of the true cross attributed to the period of Nikiforos Focas; a silver-gilt book-cover with enamels of two periods, numerous gems and a large figure of Christ in repoussé; and 12th-c icons of St George and St Panteleimon, with numerous later ones. In contrast, the library here is not as rich in illuminated MSS as some other monasteries.

After the monastery of the Great Lavra, one of the largest on Athos is the **monastery of Vatopedi**. It too was founded in the late 10th c, as although it is not mentioned in the first typikon of 972, its abbot was a co-signatory of an Act of 985; by 1072, when the second typikon was written, it was given as the second in the entire hierarchy, where it still is today.

The katholikon, dedicated to the Annunciation of the Virgin, was built on the same 'Athonite' plan as that of the Great Lavra, with its substantial W development; the exonarthex and the free-standing bell-tower are both later, dating from the first half of the 15th c. The two main doors are each covered by 44 bronze plates with a rather mechanical incised design which includes a representation of the Annunciation, and are said to come from *Ag Sofia, Thessaloniki*, and to be also of this date. (The chapels added to N and S of the exonarthex are both 18th c.) While the frescos of the katholikon date from 1312 they were largely overpainted in the 18th and 19th c and are covered in soot. Vatopedi does, however, possess the only monumental mosaics on Athos that are still in their original site; you will find them in two parts of the katholikon: one is above the two E columns supporting the cupola, with the Virgin Annunciate on the right and Gabriel on the left; they appear to be early 11th C, but are not in good condition and are very sooty. The second is over the door of the narthex, and consists of a 'Deesis' composition: the enthroned Christ between the standing Virgin and John the Baptist – this is probably 12th C. An inscription gives the information that it was installed by the Abbot Ioannikios of Vatopedi to replace an earlier damaged mosaic. Just below this is another version of the Annunciation, with the two figures on separate mosaic panels either side of the doorway; although icons are fixed over their lower part, these are clearly Palaiologue art of the 14th C, and have undergone some quite heavy restoration. It is scarcely possible that these are more than isolated donations.

Vatopedi has traditionally been one of the richest monasteries on Athos, and you will find that its funds have been used for many later buildings; there are, for instance, over 15 chapels distributed round the monastery complex. Its wealth is also attested to by the many works of art here, and you may be able to see some of these in the katholikon, where they are housed in glazed cases in the main apse. Among the monastery's many treasures are two 14th-C miniature mosaic icons with contemporary repoussé silver frames; they represent the crucifixion and a standing figure of St Anne holding the infant Virgin, and (although grimy) are certainly outstanding; among the treasures of Athos these small but delicate works must rank highly. There are also several other pre-conquest icons including a two-sided icon in one side of which a small steatite image of the Virgin is mounted, a very good steatite icon of St George and three which have quite fine 14th-C decorative silver revetments.

In the library here you may be shown two fresco fragments which probably formed part of the original decoration of the trapeza, painted in 1197–8. One is of the heads of ss Peter and Paul, and the other is the bust of an apostle; their style is heavily linear, and their interest, due to their rarity here, and date, is academic rather than aesthetic. The outstanding MSS here are an illuminated 12th-C Octateuch and a psalter of the same date. The large refectory now only has late paintings, but the 30 fine carved marble tables are original.

The **monastery of Iviron** was founded only just after Vatopedi, and is third in precedence. It acquired its name through its original association with Georgian (Iberian) monks; in 1357 it was taken over by Greek monks, who have since remained in control, although there were still Georgians here until the 1950s. Its site is one of the least hilly and more spacious of all the major monasteries, allowing a substantial open area all round the katholikon. This is dedicated to the Koimisis tis Theotokou, and takes a fairly standard Athonite form; it was built in the 11th c, and rebuilt in 1513. With the exception of the marble opus sectile floor, almost all the interior is late – the frescos were mostly last repainted in the 19th c. The most famous icon here is of the Panagia Portaitissa, and is in a chapel on the left of the entrance gate; the heads of the Virgin and Child, visible beneath a massive gilt revetment, are of high quality and in good condition, and could well be 12th c.

The treasury displays a substantial collection of objects in precious metal, although most of them are relatively late. By far the most interesting material from the Byz period is in the library, a relatively recent free-standing building; among the famous illustrated MSS here is the 13th-c Gospel Book, Cod. 5, with 37 superb illuminations, the 10th-c Homilies of Gregory, Cod. 27, and the 12th/13th-c History of Barlaam and Joasaph, Cod. 463, with its 79 brilliant and inventive narrative illuminations. If you are able to see even a page of any of these your visit will have been well rewarded.

Just standing in the courtyard here you can see something of the past that most Athonite monasteries share: the older tower to the SE, although in rather decrepit state, still has all the features of such defences and is certainly the earliest building in the complex, while the arcading of the exonarthex of the 18th/19th c has some fine earlier Iznik plates set in it.

Fourth in precedence on Athos is the **monastery of Khilandari** (or alternatively Chelandar), occupied by Serbian monks. Of the 'non-Greek' monasteries it is perhaps the most worth visiting; although it has suffered from the usual Athonite hazards of fire (the worst were in 1792 and 1891) and the repainting of its frescos (in 1803–4) the connection with rich and powerful Serbian rulers such as Milutin (1282–1321) and Stephen IV Dušan (1331–55) means that it had an unusually prosperous medieval history.

The design of the katholikon, dedicated to the Presentation of the Theotokos, probably represents an early attempt by the builders of the relatively parvenu Serbian kingdom, under Milutin, to assimilate something of the complexity and richness of Palaiologue building in Thessaloniki and CP. Built in the first years of the 14th c, its plan follows the general Athonite model (although without the w chapels), but the indulgence in rich textures of brick and stone is a feature that was developed to an even greater extent in later Serbian building. As it is, you can experience in the exterior of the exonarthex, added 1372–89, something of the inventiveness of the masons which you would otherwise have to visit modern Yugoslavia to see (e.g. Gračanica, Ravanica): the analogy with embroidery is apt – herring-bone and cross-stitch patterns in brick, and other patterns carved in marble, fill every niche and bay.

The frescos of the interior were originally painted in 1319–20, but were overpainted in 1803–4; try to look at them in good light, as something of the nobility of the original scheme (which would be contemporary with those of the *Protaton*) can still be seen in places. Fixed to the sw pier of the naos is the most famous icon of the monastery, that of the Panagia Trikherousa ('Virgin with three hands'), to which a considerable legend is attached. It is a mid-14th-c icon, and what can be seen of it through the massive revetment, coins, etc. shows it to be a finely painted variant of the Hodegetria type, and in good condition.

Of the other monastic buildings the trapeza (opposite the w door of the katholikon) is the most notable; it is a long, rectangular room, and is not cruciform, but has two apses in the short N and s sides. The main fresco decoration is of 1623, but recently some fragments of 14th-c fresco have been found over the N apse (above the high table) depicting scenes such as the Hospitality of Abraham and the Sacrifice of Isaac.

Another reason for visiting Khilandari is the small museum in the rooms above the library where there is a display of its unusually good collection of portable works. The MSS here are less spectacular than at Iviron, but there is a fine range of 12th- to 15th-c icons, including a mosaic icon of the Virgin Hodegetria, besides many later ones, some engraved hardstones, and a remarkable 13th-c wooden diptych with what would seem to be Venetian gold filigree mounts and framing for 24 small scenes painted on vellum.

The **monastery of Dionysiou** has a spectacular site on a spur of cliff above the sea. It is fifth in precedence, being first built in the second half of the 14th c; it enjoyed considerable benefactions, notably from the Emperor Alexios III Komnenos of Trebizond, whose chrysobull of 1374 (a vellum scroll about 3 m long) is still held by the monastery. The cramped nature of the buildings on their confined site no doubt contributed to the inevitable major fire in 1535, and the present katholikon (dedicated to St John the Baptist) dates from just after this event. It takes a standard Athonite form, and its frescos of 1547 have not suffered major repainting; they are the work of a Cretan painter, Zorzis, and reflect the style of a generation later than Theophanes. The paintings in the narthex are later.

One of the most interesting areas of painting in Dionysiou is adjacent to the trapeza, where it has been shown that the cycle of scenes from the Revelation was based on German prints; the 21 prints themselves were first published in 1523 in Basle, after designs of Hans Holbein, and a set found its way to Athos later in the 16th c.

The sacristy is particularly rich in precious objects; a 10th-c ivory relief of the crucifixion, a substantial quantity of vestments and other embroidery, including a 16th-c epitaphios, and (besides many other relics) a uniquely impressive silver-gilt reliquary in the form of a five-domed church; it is dated to 1515 and contains the remains of St Niphon, a former patriarch of CP who retired to Dionysiou before his death in the early 16th c. The library here, too, is unusually rich in illuminated MSS and is housed on the top floor of a new wing.

Of the other 15 monasteries on Athos, the following could be mentioned as each containing some works of pre-conquest Byz art of particular interest; while all will have numerous later icons and MSS, as well as later wall paintings, the items mentioned here could all be regarded as exceptional, and so of the standard found in any major museum.

At **Xeropotamou**, the eight monastery in order of precedence, there is a remarkable work in carved steatite; it is the so-called paten of Pulcheria, although it is in fact of 14th-c date. Its form is a circular plate (diam. 16 cm) carved with a design of figures in concentric circles; the theme is that of the incarnation related to the celebration of the liturgy. The central roundel is occupied by the figure of the Virgin, which gives it its other name of a Panagiarion. Steatite is a delicate material, and it is very rare to find pieces of this quality and date in such good condition; this must be regarded as one of the outstanding treasures of Athos. On the NW corner of the narthex of the katholikon of the same monastery you will also see an unusual 14th-c relief carving in green marble of St Dimitrios; it is in a later marble frame, but Athos does not offer any other examples of this kind of work outside.

The 15th monastery in precedence is that of **Stavronikita**, and this again has a fine medieval tower complete with its castellation. It is the only other monastery after the *Great Lavra* to boast paintings by the famous artist Theophanes of Crete, who completed the frescos in the katholikon in 1546, helped by his son Symeon; they are unfortunately severely overpainted. However, the katholikon also holds an unusual mosaic icon of a bust portrait of St Nikolaos; it is some 50 cm high, is of 14th-c date, and is fixed to a column on the N of the naos. Unlike miniature mosaic icons the tesserae are of the size used in monumental mosaics. It is an impressive work, and it is worth knowing that it is also referred to as 'Ag Nikolaos Streidas', due to a lenged that an oyster or shellfish attached itself to the forehead of the image while it was in the sea; the chief damage to the icon is in this area, but it does not detract unduly from the whole.

Mosaic icons of a different character are also the chief artistic treasure of the **monastery of Xenophontos** (16th in precedence). There are two of these, representing full-length figures of St George and St Dimitrios, and they are just 1.4 m high. They are probably 12th c, but as the tesserae are mounted in mortar it is most likely that they have been removed from an iconostasis, and therefore should be seen more as examples of monumental art. They are also interesting images in that they depict the saints with the pose and gestures of figures in prayer, and in each case a small half-length figure of Christ occupies an upper corner. In the katholikon here the frescos of the narthex, dated 1563, are by a monk called Theophanes, but he is *not* Theophanes of Crete.

Esphigmenou, the 18th monastery in precedence, possesses one of the finer miniature mosaic icons of Athos; it is of Christ Pentocrator seen in full length, and is 14th c in date. The frame of silver repoussé may well be contemporary, although slightly damaged; the image itself is in quite good condition.

In general it is wise to leave exaggerated expectations behind for a single visit to Athos, and be prepared to return several times before gaining access to any particular site or object; building up experience of this unique institution and how to use it is a lengthy process.

BEAUFORT CASTLE
See **Mani**, **Stoupa**

BEAUVOIR CASTLE
See **Katakolo**

BODONITSA CASTLE
See **Mendenitsa**

CORINTH　Κόρινθος　Korinthia. Med Chorynte, Coranto, Coranzo
Museum *. Easy access from road up to Acrocorinth.

The city of Corinth was continuously occupied during the Middle Ages, and for much of the period was of real importance. This was due partly to its position close to the isthmus (one of Justinian's most substantial contributions to the defence of mainland Greece was his rebuilding of the Hexamilion wall across the isthmus in the 6th c), partly to its commercial success as a port and a manufacturing centre of pottery and silk, and partly to its early ecclesiastical status. In the 12th c the Bishop of Corinth ranked higher (at 27th) among the bishops of the Orthodox world than that of Athens. In 1305 the isthmus was the scene of a huge tournament where a thousand knights and barons, summoned from all over Greece and the islands by Philip of Savoy, the prince of Akhaia, jousted for 20 days.

　　Although it is known that in 1309 the city had commercial buildings as well as a cathedral church of St Paul and a hospital of St Samson, nothing of this survives except where excavations have revealed modest traces of medieval building. It is only in the **Archaeological Museum**, that some Byz and med material can be seen, although its collection is mainly of classical interest. There is a case of Byz and imported pottery of 11th and 12th c, a number of Byz bronze items and a lead seal of Pope Innocent ɪv (1243–54). The two rarest exhibits are a Justinianic relief taken from the Hexamilion wall, inscribed with a prayer to protect the emperor, and a seal in fine condition of William, a Grand Master of the Hospitallers, which must be a relic of their tenure of Acrocorinth in 1400–4. (See also *Lekhaio*.)

DAFNI　Δαφνί　Athens/Attika
Monastery: katholikon and mosaics ***. Easy access by bus/car; museum hours.

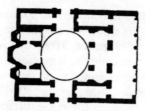

Monastery of the Koimisis: Katholikon

The peace of this beautiful site has now been largely lost to the new Athens-Corinth Highway which passes close by, but the buildings themselves with the famous mosaics are well maintained as a museum. Originally a 6th-c foundation, almost all that you see now of the **monastery of the Koimisis tis Theotokou** comes from the Byz rebuilding of *c.* 1080. In 1204 it formed part of the area of Attika awarded to Othon de la Roche, the new Lord of Athens. In 1207 Cistercian monks from Bellevaux were installed, and were the last group to leave Greece, staying here through the various changes of local rule until 1458. Burgundian dukes were buried here, including the last, Walter de Brienne, in 1311.

The design of the church is immediately impressive but simple – the great drum of the cupola is at once visible above the high surrounding wall. You arrive in the courtyard of the monastery; the range of low buildings along two sides contains monks' cells and is probably post 11th c. The stone sarcophagus that you will see has faint Gothic designs cut in it, suggesting that it was for one of the dukes of Athens, possibly Walter de Brienne. Certainly by Western builders – perhaps the Cistercian monks themselves – is the remaining arcading of a porch built on to the narthex in the early 14th c; the pointed arches strike a foreign note here. Before entering the katholikon you might care to walk round to the w and N area of the monastic enclosure where there are still some remains of the 6th-c buildings. You can also take in the superb faceted apses with their range of tall, arcaded windows offset by brick against the perfectly regulated cloisonné.

Entering the katholikon by the s door, the chief glory of Dafni, its mosaics, will immediately impress, but it is worth first looking at the architectural context so perfectly integrated with them. Although essentially a simplification of the same design as *Osios Loukas*, from the beginning of the century, with the wide cupola carried on an octagon formed by the squinches and supporting vaults, its elegance is emphasized by having no gallery and by the great height at which the squinches and vaults are set. To recapture its original appearance you should also imagine the bare masonry of the walls clad in sheets of marble, split and joined to produce symmetrical patterns.

To look at the mosaics, you may find it preferable to start in the narthex; this could be used for non-liturgical activities, and the mosaic style here is at its most free, with lucid narrative effects. The s bay has subjects relating to the Virgin's life; particularly colourful are those concerned with Joachim and Anna, the Virgin's parents, and of their bringing their three-year-old daughter to the temple. In the N bay are three scenes from the Passion not in the Dodecaorton – the Washing of the Disciples' Feet, the Betrayal and the Last Supper.

Returning to the naos, you can start by standing immediately beneath the dome. These mosaics are (with those of *Osios Loukas, Stiris* and the Nea Moni, on Chios) one of three finest examples of the middle Byz mosaic system that survive; this is the only example of them where, conforming to the concept of the church building as an architectural allegory of the Christian universe, the dome still retains its mosaic of Christ Pantocrator, whose powerful gaze meets the visitor's as he looks up into the cupola. The perfect integration of the building with its mosaics is demonstrated here, with the 16 prophets foretelling the incarnation occupying the spaces between the 16 windows round the drum of the cupola. Next in order of sanctity were the conch of the apse and the squinches supporting the dome, and these hold images of the Virgin and Child (now largely lost) and (in the squinches) some of the Dodecaorton – the Annunciation, Nativity, Baptism and Transfiguration.

You can see here how skilful use is made of the concave form of the squinch by the mosaicists: the angel talks to the Virgin across the real space of the squinch, and the cave of the nativity recedes behind the manger and the animals. Adjacent to the dome in the N and s arms of the katholikon are other of the main feasts (Birth of the Virgin, Adoration, Presentation, Raising of Lazarus, Crucifixion and Anastasis). Below these, as of lesser importance, and occupying niches and the soffits of the arches, you will see individual saints and Old Testament figures portrayed – note particularly the fine images of Aaron and Zacharias and the martyr saint, Akindynos.

In general, the style of the mosaics at Dafni, with a relatively colourful and mellifluous approach to the figure and its drapery, corresponds to the more 'Hellenistic' stream of Byz art, and contrasts in this respect with those of *Osios Loukas*, which are more severe and have a less decorative emphasis. The mosaics of Dafni remain one of the great masterpieces of Byz art.

The attitude of the Western occupants to the church and its mosaics shows some ambivalence; while the Burgundian dukes appear to have had a genuine respect for the peace and beauty of Dafni, and the Cistercians must have tolerated the rich mosaics in spite of the austerity of their rule, the restoration of the mosaics earlier this century apparently revealed Frankish lance-heads embedded in the mosaic of the Pantocrator – hardly a symptom of respect.

DESFINA Δεσφίνα Fokida
Church with frescos *

In the s foothills of Mount Parnassos, near the highest point in this small town, the grounds of the large and recent church of Ag Kharalambos contain the diminutive 14th-c **church of the Taxiarch**; it is a simple, barrel-vaulted hall some 7 m long, with a modest level of workmanship in the masonry, and some brick dog-tooth ornament round the door. Inside the frescos are in a no more than adequate state, but are still quite readable, and they are of interest in that they are dated to 1332 by an inscription over the entrance door. There are scenes from the Dodecaorton in the vault, the mandylion is over the apse, and an impressive Crucifixion over the entrance door shows some influence of the mosaic in *Osios Loukas*. The church is charming rather than impressive, but is of some interest on account of its rare and authentic inscription.

DROSOPIGI Δροσοπηγή (formerly Voulgarelli). Arta
Church and some frescos *. On left of road from Arta NE into the Pindos range, some 9 km short of Drosopigi; easy access.

The striking exterior decoration of the **Kokkino Ekklisia** ('Red Church'), dedicated to the Panagia, suggests a wealthy founder, and it was in fact even more imposing until 1980, when the cupolas over the naos and narthex collapsed. It is built on quite a simple plan of an inscribed cross with three apses and with the erstwhile cupola supported by two piers and extended sections of wall projecting from the bema. The interior, which must have been equally impressive, now has few of its frescos left, but a long inscription over the w door gives the founder as the Protostrator Theodore Tzimiskes, his brother John, and their wives Maria and Anna, and a date of 1281; Theodore must have been a general of the Despot of Arta at this time. The narthex is contemporary with the rest of the church, and there still remains on its E wall part of the fresco showing one of the *ktitoroi* with a model of the church. While the interior is of interest, it will be the exterior with its broad band of ceramic tile decoration and rich brick patterns round the windows which will remain in the mind after a visit here.

EDESSA   Εδεσσα   Pela
Church and sculpture *. Easy access on foot.

The position of this attractive hill-top town on the Via Egnatia meant that it was always strategically important. While the bridge carrying the Via Egnatia at the N of the town may be of Byz date, the **church of the Koimisis tis Panagias**, adjacent to the offices of the archbishop, is the chief survival from the Byz period. It was the old Mitropolis church, which accounts for its form of a three-aisled basilica, but is at present disused (key from the Archaeological Dept.). It is of medium size (some 20 m overall length, including a later w extension dating from the Turkish period) and the main structure is probably 12th c. It has three apses, the two side ones small and rounded, and the main one faceted externally and with two fine double-arched windows. The clerestory also has two double-arched windows on each side, and there is liberal use of brick courses in the masonry; you will see remains of what must have been an attractive external arcade built on to the s side. Inside, there are fragmentary remains of some 12th-c frescos, and a ruinous later iconostasis, but the most impressive feature of this church are four nave columns with fine double-zone caps; one on the s side is exceptionally impressive, with rams' heads and eagles in the upper zone. These, which are certainly 5th/6th c, must presumably come from a previous cathedral church, and, with the general setting, will well repay your visit here.

ELASSONA   Ελασσόνα   Larissa
Monastic church and frescos *. Easy access by foot/car.

Lying in the valley of the Elassonotikos, to the w of Kato Olympos, this town had little med importance, but was nevertheless chosen by the Emperor Andronikos II (1282–1328) as the site of an imperial foundation. Up a steep road to the acropolis just above the town the **church of the Panagia Olimpiotissa** survives of the monastery that he founded in the late 13th/early 14th c; the rest of the monastic buildings are all later, but the katholikon is in good condition.

As you enter the courtyard of the monastery you will be struck by the brilliantly varied bands of patterned brickwork lapping round the main apse; its exterior is the most striking feature of this building, of which the tall octagonal drum of the cupola rises over an inscribed cross plan. The main apse has a tall double-arched window, with further blind niches to either side displaying more virtuoso brick patterns; this is clearly closely related to *Ag Apostoloi, Thessaloniki*, but slightly less distinguished. The central bay is buttressed by broad lower aisles, so emphasizing the height of the cupola, and you will see when you enter that this has been made possible because the weight of the cupola is carried not on columns or vaults but on four substantial piers; there are only three columns, to N, S and W, and they have little weight to support. This internal arrangement leaves the narthex communicating more readily with the side aisles, so forming an ambulatory, than with the central bay, which on this account has a self-contained quality.

The w doors must be contemporary with the foundation, as they have an inscription dating them to either 1295 or 1305. The frescos must also originally have been of this date; their high quality can still be seen in some areas, but for large parts you will be looking at a good 17th-c repainting of the Palaiologue originals. The subjects depicted include a Virgin cycle and some of the Akathyst Hymn – one of the earliest extant versions of this theme. The caps have 14th-c carving, but of no great distinction: clearly the major decorative effort here went into the highly inventive exterior brickwork. A carved wooden polychrome door in the sw corner is dated 1640.

With its imperial associations, and its reminiscences of major buildings of the same period in Thessaloniki and Arta, this is a rewarding church to visit.

ELLINOEKKLISIA   Ελληνοεκκλησία   Samari, Messinia
Church, with sculpture and painting **. Some 7 km NW of
Androusa; easy access by car.

The **church of the Zöodokhos Pigi** is in an attractive rural setting, but
easily reached from the road. It is an impressive, medium-sized,
inscribed cross, single domed building with three faceted apses; it
has recently been sensitively restored. Built in the 12th c it has
remained almost unaltered; among its external features are the use
of massive marble blocks up to about 2 m, with high quality
cloisonné only used above this, a substantial porch adjoining the
narthex at the w (other examples have often been blocked up later),
an integral and contemporary chapel adjoining the N wall, and a
belfry built over the narthex, and given the form of a baldacchino.
So many belfries that can be seen on other 12th-c churches could
easily be either additions or replacements, but this one looks
completely original.

Inside, the most interesting feature is the carving of the marble
icon frames on the E piers, and it has been suggested that there was a
workshop in the vicinity for this kind of work, from which examples
were exported to *Mystra (Mitropolis)* and *Stiris (Osios Loukas)*.
There is also a masonry iconostasis, with carving and frescos, and a
considerable number of other frescos, although poorly preserved.
Of interest are those of the Passion subjects in the s vault, the
Ascension in the vault of the bema, and, in the apse below the
enthroned Virgin, an unusual symbolic image of the Eucharist, in
the form of the body of Christ lying as in the tomb.

FANARI   Φανάρι   Karditsa, Thessaly
Byz fortress **. 8 km NW of Karditsa; easy access by road.

Considering the scarcity of Byz military buildings that have not been
adapted or rebuilt, the **fortress** here must be one of the more
neglected of such sites in Greece. It is not mentioned by Prokopios
among the Thessalian forts restored by Justinian, but the masonry,
with some reuse of larger stones from earlier building, is certainly
Byz. On the borderland between Epiros and Thessaly, the area was
something of a no man's land, never fully under Frankish rule, but
always coveted by the rulers of Epiros. There was a form of Greek
control late in the 13th c, with Michael Gabrielopoulos, a local
archon, establishing his base here in 1295, and telling the local

populace that he would not let the Franks install a garrison. Although the area was part of the territory under the control of the dukes of Athens, in 1302 another Greek had been left in charge there as a marshal by Guy II de la Roche, and in that year there was an attempt at a coup to establish full Greek control from the despotate of Epiros; the fortress of Fanari was seized as part of this move, but full Greek possession was never achieved. Later in the 14th c it was to pass into the hands of John Orsini, despot of Arta.

The site is a hill-top one with spectacular views over the plain N to *Trikala* and SE to Karditsa. The main fortress area is an oval polygon, and this is enclosed by massive walls some 14 m high; you arrive at its S end, and it is here that the only traces survive of buildings outside the walls. The only gateway is at the N, but a breach in the wall at the E allows a scrambling entry if the modern gate is shut. Square towers flank the gate, and there are four others, one of which may be later, as it contains no brick and has a slight batter, not visible on the others. There is little left standing inside the enclosure of some 40 by 60 m; what may be the remains of a church building are embedded in the N wall and tower, and there is a massive rectangular cistern in roughly the centre of the enclosure. It may be the lack of sophistication or subtlety in its construction (at least as it now appears) that accounts for the apparent neglect by historians of this uncommon and genuine example of Byz military architecture.

FERES Φέρες Rodopi. Med Vira, Bera
Church and frescoes *. 30 km NE of Alexandropolis; easy access by car.

The **monastery of the Theotokos Kosmosoteira** ('Virgin, Saviour of the World') was founded by the Sebastocrator Isaac Komnenos in 1152, and his typikon for it still exists. The church is of an inscribed cross plan, with a large central dome on a twelve-sided drum and four smaller ones; from its size, relative complexity of design and richness of brickwork decoration it was clearly intended to be an impressive project (there are few other five-domed churches in Greece, outside Thessaloniki). The niches above the apse windows no doubt refer to current practice in CP. Its frescos, dating from its foundation, must also have been impressive, but were covered during the Turkish period and are not now in good condition. The figures of St Dimitrios and St Theodore suggest the grandeur that must once have been more evident, aided by fine carving on caps and cornice. The building in any case still retains exceptional status as a surviving substantial imperial foundation.

GALATISTA Γαλάτιστα Khalkidiki
Byz tower. 40 km SE of Thessaloniki; easy access from main road.

Just a stone's throw N of the main road through the village you will find a tower some 20 m high; its plan is some 13 by 10 m, and its most unusual feature is a series of deeply projecting pilasters (three on N and s sides, four on E and w). Its only entrance is some 5 m from ground level, and it seems never to have been attached to any larger structure. Built mainly of dressed stone, there is quite a lot of brick used, notably in the arch over the entrance. It doesn't fit into the pattern of Western med towers (such as at Ierissos, 80 km to E) and is most probably a Byz defensive or signalling tower of the 11th/12th c, linked to *Stagira*, although there is a lack of comparative material.

GARDENITSA
See **Mani**

GASTOUNI Γαστούνι Ilia
Church *. 5 km s of Andravida; easy access by bus/car.

The name is due to the Frankish baron Gastogne who built the 13th-c castle, of which there is now no trace. The **church of the Panagia Katholiko** is an earlier 12th-c building on a fairly conventional inscribed cross plan with two columns but only one apse. The exterior is the main attraction here, with unusually fine cloisonné masonry and rich and inventive brick patterns round the N and s windows, including distinctive wheel motifs either side of the apse. The interior is slightly unusual in that there is a single column placed centrally between the naos and the narthex, creating a more positive division than would otherwise be felt. Plentiful soot allows a few shadowy frescos to be seen only in the narthex, and there is an amusing later oil painting of events concerning the church under Turkish rule, during part of which it was a mosque.

GAVROLIMNI Γαυρολίμνη Etolia-Akarnania
Church *. 25 km w of Naupaktos. Access by car down rough track.

The **church of the Panagia Panaxiotissa** ('Virgin worthy of all') lies about 2 km to the N of the town; there is no obvious reason for its rural siting. It is a later 10th/11th-c church, with a large single dome over an inscribed cross plan with three externally curved apses. Its most striking characteristic is its exterior, where the impressive circular drum of the cupola is decorated with unusually bold brick and tile ornament.

Its interior has little of interest, but you will find that the remote rural surroundings increase the impact made by this quite sophisticated building and its imposing cupola.

GERAKI Γεράκι Lakonia
Castle, nine churches and paintings ***. Allow a clear half-day; one guard has keys for most of the churches.

This town, which has a very ancient history, was one of the smaller of the twelve Frankish baronies, being worth six knights' fees in 1205; it was awarded to Guy de Nivelet, whose task was to watch over the plains of Lakonia. It was held by the Franks for only a short time, as it was one of the four castles that had to be ceded to Michael VIII in 1262 as the price of Guillaume de Villehardouin's freedom; it

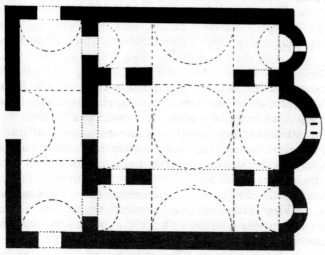

Gavrolimni: Panagia Panaxiotissa

thus became in effect a Greek outpost of *Mystra*, and was to remain in Greek hands until the mid-15th c.

The area today is divided into two distinct parts. There is the steep hill outside the modern town, now uninhabited, surmounted by the castle built by de Nivelet and with a number of buildings reaching down the hill from outside its walls; this will be dealt with first. (Access is fairly easy, with a rough road going up close to the ruins, then a steep track.) Then, on the neighbouring hill, there is the town itself, mostly of later building, with some churches in the country to the s. (Access is easy to all of them.)

The site of the Frankish **castle** is a fine one, not unlike that of *Mystra*, with steep cliffs protecting it from the s and e. The bailey is a polygon of some 60 by 80 m, and considerable amounts of the enceinte are still standing, some with its original castellation; the surviving sections indicate that there was a sentry-walk round the walls at the height of the castellation (as e.g. at *Passavas*). There are no towers or keep now, but a large, plastered cistern is still mainly intact against the se enceinte. The castle is said to have been built in emulation of that at Mystra, and if so it must have been started after *c*. 1254.

Easily the most prominent feature of the castle bailey is the **church of Ag Giorgios tou Kastrou**. Externally it appears to be an undistinguished, three-aisled basilica, with three rounded apses and quite a substantial narthex. Inside, however, it is clear that the building is the product of two distinct phases, with the s nave and narthex added to an existing double nave structure. This is emphasized by the supports for the barrel vaults, which are on one side a pier and on the other a column. Given the historical background of the site, it is most probable that the first phase was a basically Frankish building, probably forming the castle chapel, and so dating from the later 1250s, while the later phase would be from after 1262.

The interior has decoration of considerable interest, although not of the highest quality. The fresco decoration is only in fair condition, but is quite extensive, covering much of the two barrel vaults of the original nave, with a large crucifixion scene over the door, and scenes from the Dodecaorton in the vaults; as is very common in the area, the Virgin Platytera occupies the conch of the apse. There is a rather fine marble templon with a 10th-c Byz marble relief panel on one side, balanced by French decorative painting on the other, and with French caps and Byz paintings of Christ and Virgin Glykophilousa ('Sweetly embracing') in the upper part.

But the most interesting item of the interior is a large pierced marble shrine (or *proskynitarion* – neither term is quite satisfactory) against the N wall. Often said to be the tomb of Guy de Nivelet, although the chronology makes this uncertain, it is decorated with many different motifs. The central opening is framed by two pairs of knotted marble colonettes (a Byz theme) but you will find that the other pierced decoration is partly of abstract interlace designs, of Frankish or other inspiration – a fleur-de-lis and rosettes, a crescent and six stars, and even two Maltese crosses long before the Hospitallers arrived in Malta and made this their symbol. An armorial which may be that of de Nivelet can be seen at the top of the screen, and if so this may be the tomb of a member of the family. If these problems attract you, you should enjoy your visit here, and in any case the outlook from the castle is spectacular. (An armorial over the entrance door into the naos is apparently *not* that of the de Nivelet.)

Just below the castle wall to the w is the small **hall-church of Zöodokhos Pigi**. Oriented N–S, its N end is ruined but the remainder is roofed and in a fair state. It is notable for a carved Gothic doorway, which must be 13th C, and some 14th-C Byz frescos in fair condition; besides predictable subject-matter as in Ag Giorgios, there is beside the door a painting of Christ Elkomenos – probably a reflection of the icon that must have been in the church of that name in *Monemvasia*, p. 151.

You will see two other small, half-ruined hall-churches further down the slope, but the other most complete church is that of **Ag Paraskevi** at the foot of the path up to the Kastro. It is a small, domed, 14th-C inscribed cross design, with a masonry templon and most of its frescos still surviving. The most interesting is a group portrait of the founding family on the w wall.

The five churches mentioned below are readily accessible and are attractive examples of their period, with well-restored exteriors. All except the last two are within the area of the town, and collectively they present an unusually interesting range of middle Byz church architecture; their interest is also increased in some cases by well-restored interior paintings.

The first church that you will reach on entering the town from the direction of the castle, beside the road, is that of **Ag Athanasios**; it is a medium-sized, inscribed cross, single dome design. Its most notable feature is a liberal use of chunky spolia in the s and w façades; it has no later additions and no separate narthex. Inside, you will find that the dome is carried on four piers (no columns used) and the templon has been removed. There are the remains of some frescos, mainly in the bema, with interesting images of the Last Supper and the Presentation of the Virgin, with one of St Michael in Khonae in the s tympanum. The style of the frescos is 14th c and the church is often given this date; however, it could equally well be later 12th c, with the templon perhaps removed during the Latin occupation.

The **church of the Evangelistria** is the earliest in Geraki, being of the middle or early 12th c; it is quite a small (6.4 by 4.6 m) domed, single nave, inscribed cross design, with no columns or piers – the dome is supported by sections of wall. Again, chunky spolia is used liberally in the s wall, but not elsewhere; as in this case, and in *Ag Athanasios* and *Ag Ioannis Khrysostomos*, these are the most prominent external walls, it seems that the spolia were a point of which the builders were proud. The 12th-c frescos are some of the most interesting and better preserved in the town; note particularly the Pantocrator in the cupola and the Ascension in the vault of the bema, fine versions of the Nativity and Anastasis on the N wall with the deacon saints Euplos and Stephen on the painted masonry templon.

The small **church of Ag Ioannis Khrysostomos** is a simple, barrel-vaulted, single nave building of the 13th c. Its most noticeable external feature is four massive, squared marble slabs covered with an inscription; this is one of the surviving examples of the *Edictum Diocletianum* dating to 301 AD, which consists of a list of maximum prices to be applied throughout the empire; three of them form the jambs and lintel of the entrance door. (How easy life would be if prices could be fixed for ever just by carving them in marble!) The interior is a simple hall with early 14th-c frescos in good condition. There are fine images of ss Dimitrios, George, Nikolaos and Symeon Stylites, an unusual short series of portrait roundels of queens, and a complete cycle of the Dodecaorton with two Passion scenes inserted; on a small later fresco layer in a corner of the w wall is a portrait of the priest Kontoleon, who contributed renovations to the church in 1450.

Two further churches lie a short distance outside the town, in fields to the s. They are signed from the roadside, and can easily be reached on foot. The **church of Ag Sozon** is one of the larger churches of Geraki, comparable with *Ag Athanasios*; it is built on an inscribed cross plan, but is unusual for its date and size in having the dome supported by what are really pierced wall sections rather than piers. The upper walls are formed from good local stone with quite ambitious use of brick in the gables and cupola, and there is a lot of chunky spolia in the masonry of the lower walls. The frescos surviving inside are of less interest here; most are of later 12th/13th C, and some are in poor condition, but provide the date for the building; note particularly those of the reception of the Virgin into the Temple, and the Flight into Egypt on the N wall.

A short distance further on is the **church of Ag Nikolaos**; it has no dome, and is one of the three barrel-vaulted, double-nave churches in Geraki, although its plan is more that of a single nave with apse and bema to which is added a parekklision without either apse or bema. Its (badly damaged) frescos are later 13th C, after the return of the town to Byz control, and this is probably the date of the building. It retains a masonry templon, and the paintings which survive on this, of St Mary of Egypt and St Zosimos (quite a common subject in this location) and in the bema, are of unexpectedly good quality in such rural surroundings.

GLEZOU
See **Mani**

GLYKI Γλυκή Thesprotia
Ruins of church; unenclosed.

In the centre of this village in the valley of the Akherontas is a ruined 10th-C basilica; it still impresses as a substantial, three-aisled building with an atrium and narthex, totalling some 40 m overall length. It is known to have been the seat of a bishop, which accounts for its basilical form. Building is of local stone except where some classical blocks were used in the construction of the apse. The best of its caps are now displayed in the *Museum of Ioannina*, but you can find one here, with some other sculptural fragments. The setting is attractive.

While hardly warranting a special journey, you might feel that a visit here repays using the slower and more attractive inland road from or to Igoumenitsa.

IOANNINA Ιωάννινα Épiros

Castle, monasteries, museum **. All easily visited on foot.

The med importance of the city began with the establishment of the despotate of Epiros in 1204/5. Refugees from CP and the Morea settled here, and an archbishopric was created at the end of the 13th c. Michael I Dukas (1204–15) built the original castle, which remains the chief survival of the med period in the town itself. From 1348, with the Albanian despot in Arta, the Serbian Symeon Uroš ruled in Ioannina, and from 1355 was styled Emperor of the Greeks and Serbs in Thessaly and Epiros. This period imparted a Balkan flavour to Ioannina which it still to some extent retains. In 1412 it was in the hands of Carlo Tocco and shortly became again part of the reunited despotate of Epiros; from 1429, when it surrendered to Murad II (the father of Mehmed II) the town was under Turkish rule. (For the despotate of Epiros, see pp. 23–27).

The **castle**, built on a low promontory jutting out into the lake, has no natural defences except the water. Its defenders must always have relied on the massive walls, which are its chief surviving part; virtually all of what can now be seen, however, must date back only to the late 18th c, when they were virtually rebuilt by Ali Pasha. There would certainly have been some surviving buildings from the Byz period in the castle, but in 1618, in reprisal for a Christian revolt, all the churches there were completely destroyed. Although of Byz origins, this is really now a Turkish stronghold.

The most impressive Byz exhibits in the **Archaeological Museum** are a set of four fine 10th-c caps from the ruined basilica at *Glyki*. Other modest sculptural fragments are probably the only remains of the Byz buildings that could once be seen in the town, both inside and outside the castle. Part of the complex history of Ioannina is represented by a case of Byz and Venetian coins, and there is a group of later icons.

The chief survivals of Byz interest are all to be found on the **Island in the Lake of Ioannina** (frequent ferry boats leave from beside the castle for the 15-minute trip). They take the form of four monasteries, Stratigopoulos (or Nikolaos Dilios), Philanthropinon (or Nikolaos Spanos), Ag Panteleimon and Ag Ioannis Prodromos. The earliest is the **monastery of Stratigopoulos** which was founded in the 11th c. The church is a simple hall, with wooden roof and no dome. The exterior is largely untouched, with arcaded walls on both

N and S, large chunks of local limestone set in 'double cloisonné' and simple brick decoration round windows and zig-zag round the large apse. The interior has 16th/17th c frescos, which include a Last Judgement on the w wall, but these are in a poor state; the wooden iconostasis is late.

The **monastery of Philanthropinon** contains the richest and most varied fresco painting on the island. The exterior is very plain, and again there is no dome; the plan is basically simple – a long, barrel-vaulted hall, with a narthex and two parekklisia to N and S. Its great attraction is the large areas of varied and colourful frescos which cover all the walls and vaults; they contain no less than eleven inscriptions, making it one of the best documented Byz painted churches. The earliest of these is of *ktitoroi* which gives the information that the building was renovated in 1291–2; the original foundation must have been prior to this. Two more of 1560 are in the narthex and the N parekklision, and these establish the other main phase of renovation and painting. Three more of this period are unusual in that they include a record of the deaths of the artists who did the paintings, so suggesting that they were highly regarded.

You enter first the N parekklision, and you will find that the frescos here (all from the phase of 1560) include a fine sequence of portraits of 14 bishops and two stylites (hermits who lived on top of columns), with other monastic saints; there is also a lengthy series of martyrdom scenes. The paintings in the naos contain the earliest and artistically most impressive in the whole church. They are largely from the group carried out in 1291–2, and contain a long series of miracle scenes of Christ, with some subjects from the Dodecaorton in the vaulting and an impressive cycle of Passion frescos; these are of very high quality, and contain a vivid scene of the suicide of Judas. In the S parekklision there are frescos of the uncommon subject of the Greek sages, including Thucydides, Solon, Plutarch and Aristotle; this subject is mostly found in frescos of the Turkish period, usually in places which may have been used as schoolrooms for children, suggesting that it formed part of a teaching tradition of Greek nationalism. Take your time here, as the various fresco cycles are the most interesting Byz feature and repay study.

The other two monasteries are much smaller, and of only slight Byz interest; both are 16th c foundations. That of **Ag Panteleimon** has a simple, wooden-roofed hall-church with a rounded apse and no dome; there are no paintings and the iconostasis is 18th/19th c. (You will find that the association of this monastery with Ali Pasha, the 'Lion of Ioannina', who was assassinated here in 1822, is inescapable.)

Of the nearby **monastery of Ag Ioannis Prodromos** only the small church survives, but it is architecturally more interesting. It is quite tall for its ground-plan, which is a central one formed from two crossing barrel vaults, but again there is no dome; the transverse gables have attractive triple windows with good dog-tooth brick courses. The apse does not project to the E, and a later narthex has been built on to the w, joining the church to the cliff behind. Again, the interior is of no great interest.

ISOVA   Ισοβα   Trypiti, Ilia

Ruins of Western monastery and church **. Just outside village of Trypiti, nr Kallithea; easy access by car. Unenclosed.

Although there is not now as much to see here as there is of, say, Fountains Abbey or of the Welsh border abbey of Tintern, it may be these sites which come to mind when you look down on the surviving buildings of the Western **monastery of Notre Dame** in its peaceful valley near the Alfios. There are in fact the ruins of two separate foundations here: one is that of the monastery of Notre Dame and the other is of the later church of St Nicholas. The church is the first building that you will come to, but as the monastic buildings are earlier, you may feel that it is preferable to look at them first.

There has been some discussion as to whether the monastery housed Cistercian or Benedictine monks; there are known to have been several more Cistercian houses in mainland Greece and Evia, but only two in the Peloponnese, one of which is at *Zaraka*, so this may have been the second – certainly the remote site is of the kind favoured by the Cistercians. The church was probably built *c.* 1225; although it was in 1210 that Pope Innocent III wrote to the Cistercians in Hautecombes saying that Geoffrey de Villehardouin would build them a monastery in the diocese of Patras: this may have been the result, but we cannot be sure. One of the few certain facts about this beautiful site is that in 1263 the building was burnt down by the Greeks, apparently employing Turkish mercenaries.

The overall length is some 43 m and the building was clearly a fairly standard, Western basilical single nave plan; there were pointed Gothic windows and from the surviving profile of the w façade it must have had a pointed wooden roof. There are no signs of a door in the w wall, the entrance probably being in the E end of the s wall. It is clear that the construction was the work entirely of the monks or of Western lay masons; you will not find any trace of local Greek building practice here. Nothing now survives of the other monastic buildings and cloister which would have adjoined the N side of the church; you can see corbels in the outside of the N wall showing where the wooden roofing of the cloister and dormitory would have been supported before they were burnt down.

While the destruction of the monastery would have prompted the building of the adjoining **church of St Nicholas** to the s, there is no certainty as to the identity of the new arrivals; they were certainly Western monks, but probably not Cistercians. It is altogether a less ambitious building than that of Notre Dame, being only some 15 m long; it was a three-aisled basilica, with a single externally rounded apse. It retained pointed Gothic windows and a pitched wooden roof, but you will see at once that these Western features are combined with what is clearly Greek masonry. As a rib vault from the monastery was found built into St Nicholas its foundation must date from after 1263, and may well be quite shortly after; apart from this, there can be no certainty as to either the date or the builders of St Nicholas. While you may well find that the modern farm buildings are rather obtrusive, they should not detract too much from your enjoyment of this peaceful and atmospheric site.

KALABAKA Καλαμπάκα Trikala

Cathedral church **. Upper part of town. Easy access by car/foot.

While visiting the monasteries of *Meteora* be sure to leave time to see the **mitropolis of the Koimisis tis Theotokou** here; the present building is 14th c, but there was certainly an EC church here originally (the place and its diocese is referred to as *Stagi* in all the documents before the 14th c.) This church would certainly have been in existence for centuries before the earliest of the Meteora monasteries. The choice of a basilical plan may be due to a preference for a design with more venerable associations, and (as elsewhere) it could be that the bishop here wanted to conform to this standard and more archaic type. Inside you can see preserved on the N wall of the narthex the text of a chrysobull issued by the Emperor Andronikos III Palaiologos in 1336 when he visited Thessaly, confirming the rights of the bishop and his people. A further document, a charter of 1393 issued by the patriarch Antonios IV, is also reproduced among the paintings.

This is an immediately impressive building; the choice of a three-aisled basilical plan could not have been dictated by cost, as the detail, and finely coffered timber roof, are of high quality. After entering through a large, later wooden-roofed exonarthex, you will at once be struck by the most prominent feature of the basilica itself: a large EC ambo, with steps leading up from both W and E, almost fills the entire central area of the nave. There is nothing comparable to this in Greece, and it must survive from a substantial EC building previously on this site; from the earlier building, too, must come the ciborium, the altar canopy, as well as a portion of mosaic flooring now visible in the N aisle. You will also see that in the curve of the apse are the remains of the stone seating of the synthronon – again a sign of diocesan rank. All these are 5th/6th-C survivals from the earlier building. There are substantial areas of fresco remaining in all parts of the church; some of it is 13th/14th C, with a further phase dated to 1573 by an inscription, and this has been found to be close in style to that of the famous painter Theophanes of Crete, with the frescos in the trapeza of the *Great Lavra, Mount Athos*, being very comparable; some 11th/12th-C paintings also survive on the N wall of the diaconicon. An interesting and rewarding church to visit.

KALAMATA   Καλαμάτα   Messinia. Med Calamate
Castle and church *. Easy access by car/foot from town.

Kalamata was a town with ancient origins when it was granted to Geoffrey I de Villehardouin in 1208. It already had a Byz fortress, but this had apparently not been worth maintaining, and the building had been made over for use as a monastery before 1205. Guillaume II de Villehardouin, the most Hellenized of the Western leaders, was both born in the castle that Geoffrey built here, and died in it in 1278. It was occupied briefly by the Slavs in 1293, but was soon returned to Frankish control by Florent of Hainault, passing by marriage to Guy II de la Roche, Duke of Athens. Held successively by the Florentines and the Angevins, it was in the possession of the Palaiologoi by 1425.

It must be said that the **castle of Kalamata** does not have a spectacular site, and it must always have been hard to retain against a determined assault; the readiness with which it passed from one occupying power to another throughout the later med period without great damage may be partly due to its unsatisfactory defensive position. Indeed, there would probably have been no castle here at all if the Byzantines had not had a use for the port. Geoffrey's building operations produced a standard Frankish castle of a keep, inner bailey and single outer enceinte. The part of greatest med interest is perhaps in the SE corner of the keep, where Geoffrey enclosed and built on an existing Byz church, presumably dating from when the site was used as a monastery before 1205. Recent earthquake damage has forced the closure of the bailey area, but you will see a Venetian outer wall and entrance gate built at the turn of the 18th c; once again, their interest in safe sea routes for their ships must have been the reason. The **Museum**, which displays a small collection of icons, was also closed in 1989 on account of earthquake damage.

The **church of Ag Apostoloi** has two clear phases of building, with the E end (bema, barrel-vaulted crossing and dome with octagonal drum) forming the original church. From the cloisonné masonry, arcaded windows and decorative brick patterns this is probably of the early 12th c. On to its w bay was joined the larger domed building, with its octagonal drum pierced by four windows; also at this time the bell-tower must have been built against the NE corner. All this later phase appears to date from the 17th c. The older part of the interior has some 14th-c frescos: the Pantocrator and prophets in the dome, and evangelists in the squinches are the best preserved; the rest are largely destroyed.

KALAVRYTA Καλάβρυτα Akhaia. Med La Grite, Kastro Tremolo

Castle ruins (unenclosed) and two monasteries *. Easy access by car. Allow half a day for visiting all three sites.

Some 18 km up the winding road from the coast you will see the modern buildings of the **monastery of Mega Spilaion** (Μέγα Σπήλαιο 'Great Cave'); none of the med structure survived the fire of 1934. While the original cave can still be seen, the main Byz interest here is the collection in the small museum (the icon in the katholikon attributed to the hand of St Luke is certainly of considerable age, but impossible to see properly for revetment and varnish). The earliest items in the collection are four illuminated Gospel MSS of 11th and 12th c, all displayed open at full-page author portraits, and one with a lavish facing headpiece; there are also numerous

16th- to 18th-c items such as icons, silver liturgical objects, an epitaphios brought from Asia Minor and other embroidered vestments – *epimanikia, omoforoi* and *sakkoi*. A separate room houses a display of Byz relics in 18th-c and later silver and silver-gilt reliquaries.

Some 10 km further on is the **castle of Kalavryta**, above the village; access to it is up quite a steep track. This was one of the more important of the Frankish seigneuries, being worth twelve knights' fees. It was held first by Othon de Tournai, and then passed in the early 14th c to the La Trémouille family, barons of Khalandritsa (hence the name Tremolo); the Greeks were able to dispossess the Franks here and remained for over a century before it was bought by the Hospitallers in 1400; they were here for four years before it reverted to Greek control.

The energetic who climb the steep hill up to the plateau overlooking the town will be rewarded with a fine view down the valley toward the *monastery of Mega Spilaion* and some modest remains of what must have once been an impressive castle. There are the ruins of two cisterns and quite a large keep – over 6 by 10 m in plan; you can also see the 'Queen's rock' from which a princess is reputed to have thrown herself to escape her enemies. It was in this castle that a substantial library was housed belonging to George Kantakuzene, and from which, in 1435, he lent the visiting fellow antiquary Cyriacus of Ancona a copy of Herodotus and several other books. *Sic transit* . . .

Further on still is the **monastery of Agia Lavra** * (Αγία Λαύρα), where there is another small collection of Byz material displayed (access by car is easy up a winding road). The buildings here are unexceptional, but as in the *monastery of Mega Spilaion* lower down the valley, the small museum preserves the most interesting material on this site. Besides numerous small Mycenaean and classical items, there are some EC terracotta ampullae and a marble head from a relief, 10th- to 12th-c bronze objects including crosses and two 12th-c Byz Gospel MSS, both displayed open at author portraits, besides many later icons and embroideries; there are also Turkish and Venetian documents of significance to the history of the monastery.

KAMPOS
See **Mani, Stavropigi**

KARDAMYLI
See **Mani**

KARITAINA Καρίταινα Arkadia. Med Caritène, Carentaine
Bridge, castle and three churches **. Easy access by car/foot.

Karitaina was made one of the larger baronies in 1205, being worth
22 knights' fees. It was awarded, according to the *Chronicle of the
Morea*, to '. . . vaillans homs que on appelloit monseignor Geoffroy
de Bruieres qui sires estoit de l'Escorta, lequel fit fair le chastel de
Carentaine'.

The road by which you will approach the town crosses a modern
bridge over the Alfios, but if you look down from this you will see
below a Frankish **bridge** that was renovated in 1439, and was still
used until recently; you can reach it by an easy track. Nothing quite
like it exists from the Frankish period, with four arches surviving
from the med structure, taking it to about half-way across the gorge;
a chapel has been built against the fourth pier.

The town is dominated by the **castle** (Kastro), reached on foot up a
steep path; it has a spectacular site, from where you can look down
over the town and the river Alfios. It was probably built *c.* 1254
not for Geoffroy de Bruyères, the 'seignor de Carentaine', but for
his father, Hugues, and was eventually sold by its treacherous
commander in 1320 to the able Byz General Andronikos Palaiologos Asan.

The remains of the castle, which you enter on the E side, indicate a
long and roughly triangular enceinte with two towers; there seem to
be few later modifications, and it is hard to identify any 14th-c Byz
building; this being so, most of what you see must be taken to be the
Frankish building of the mid-13th c. Some use was made of ceramic
filling for the mortar, but not as much as in other Frankish sites;
there are two cisterns still visible, one unusually large and constructed on a double-nave principle. Besides these you will find the
most prominent survival are the walls of a rather enigmatic rectangular structure, oriented E–W, which may be the remains of the
main hall of the castle.

On the way up a short detour will take you to the small **church of the
Panagia tou Kastrou**, on the slope just below the walls. It is a simple,
inscribed cross, domed church; it has no frescos and must date from
the Turkish period, but the two unusual and finely carved caps on its

columns make it worth visiting; the only comparable type is in the Smyrna museum, and the patterned bosses suggest an 11th-c date.

A short distance from the bottom of the path to the Kastro is the **church of Ag Nikolaos**. Your first view of it will be from above, and the eye is caught at once by its five cupolas, with quite a prominent E semidome; its size does not appear to warrant this, and as the four corner cupolas are low and blind, they may have been intended for external effect. It is built on an inscribed cross plan with four piers; the slit windows confirm other signs of 14th-c date. The frescos inside are of several periods, and are in a generally poor state; the best preserved are of quite a fine saint in the SE cupola and the Ancient of Days in the s vault.

On the w edge of the town, just above the road, is the **church of the Zöodokhos Pigi**. The church itself is unexceptional, being of the 15th c (although the E end may survive from an earlier building) and without any paintings visible, but the free-standing bell-tower beside it is a different matter. This has in the past been described as Frankish, as the concept is certainly Western, but the execution here is an entertaining example of Byz cloisonné technique, with quite lavish and engaging use of brick patterns and dog-tooth ornament. It must date from the later 13th/14th c, and suggests an interesting use of Western forms by Greek builders.

KARYSTOS   Κάρυστος   Evia

Castle ruins **. s end of island; easy access by car, then steep, rough track.

The island of Evia (so close to the mainland that it was regarded more as part of Greece than of the archipelago) had originally been taken by Jacques d'Avesnes in 1205; he died without heirs, and Boniface divided the island into three parts which he awarded as fiefs to three gentleman adventurers of Verona, thereafter known as the triarchs. As usual, the Venetians took no interest in inland territory here until the security of their ports was threatened. They clung tenaciously to the two that they had been awarded in the partition treaty of 1204: Khalkida and Karystos. The latter was an ancient site and a fine addition to their holdings of all the best harbours in the Aegean, but they must always have been uneasy at the presence of a large and well-built castle on the hill just outside the town. In 1261 the Latin Emperor Baldwin II took refuge here when driven out of CP, and on the death of the triarch Boniface of Verona in 1317 the castle was seized by the Catalan leader Alfonso Fadrique, who had married his daughter, Marulla. The Venetians only recovered it in 1365, but were then to retain effective control until the Turkish conquest.

The name of **Castel Rosso** bears no relation to its appearance; it is built of greyish-yellow sandstone (no brick used at all) and is easily the most massive and eloquent reminder of the Frankish/Lombard presence in the island. Its strength was so great that it was said that it could be defended by only 30 fighting soldiers. It was built in the period after 1205 by Ravano dalle Carceri, the triarch who had been awarded the S third of Evia. The site has impressive natural defences, with cliffs to N and E; the outer enceinte has now largely disappeared, but the inner bailey – a broad polygon of some 50 by 70 m – is entered through a rebuilt gateway. There are still substantial internal walls standing amid much rubble, and what appears to be the remains of the apse of a small chapel can be seen in the NW ramparts. The bailey slopes upwards to the NE, where the remains of the keep are obscured by a small modern church; a cistern and a further barrel-vaulted chamber survive close by. The only later fortification is a square tower built on to the SW corner, with provision for artillery; this is probably Turkish. The view from the ramparts S towards the harbour and bay of Karystos is a fine one, and emphasizes the desire of the Venetians to retain control of the S of Evia for as long as they were able. On several counts a visit here is well rewarded.

KASTORIA Καστοριά Kastoria/Macedonia
Churches and frescos (six described here); museum.

Due to a happy accident of history this attractive lakeside town still retains a unique range of small, highly picturesque churches; what is even more remarkable, they contain between them the most complete record of middle and later Byz fresco painting anywhere in Greece. There are still 12 churches of the Byz period, almost 30 post-Byz and over a dozen 19th C, and the great majority still retain some or all of their fresco decoration. There were other churches which did not survive the centuries; one must assume that there was once a mitropolis – a population of this size would have had its own bishop – but its only trace now is in the name of one of the many smaller churches, that of the Taxiarchs by the mitropolis.

As it is, a striking feature of the town is how, of over 50 Greek churches, only one has a cupola. This can probably best be explained by a deference to local convention and custom, perhaps also to the appearance of the hypothetical mitropolis church; other reasons may have been lack of finances and other resources (*Veroia* is a very similar case). In general, the modest size of almost all these churches, with their highly individualized approach to design, construction and decoration, suggests that they served to a major extent as private chapels; certainly no surviving church in the town could have sheltered a large congregation. Those described here represent the most significant of the Byz group; although the 11th c was one of the most prolific periods here, following the reconquest of N Macedonia by the Emperor Basil II in 1018, the earliest building is now thought to date from the 10th c, and so anticipates the reoccupation. There is no logical route to follow within the town, so an approximately chronological sequence is given here. There are official guards with keys; it is worth having a torch with you.

The **church of Ag Stephanos** ** makes a good starting-point; its exterior has an attractive combination of rough-cut masonry set in bands between double horizontal courses of brick, and with distinctive cart-wheel brick patterns in the E end. The forms of the building itself are highly individual: the nave is very tall for its width, with a galleried narthex protruding from the w and, lower still, aisles to N and s. All this tends to give the silhouette a rather lean-to, miniature quality, but there are in fact no additions to the original design; this has been dated later, but is now thought to be 10th c, and perhaps as early as *c.* 900. The frescos inside are not in good condition, but are a valuable source for a knowledge of Byz art in Greece, as the oldest are contemporary with the building.

The earliest are in the vault of the narthex, and form the main part of an impressive version of the Last Judgement; although damaged, its date makes this of considerable interest. Do not neglect to go up into the gallery from here, as the stairs take you close to the fresco surface. The constriction of the stairway may be due to the reinforcement that was needed to support such a high vault on the nave. The tall barrel vault of the nave has a 12th-c fresco which shows an adaptation of a cupola scheme to the basilical form, with a sequence of three busts of Christ, as Emmanuel, the Ancient of Days and the Pantocrator.

The **church of the Taxiarchs by the Mitropolis** ** is of comparable plan and date to Ag Stephanos, but it has a somewhat more

1. *(above)* Arta: the Parigoritissa from the NW.
2. *(left)* Arta: church of St Basil, E façade.
The individuality of the despotate of Epiros and its rulers is finely expressed in these two buildings: the huge but eccentric 'palace-church' and the smaller building with its startling ceramic decoration.

3. Kyllini: the church of Vlakhernae, seen from the SW, displays an enigmatic fusion of Byzantine and Western building forms.

4. Khrysafa: the profile of the church of the Panagia Khrysafiotissa, seen from the SW. is dominated by the later tower built over the apse.

Two churches built by Western orders.
5. *(above)* Andravida: now only the E end of the Dominican church of Ag Sofia survives with its Gothic vaulting; the nave and aisles would have had wooden roofing.
6. *(left)* Isova: the interior of the w wall of the monastery of Notre Dame, where Western chants would have been heard during the four decades of the building's life.

7. Porta Panagia: the two phases of the church's building are easily seen in this view from the SW.

8. Amfissa: the church of the Virgin, seen from the NE, occupies a rural site above the town and its castle.

9. Orkhomenos: the 9th-C church of the Koimisis, seen here from the W, is one of the outstanding churches of central Greece.

10. Athens: the church of Ag Apostoloi in the Agora is architecturally the most inventive of the surviving churches in the city.

11. *(top)* Thessaloniki: the mosaic of the Ascension in the dome of Ag Sofia.
12. Thessaloniki: the fresco of the Koimisis in the church of Ag Nikolaos
Orfanos. These two images convey the range of period and medium to be
found in the churches of 'the second city'.

13. Arta: part of the relief on the tomb of the *basilissa* Theodora Petralifina in the church of Ag Theodora; she is shown with her son Nikiforos, both wearing full court dress.

14. Orkhomenos: a sun-dial in relief on the church of Koimisis; these can be found quite commonly on the s wall of churches.

15. Khlemoutsi: the echoing halls of the castle keep have much of their fabric still intact; this is the most complete and the most advanced in its design of all the Frankish castles.

16. Livadia: the carefully-cut ashlar of the castle gateway is still in fine condition, although the bailey is now overgrown with pine trees.

Two views of Acrocorinth.
17. *(top)* The castle's history is told here: of the towers flanking the third gateway, that on the left is 12th-C Byzantine and that on the right 4th-C BC with Byzantine additions, while the keep on the skyline is Frankish.
18. The curtain walls of the castle climb the steep hillside towards the first two entrance gates.

19. Nikopolis: the main gateway in the fortified walls built by Justinian; these form the most extensive such system in Greece.

20. Karitaina: the Frankish bridge, fortified by a small chapel, still spans the Alfios, the sacred river of antiquity.

Four capitals from Greek churches.

21. *(left)* Karitaina: a re-used capital in the small church of the Panagia tou Kastrou.

22. *(below left)* Thessaloniki: a re-used capital of the 'wind-blown acanthus' type, in Ag Sophia.

23. *(below right)* Thebes: an unusually inventive early Christian capital in the Museum.

24. *(bottom)* Lekhaion: a 5th-c capital still on the site of the huge early Christian basilica.

25. *(top)* Kastoria: the church of Ag Stefanos from the E.
26. Mount Athos, monastery of Khilandari: the roofs of the katholikon show this Serbian foundation to be on a more compact plan than those of other Athonite monasteries.

27. *(top)* Elassona: the apse of the katholikon of the Panagia Olimpiotissa. Byzantine masons used brick to create a rich variety of patterns on church buildings of all kinds and periods.

28. Molyvdoskepastos: the tall dome of the katholikon suggests influence from Serbia, not far to the north.

Two views of Mystra.
29. *(right)* The hillside from the N, showing the cupolas of the Afendiko and, at the summit, the castle of Villehardouin.
30. *(below)* The apses of the Evangelistria, one of the smaller churches of the city.

Two views in the Mani.
31. The church of Ag Theodoroi at Vamvaka, where the interior can boast the
rare signature of a medieval sculptor.
32. Some ruins of Villehardouin's castle of Great Maina on the Tigani headland;
it could only be easily serviced from the sea.

33. Philippi: the towering ruins of the w wall of Basilica B here frame a medieval tower on the skyline.

34. Geraki: the hillside below the castle, with its ruined houses and small churches, carries echoes of Mystra, not far away.

sophisticated character; the nave still seems high, but the exterior arcade to the s is certainly later, as is the inner addition on the N, and the narthex does not project. The masonry is not quite so decorative, with just modest dog-tooth bands relieving the windows and apse. Its original plan was a simple, three-aisled basilica, with three bays in the nave, a rounded projecting apse and quite a broad narthex. You may find the frescos here of greater interest; there are impressive images of the archangels Michael and Gabriel on the exterior of the w wall, besides later frescos under the s arcade. Inside, the w wall has a fine version of the Koimisis below the Ascension, and (more unusually) there are six Passion scenes in the nave; of particular interest are the frescos of icons, painted on the walls of the nave above the arches as if they were panels hanging on the walls.

A third church which may also originally date from the early 10th c is that known as the **Panagia Koubelidiki ****, or the 'church of the Virgin with the little cupola'. Its construction makes it the most sophisticated in the town, as it is the only one with a cupola; the plan is that of a triconch, with the cupola supported by a main apse and two further apsidal forms of the same size to N and s. But even from the outside you can see how this gives way to the rather uncertain form of the w part built on to the domed area; there is a narrow vaulted space between the naos which may have been a tiny narthex. To this was added the present square narthex, which is slightly later. It is as if the function of the church may have changed early on – soon after the main domed naos had been finished. The masonry has the same rows of irregular stone divided by thin brick courses; the main ornament is provided by quite modest lines of dog-tooth brick patterns let into the cupola and walls. (The cupola was in fact rebuilt earlier this century, but accurately reproduced the original form, and even used some of the old materials.)

The fresco decoration here is interesting but less important, with none of the paintings as early as the 10th c; they were installed at several periods, and the latest are probably those remaining on the exterior of the w front. Inside, over the w door there is a fine Nativity fresco, probably 12th c, with colourful detail; near are fine figures of the two ss Theodore receiving crowns, with scenes of their martyrdom above. In the narrow barrel vault next to the naos a fresco of the Ancient of Days must relate to the Pantocrator in the dome, and on the w wall of the naos there is a painting of the Koimisis that has become integrated with the Ascension of Christ in

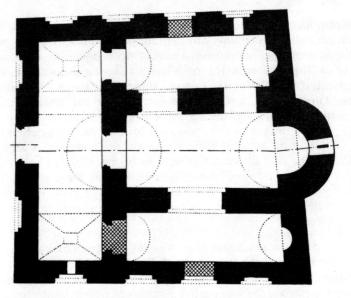

Ag Anargyroi

a way which seems to be something of a local tradition; the paintings in the main apse are probably the earliest, but are the least well preserved.

With the **church of the Ag Anargyroi** * (or 'moneyless healers' – doctors who took no fees) we are in a later generation of buildings, dating from the 11th c, and after Basil ɪɪ's conquests. It has the finest of the carved doorways in the town; the relative scarcity of decorative carving of this kind is emphasized by the interest in exterior masonry in many of the town's churches. Its plan is still very simple – a three-aisled basilica, with a narthex extending its full width – but the proportions are now broader and more generous; the aisles, with their separate, lower roofs, are as wide as the nave, itself a more comfortable width relative to its height than in the earlier churches. This means that the exterior, with the nave rising above the narthex and aisles, has a maturer quality. The masons have enjoyed giving the wall elevations a richly decorative surface with a variety of brick ornament, and the nave clerestory windows are now larger than in the earlier buildings, although lacking in the aisles.

Inside, the frescos are of several periods but repay careful viewing. In the narthex you can see how a 12th-c fresco layer has partly fallen away from a figure of St Nicholas, revealing the original

11th-c painting beneath. In the N aisle there are frescos from the 11th, 12th and 13th C (torch needed here); both aisles originally had barrel vaults, but these (presumably with their paintings) are now gone. The frescos in the nave are mostly uncleaned and very obscured, but the founders' portrait, two fine figures of ss George and Dimitrios and the fresco of the Lamentation have been cleaned and show the riches that must still be here.

From the second half of the 12th C is the **church of Ag Nikolaos tou Kasnitzi *** – the suffix deriving from the founder, Nikiforos surnamed 'of Kasnitzi', whose inscription you can see on the w wall inside. The plan here is even simpler: a single apse, aisleless wooden-roofed hall, it has only a modest narthex breaking up the interior space. By contrast, the brickwork on the exterior is again engagingly decorative, but it is the frescos here which provide the principal interest; they are some of the best preserved and most impressive in Kastoria. See in particular the w wall with the Koimisis and Transfiguration forming a single composition with the Ascension, and fine warrior saints and St Nicholas in the nave. The apse frescos are in the least good condition.

While in Kastoria, do not omit a visit to the interesting and attractively sited lakeside **church of the Panagia Mavriotissa *** (a short drive or about an hour's walk). The 'core' of the church here (rather casually oriented NE–SW) is a simple, wooden-roofed hall with a large rounded apse; this is probably of 11th-c origin, and at an early point a substantial narthex was added; a large parekklision, again of much the same size as the narthex and the naos, and dedicated to St John Theologos, was built against the s side probably in the 14th C. The principal interest of the complex here is undoubtedly the extensive frescos, which survive both on the exterior and (mostly in better condition) on the inside, from several different periods. Opinions vary quite widely about them; most of those in the main church, including the impressive painting of the Koimisis on the w wall, are probably from the middle and later 12th C. Among the *grafitti* on the exterior frescos, which include a good rendering of the Tree of Jesse, is apparently one of 1265; another group, which included this, the Ascension in the naos and the two imperial portraits is of the mid-13th C; those on the N and S narthex walls include areas which are likely to be of the 15th C. In the parekklision a fine series of 12 miracle scenes of Christ may also be of this date, while those on the exterior of the w wall are probably of a later phase again.

A new **museum** * has recently been built, and although the display of exhibits was not completed in 1989, the two rooms of icons already on view form an impressive collection. They offer an interesting cross-section of Greek icon painting from the 12th to 18th c; among them in particular a fine icon of the prophet Elijah of the late 12th c, icons of local subjects – the Panagia Faneromeni, the taxiarchs of the Gymnasium, and St Thanasios – all of the Byz period, and a striking group of three double-sided icons of 15th/16th c; these would have been carried in procession so that both sides could be seen.

Kastoria is the centre of an attractive area, and while there try to make a visit to the very different church at *Omorfokklisia*.

KATAKOLO   Κατάκολο   Ilia. Med Beauvoir

Ruins of Byz fortress *. Easy access by road, turning off to Ag Andreas approx. 2 km N of Katakolo; then a short walk up a steep track on the left to ruins.

Do not be deceived by modern maps showing two castles on the Pondiko headland in the NW Peloponnese, s of *Andravida*: there is only one, that was later called **Beauvoir castle**. A position on the low tip of the headland, now occupied by a lighthouse, would have served no conceivable purpose. The Byz fort on this promontory in 1205 was called 'Pontikokastro' (or 'Mouse Castle') and it was easily taken and held by Geoffrey de Villehardouin and Guillaume de Champlitte in the early days of their conquest of the Morea. It was here that in 1217 the marriage was rapidly arranged between the young Geoffrey de Villehardouin and the daughter of the Empress Jolanda, wife of Peter of Courtenay the new Latin emperor of CP.

The approach to the site is quite steep, but not precipitous from any aspect; there are now no signs of any outer circuit wall, but the level top of the outcrop is some 50 by 60 m, and was enclosed by a wall and towers. Two tower bases remain to NW and E (now best seen from below at Ag Andreas), and these are clearly in Byz building technique – cloisonné masonry of dressed square limestone blocks. The area enclosed is completely overgrown, and there are holes in the ground through which the unwary can fall into chambers below. Visitors here early in this century still wrote of cisterns, and of entry through a tower with a pointed arch; the cisterns, probably remain underfoot, but the entry tower (which may have been Frankish?) has gone. The chief interest of the remains here is that the Franks seem only to have done minimal subsequent building – perhaps because the site was not sufficiently well endowed; certainly what you now see must be substantially 12th c Byz military fortification. In spite of the 'low walls' which it was said to possess, and which no doubt made it easier for the Franks to take, they may have given it the name of Beauvoir on account of the prospect from the summit, which offers a fine outlook to both sides of the promontory and inland.

KAVALA   Καβάλα   Kavala Thrace. Byz Neapolis
Byz fortress and museum *.

The citadel, built on an ancient acropolis, still has its **Byz fortress** (Frourion). The road by which you approach it passes through remains of outer fortifications; the fortress itself, which is reported by Prokopios as having been restored in the 6th c by Justinian, takes the form of two courtyards, the first polygonal of some 50 by 60 m and the second longer and narrower; a substantial round tower straddles the wall that divides them. The first that you enter has the ground steeply sloping away to the NE, and a sentry-walk survives round most of the enceinte. The second courtyard that you reach has a cistern some 10 m long formed from two adjacent barrel-vaulted chambers, and there is a further large underground barrel-vaulted chamber. It is not easy to distinguish differences in the masonry, but all the NE sector of the first courtyard is typical Byz construction, as also the two gateways in the first courtyard with their brick arches, the lower part of the tower and much of the lower areas of the rest of the walling; the upper part of the tower and much of the castellation appears later, presumably Turkish, rebuilding. The enthusiast for Byz military architecture will find more here to see than in most of the other surviving Byz strongholds. (The impressive aqueduct is entirely Turkish 16th c.)

In the **Archaeological Museum** the med holdings are limited to a limestone slab from nearby Christopolis with an inscription referring to the rebuilding of the city walls by the governor of the Strymon theme in 926, and two fine 5th-c double-zone caps from Basilica c at *Amfipolis*, with birds, foliage and the heads of rams and lions in the upper zones.

KENTROKALOSPITO
See **Mani**

KHALANDRITSA Χαλανδρίτσα Akhaia
Church and tower. Easy access on foot from village.

The barony here was first held by Robert de la Trémouille during the Frankish period, and at only four knights' fiefs was one of the smallest; although it survived longer than almost all the others, it has left very little behind. You will find that the **church of Ag Athanasios**, an 11th/12th-c Byz, domed, inscribed cross church in the middle of the village, has been given a later apse, built on a rectangular plan and with a quite clear groin vault; this is most probably a Frankish 13th-c replacement, and although only matched in the Peloponnese at *Andravida*, lacks the latter's charm. The church is otherwise of little interest, only having a damaged later Byz painting in a niche of the prothesis.

Some 50 m N of the church, across a small valley, the base of a square tower stands 3–4 m high; this was thought earlier this century to be the remains of the castle of the de la Trémouille family, but is far more likely to be one of the many medieval towers used for agricultural or storage purposes (see pp. 46–47).

KHALKIDA Χαλκίδα Evia. Venetian Negroponte
Church * and castle.

This town was the capital of the island of Evia, and although joined to the mainland by a bridge, it was always easier to defend on this account. The history of Khalkida was linked for much of the later med period with that of *Karystos* and its strength as a port attracted the Venetians from the start, as any who held it was able to control a large area of local and maritime trade; they made sure that they were awarded it in the partition treaty of 1204, and clung to it until 1470, when it finally fell to Mehmed II.

The chief surviving feature of the long Venetian presence in the town is the impressive **church of Ag Paraskevi**, which is an intriguing architectural hybrid. Its form is now that of a wooden-roofed, aisled basilica, some 40 m long; it can never have been domed. The four W bays of the nave carry an arcade above, but no gallery; the two E bays have higher and more pointed arches, but no arcade. The presence of two unequal piers dividing these two parts of the nave give some support to the idea that there might once have been a dome, but their span would suggest one of impossible size. Rib vaults in the chapels flanking the square apse, with the pointed nave arches, show that a radical extension was made in the 13th/14th c; a dated 14th-c wall-tomb, recorded earlier this century in the s chapel, is no longer present.

Re-use of earlier materials throughout adds to the complexity: the w bays of the nave have three fine wind-blown acanthus caps, with one 6th-c marble one, while there are two classical columns in the w bays with cabling partly cut out in a way that suggests this might be their third period of use. The rich carving over the entire central w arch, with half figures among foliage, is surely Venetian, recalling comparable work of the mid-14th c in Aquileia and (in a more developed form, and in profile) from the 15th-c on the façade of San Marco in Venice itself. The evidence points to the presence of a considerably earlier church of basilical form (and, from its nave width, of some size) which was converted and extended in the 13th/14th c under the Venetians. The later bell-tower rests on a base that must also be of this date.

The **castle of Karabamba** on a hill on the mainland immediately overlooking the straits is now almost entirely Turkish rebuilding, with only a little earlier masonry visible in the s and SE sectors.

KHAROUDA
See **Mani**

KHLEMOUTSI Χλεμούτσι Ilia, s of Kyllini. Med Clairmont, Clermont, Castel Tornese
Castle ***. Easy access by car to gate, and easy internal ascent.

If Acrocorinth is the most extensive of the Frankish castles in the Peloponnese, then the **castle of Khlemoutsi** is both the best pre-served and the most accurately dated. Its preservation may be due to the lack of powerful natural defences at the site; it can never have been regarded as the best place in which to make a last stand. (In antiquity the name of the headland on which the castle is built was Cape Chelonatas, from its resemblance, when seen from the sea, to the shell of a tortoise; this certainly describes the hump of land, with no cliff or ravine, on which it rises.)

The origins of the castle lie in a feud that developed c. 1218 between Geoffrey I de Villehardouin and the Latin clergy of Akhaia. It was pointed out to Geoffrey that the clergy 'who need have no fear of battle' owned almost a third of his lands; in order

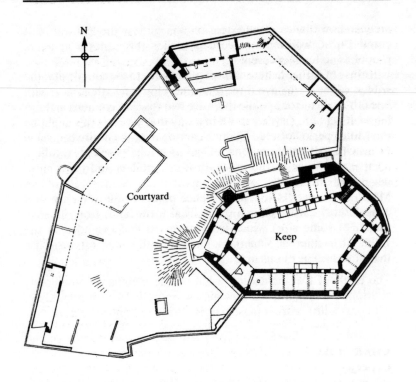

N

Courtyard

Keep

Castle of Khlemoutsi

to drive the Greeks out of Monemvasia he asked the clergy to contribute, in place of military service, funds from their ample revenues. They refused, saying they belonged to the Pope, not themselves. Geoffrey then confiscated all their possessions, and in February 1219 Pope Honorius III was complaining that the property of the church was by then illegally alienated: 'pro bonis ecclesiasticis iniuste occupatis'. Geoffrey at once used the revenues to build Khlemoutsi, remaining for a time under excommunication as a result (the acrimonious correspondence over this is why the date is, for once, accurately verifiable). It was largely completed by 1223. It was here that a mint issued the French currency (the *tournois*) for Akhaia, hence the Venetian name of Castel Tornese.

In 1313 Guillaume de Villehardouin's younger daughter, Marguerite, in order to find support for her claim to their lands, married her daughter to one of the leaders of the Catalan Company, Ferdinand of Majorca, who had so decisively defeated the French two years earlier at Kephissos. Although Marguerite was imprisoned in Khlemoutsi for her supposed perfidy, and died soon after, her gamble was successful for a time. Ferdinand captured the castle in 1314 and held it until 1316 when Louis of Burgundy arrived; with an alliance of French barons and Greek troops from Mystra Ferdinand was defeated, and Khlemoutsi reverted to the Angevins. In 1427 Constantine Palaiologos, despot of Mystra, lived here while preparing to attack Patras; he had married the daughter of Carlo Tocco, who had brought Glarentza with her as her dowry, and a modern plaque by the entrance to the keep records his presence here over five centuries ago.

The design of Khlemoutsi is unlike that of any other of the Frankish castles in Greece, and the castle is among the earliest of a group of French castles centred round that of Boulogne; this places it in the forefront of European military architecture of its period. Most of what you see here dates from the original construction of 1219–23, with only small later modifications and additions, mostly made by the Turks to accommodate artillery. Its dominant feature is the huge keep, built on the plan of an irregular hexagon; this is not enclosed by an enceinte, as is usual, but projects from the curtain wall on three of its sides to the SE. The curtain wall runs downhill from either side of it, enclosing a large apron-shaped bailey; there is one projecting tower in the W sector which is uncommon for being rounded. There would have been other buildings against the inside of some of these walls, of which various remains are still visible; a cistern can still be seen not far from the entrance to the keep, and what may be another is on the left as you enter the main gate.

The keep is large enough to enclose a spacious, level courtyard, some 60 m long and over 25 m wide. You may find its huge, echoing halls, with their finely-cut limestone vaulting, to be the most memorable feature of this castle; some are only partially roofed now, and the original flooring at ground and upper level is gone, but the space and increased height which this gives them are immensely impressive, and unique in Greece. Original steps lead up on to the flat roofs, still largely intact, from which you can gain an excellent view of the surrounding country, with the sea and harbour away to the NE; the forms of the land will not have changed greatly since it was built. Khlemoutsi must be regarded as the most outstanding work of secular building in all of Frankish Greece.

KHONIKAS Χώνικας Argolida
Church *. Easy access.

The **church of the Koimisis tis Theotokou** is built on an inscribed cross, four-column plan, and with an unusually tall drum for its early 12th-c date. The windows in the drum and elsewhere in the church take the attractive form of tall slabs of marble pierced by a cross and circles; the most striking feature of the exterior is the use of spolia in the form of large cut stones let into the w front forming two crosses. Some simple brick ornament is used to give relief to the well-cut stone of the walls, and a small belfry (though probably later) rises above the single w door. The church here, with those of the *Ag Moni*, *Areia* and of the *Panagia*, *Merbaka* form a small but coherent 12th-c group which can readily be seen in a day; you might like to add a visit to *Ag Ioannis*, *Lygourio*, where the building is less sophisticated but earlier, and may be regarded as the starting-point of the group.

KHRISTIANO Χριστιανό Messenia
Cathedral church **. Easy access by car.

The **church of the Metamorfosis tou Sotiros** was radically but carefully restored in the 1930s after major earthquake damage. It is an immediately impressive building, its size being completely unexpected in this quite remote little village; the explanation for this is

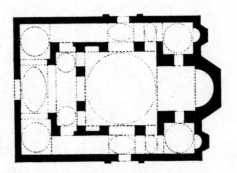

Khristiano: Metamorfosis tou Sotiros

that it was formerly the seat of an archbishop, and so is in fact a cathedral. It was built in the later 11th c, and its design and contructional principles, with the short arms of the central cross supporting corner squinches, which in turn carry a massive 16-sided drum for the cupola, has similarities with other major churches such as *Ag Sofia, Monemvasia*, and that at *Dafni*, near Athens. The bold and impressive monumentality of the design is relieved by carefully laid cloisonné masonry which is emphasized by double-tile divisions, quite rich brick patterns round the arcaded windows, and the plinth formed from a repeated cross pattern provided by large slabs of dressed marble. Inside you will see minimal fragments of fresco remaining in the bema and conch of the apse, but little else of decorative interest; the drum and cupola are completely rebuilt, recreating the impressive interior space.

There was originally an episcopal palace attached to the church, and there is an interesting and rare opportunity here to see quite substantial remains of (in effect) secular building attached to the w end. A visit here provides an uncommon glimpse into the architectural context and surroundings of a Byz provincial bishopric.

KHRYSAFA Χρύσαφα Lakonia, e of Sparta
Three churches *. Easy access by car.

There are two centres of interest here; the first is a church within the town, and the second is provided by two others, lying 2 to 3 km. outside in the countryside.

Within the town is the **church of the Koimisis tis Theotokou**; it is a 14th-c cross-domed building on an unusual plan, with three rounded apses to the e and the cross arms projecting to n and s as two further apses. Besides this original aspect of its plan (which made four interior columns necessary) there is also some fine and inventive brick and tile ornament, particularly round the apses; a limited amount of later rebuilding does not detract from this. Note also the carved heads (rather like embryonic gargoyles) at the corners of the octagonal drum and the roof – a local habit here, repeated occasionally elsewhere (e.g. *Stiris, Theotokos* and the *Mani*). The narthex may be a bit later, or at least enlarged, and the belfry is certainly a later extension, as it has some rather fine Iznik bowls inset at its apex that must be no earlier than 16th c. Inside there is a substantial amount of fresco painting still surviving; much of it is an unusual, almost monochromatic, technique using a lot of burnt umber. The condition is not good, but there are extensive cycles of martyrdoms, miracle scenes, a Virgin cycle and a fine enthroned Virgin in the apse.

In fields outside the town to the s a short way down a tractor track are two further churches, which must have formed part of a monastic complex; there are still some remains of other buildings to the s. Most prominent is the **church of the Panagia Khrysafiotissa** (13th c). The basic plan is that of an inscribed cross, triple-apse church, with narthex and exonarthex, and with two piers supporting the single dome, but the exterior is dominated by a substantial later tower built over the E end; this has absorbed half the drum and cupola, and caused the upward extension of the apse. Its function must presumably have been for defence, but it is not possible to be certain when it was built. Inside the church there are frescos that are probably contemporary with it, although not in good condition.

A few paces to the N you will find the much smaller 14th-c **church of Ag Ioannis Prodromos**. This attractive but modest little building – a domed, inscribed cross plan, with one apse, two internal piers and no narthex – has avoided any later additions, and you will see both it and its peaceful surroundings in much their original state. Inside there are traces of contemporary frescos, and the masonry icon-ostasis has a painted inscription on its E face.

A visit to Khrysafa will provide you with the experience of a small range of different forms of Byz building in an unusually attractive rural setting.

KONTARIOTISSA Κονταριώτισσα Pieria
Church *. Easy access.

Avoiding at all costs the truly hideous modern monastery dominating the area to the w, you will find the **church of the Koimisis tis Theotokou** on lower ground, but still in an attractive rural setting just uphill from the village. It has a typically severe exterior for its 10th-c date, and its interest lies in the combination of its early date and its 'domed basilica' design, comparable on a much smaller scale, and no doubt consciously, with *Ag Sofia, Thessaloniki*. It has three substantial rounded apses, and the central one had three large windows, now blocked up, implying a lighter interior than was usual later. Although a lot of brick was used, particularly in most of the apse construction and the drum of the cupola, there are no brick

patterns beyond some herring-bone round the main apse. A later
chapel has been built on to the sw corner.

Inside, the dome is supported on a combination of piers and six
columns, which in some cases have EC caps, perhaps taken from
nearby Dion. The iconostasis is a late wooden one, and the few
surviving frescos, although in poor state, appear to be 14th c; there
are also some later paintings on the exterior of the s wall, where a
later additional chapel has been dismantled. There are few churches
in Greece of this date, and its survival in almost untouched state
makes it a rewarding building which you should find 'vaut le détour'.

KORONI Κορώνη Messinia. Med Coron
Castle *. Access on foot from town, then easy paths.

Unlike most of the castles of the Morea, that at Koroni was never in
Frankish hands; the port was ceded to the Venetians in 1206,
immediately after the Fourth Crusade, and it had no other occupants but the Venetians until it fell to the Turks, which was not until
1500. Some parts of the town close to the sea still have a planned
quattrocento piazza layout, and the castles here and at *Methoni*
were known as 'the eyes of the Serene Republic'. The bishop was a
suffragan of the Latin archbishop of Patras.

The substantial **castle** is roughly triangular in plan, occupying the
headland to the E of the town, and almost all that you now see (such
as the massively impressive rounded bastion rising from the sea) is
predictably Venetian and certainly quite late; the towering gateway
is probably the earliest of the Venetian building. The interior of the
castle area is fully inhabited, and towards the centre of the triangular area you will come across the ruins of quite a large Byz church (in
the grounds of the modern Moni Ag Ioannis Prodromos). It would
seem to be 11th/12th c and indicates a clear med Greek presence
here; its s apse was transformed into a mosque, but has now
reverted to use as a church, and the N apse contains a ruined cistern
and the base of a minaret. A ruined gateway in the E defences allows
a visitor to walk through to the grassy headland not enclosed by
them, and looking back from here you can gain a good idea of their
seaward aspect. For the medievalist this is a memorably picturesque
site to visit, if otherwise not very rewarding.

KYLLINI Κυλλήνη Ilia
Church *. Access by dirt road 3 km to s of town.

For much of the later med period this was the chief port of the
Morea, prospering as the point of transit for Venetian and Genoese
galleys crossing from Taranto or Brindisi. The *Chronicle of the
Morea* describes the court life developed by the Angevins here.

The beautiful **church of the Convent of Vlakhernae**, to the NE of
Kyllini, presents such a successful marriage of Byz and w
architecture that its resulting style demands the coining of a new
name. Some 40 m in overall length, its main elements of porch,
three-bay narthex and three-aisled barrel-vaulted basilica with
externally faceted apses are built in what would normally be regarded as 12th-c Byz cloisonné technique; decorative dog-tooth
string-courses and window surrounds reinforce this impression, as
does the inclusion of attractive carved Byz marble spolia at the s
door and on the s end of the narthex. Yet the forms of the building,
particularly the high w porch integrated with the narthex, can only
be seen as a Western concept; the simple carving on interior caps
and a keystone of the narthex is also purely Western. Other parts of
the building further combine the two traditions.

Of the various suggestions made to account for this building,
perhaps the most convincing is that when the Franciscan monks
arrived after 1205 they took over an unfinished 12th-c Byz church;
using local builders they continued and completed it in what would
then have been an archaic but homogeneous local style. It is even
possible that the porch is later still, representing yet a third phase.
Although closed in 1989 due to recent minor earthquake damage,
be prepared to take your time over this attractive architectural
conundrum, and do not be deterred by the friendly patients housed
in the adjoining modern buildings.

For the huge castle nearby, see *Khlemoutsi*.

KYPARISSIA Κυπαρισσία Messinia. Med Arkadia
Castle *. Access by steep but easy footpath.

This was not one of the largest or the most important of the Frankish
fiefs, but still has some points of interest to offer. It was given, with
Kalamata, to Villehardouin by Champlitte in compensation for his
original fief of Koroni which had been lost to the Venetians; it fell to
him after a short siege in 1205. It changed hands several times but
was still in the possession of the then prince of Akhaia, Centurione

Zaccaria, in 1430 when he was forced to make peace with Thomas Palaiologos; he gave him his daughter, Catarina, in marriage, and what was left of the Frankish principality as her dowry.

The **castle** is not on a large site, considering its history as the longest surviving of the baronies of the Morea; the central bailey is a rough oval approximately 60 by 80 m, but it is precipitous on two sides and must have been easy to defend before the age of cannon. Its interest lies in the fact that it is a Frankish castle built on a Byz acropolis, and that the central keep has survived as evidence of Byz military construction. You enter the Frankish circuit wall, of which considerable amounts remain, in the SE corner; the masonry is similar to much other Frankish building, and it has been little altered since. The Byz keep, although partly encased in, and supported by, later masonry can be seen in the N and W faces to be of limestone blocks with sporadic tile courses, and there is a more abundant use of lime mortar in the filling than Western builders usually seem to have used. Part of the circuit wall in the SW also appears to be earlier than 13th C. Interesting, if not spectacular.

LAMIA Λαμία Fthiotida. Med Zetounion, Gipton and la Citó Castle *. Easy access.

The rocky acropolis dominating Lamia must always have been coveted, and its long history involves assaults by many different powers. It was near here that the first Frankish parliament of Ravennika was held in 1209; the castle was captured by Theodore of Epiros early in his campaign of 1218, but in 1280 it formed part of the dowry of the daughter of John Doukas of Neopatras when she married Guillaume de la Roche, Lord of Livadia, and so became part of the Duchy of Athens. In 1319 it was taken over by the Catalan leader Alfonso Fadrique, for the Duchy of Neopatras, and only a century later had a Greek governor for a short period before the Turkish occupation began.

The outlook from the **castle** is very impressive; the castle itself cannot at present be entered as a large Turkish building that occupies most of the interior is being restored. The walls of the enceinte form a rough quadrilateral, with towers at the corners; there is a short N wall, and the W wall is the best preserved where some 60 m of masonry incorporate both polygonal and rectangular blocks of earlier building. Most of the enceinte would seem to date from the 14th-C Catalan occupation, with some later Turkish modifications.

LANGADA
See **Mani**

LARISA   Λάρισα   Larisa/Thessaly. Med Larsa
Remains of Byz fort *.

There was already a fortress here in the 6th c, which was rebuilt by
Justinian, although it apparently fell quite readily to Bulgars invading in 985. The Byzantines recovered the city, and its fort withstood
a siege by the Normans in 1096. In 1204 the town was occupied early
by Boniface of Montferrat after Leo Sgouros had withdrawn, and he
bestowed it as a fief on one of the Lombard barons who then called
himself Guglielmo de Larsa. By 1214 Michael i Doukas has
captured the town and added it to his Epirote holdings, and in 1386
it became one of the first towns to be occupied by the advancing
Turks. Throughout the Byz period it was the seat of an important
bishopric, and during the Latin occupation it was to the Bishop of
Larisa that the Pope would often write when complaining of the
misdemeanors of the secular rulers.

In the centre of the town there is certainly a small and massive Byz
construction on the plan of a hollow rectangle, but although it is
called the Frourion it would be hard to sustain a case for it being
anything more than an adjunct to a **fortress**. (A small park adjoins it
where you can take refreshment while pondering it.) Its external
size is some 25 by 35 m, and its height 8 m, and it was built with
gateways in all four walls; although those on e and w are now
blocked up, it is these which make it so unlikely that this was a real
fortress: just one gateway would surely have been both adequate
and prudent. The n wall has remains of further building against it,
and although there are repairs to the top of the wall, it does not give
the appearance of having been much higher. The construction of the
walls is interesting in that they incorporate brick arches (five on the
shorter sides and seven on the longer) with triple rows of brick
across their base; you can look inside, but cannot enter it. While
clearly only a fragment of a larger complex, the rarity of this kind of
Byz military building means that it will repay a visit. There is also a
7th-c Byz church being excavated just across the road.

LEKHAIO   Λέχαιο   Korinthia
Ruins of basilica **. Some 3 km along coast road w of Corinth, turn
right just before road goes under bridge.

The magnificently sited **basilica of St Leonidas**, lying within a few paces of the Gulf of Corinth, is one of the major showpieces of the EC period in Greece, but has escaped the fame of *Philippi*. Of truly vast extent, with the worshipper originally approaching through a forecourt and atrium before entering the basilica proper, the overall length is almost 190 m, of which 120 m would have been inside the basilica itself. Although no walling stands to more than knee-height, you cannot fail to be impressed by its scale and setting. It was probably begun in the mid-5th C but construction may have lasted into the 6th, with a number of complex features in its design; still very evident are the differing floor levels for aisles, nave and transept. A huge apse originally carried a mosaic, and the transept on a tripartite plan still has traces of lateral benches for the officiating clergy.

Surviving areas of floor mosaic have been covered with gravel, but you will find large sheets of white and grey marble still in place in the floor of the nave and atrium, and much fine sculpture, with 5th-C caps in brilliant condition. Graves, with crosses still painted on their plaster walls, have been excavated near both the SE and NW corners. The unencumbered, treeless surroundings add to the impressive grandeur of this site.

LEONTARI Λεοντάρι Arkadia
Fortress ruins and two churches **. Easy access by car/bus.

The small town of Leontari was (like *Moukhli*) a relatively late Byz foundation; it was established in the late 13th or early 14th C by the despotate of Mystra, but its **fortress** was soon occupied by the Turks on their invasion of the Morea in 1395.

A certain amount still remains of the fortress – enough to suggest that the Byz builders had learnt something from the Franks about this kind of building. Its layout is comparable to that which would have been expected from Western builders, with a central keep and a surrounding circuit wall; only a little of the latter survives, but there is quite a substantial keep on the small summit, and a large cistern.

The sizeable **church of Ag Apostoloi** lies towards the E edge of the town, and is of a scale and sophistication which makes it a surprising building to find here. It is an early 14th-C structure, and although it was used as a mosque under Turkish rule (the minaret has been turned into a bell-tower – why did this not happen more often?) it has retained much of its original architecture. The immediate impression made by the exterior is one of relative complexity; there are two quite tall cupolas, one over the inscribed cross of the naos, the other over a w gallery, and four more tiny blind ones on either side of the N and s gable. The outline of the larger domes forms a series of 'eyebrows' as it rises over each of the eight windows in both drums. Even richer in surface relief are the three apses, where two rows of blind niches form an undulating screen round the upper storey, reminiscent of the apse of the *Hodegetria, Mystra*.

The interior, although spacious, with a wide naos merging with the narthex, is initially disappointing, the wall surfaces being mostly covered in 19th- and 20th-c soot; only very shadowy traces of fresco have survived on the N wall. The four columns are all different (presumably reused) and have flat, rather 'Egyptian' caps. In the gallery, however (reached from outside), the pumpkin dome has considerable remains of fresco, with figures of cherubim and saints occupying the curved vertical sections. They are of high quality, and are in a manner and style very reminiscent of the Kariye Djami in CP; they have been recently restored, and afford a distinct glimpse of metropolitan sophistication. This church, with the further decoration that it must be assumed to have had (destroyed during its period as a mosque) suggests that the village had quite important connections in the 14th c. (The papas will open the gallery for you, although you can see some of the frescoes from outside.)

The much more modest **church of Ag Athanasios** suggests that there was a small village here before the 13th c; it is a simple cross-vault building with no dome, but attractive brick patterning, and is probably 12th c in date. The interior is undistinguished, with the 14th-c frescos, although extensive, in a badly damaged state.

LERNA CASTLE
See **Myli**

LIVADIA   Λειβαδειά   Viotia
Castle **. Access by car almost to entrance, then steep tracks.

The town occupies a strategically important position, guarding the entrance to Thessaly from the s; its most active occupants during the later Middle Ages were the Catalans, who held Livadia and its castle as part of the Duchy of Athens from 1309 until 1380, when it was betrayed to the Navarrese; it also formed part of the bequest of Nerio Acciaiuoli to his son Antonio I in 1394.

The town is dominated by its only surviving building from the Middle Ages – the **castle** (Kastro), occupying a site almost as impregnably magnificent as Acrocorinth, although on a less dramatic scale. It is easy to see why the site of the Mount of Ag Ilias attracted the newly arrived Frankish rulers of Thebes; it is bounded to the w and n by the curve of the precipitous gorge through which the Erkinas river flows, and the terrain here would make any attack impossible; only from the s and e could a determined assault be contemplated. The castle was begun in the 13th c, but most of what you now see must date from the Catalan occupation of the 14th c, with only restrained recent restoration.

The long curtain wall runs steeply down, right across the n face of the mountain, ending at its lower e end with a substantial tower; the only entrance is towards the uppermost end, just before it meets the precipitous and craggy gorge which forms the only (and natural) defence of almost two-thirds of the enceinte. The masonry technique is largely indistinguishable from that of Frankish builders, with ready use of ceramic tile fragments for filling in the mortar; a yellowish growth on much n-facing masonry gives the grey local building stone the appearance of limestone. The main distinguishing feature here is the finely cut ashlar blocks from which the gateways are formed; these would seem to be a Catalan speciality, and are not found in quite the same form anywhere else. (Even at *Khlemoutsi*, which had fine masons, the gateways do not have this feature.) Part of the keep still survives, as a modest tower on the topmost crag of the mountain. A small late church is said to occupy the site of a temple to Zeus.

The reason why this castle retains so much of its 14th-c masonry is perhaps that, although it would always have been hard to capture on foot, the invention and development of gunpowder meant that well-placed cannon on the opposite side of the gorge could have rapidly decimated even the most determined defenders; not just its usefulness but also its siting and its design may simply have gone out of date. Unlike nearby *Khalkida* it seems neither to have caused any problems for Mehmed II, nor to have been of any great interest to him – hence its current state of relatively good preservation.

LOUTRA ELEUTHERO   Λουτρά Ελευθερώ   Kavala
Byz tower. Beside the road, 3 km E of village.

If you take the coast road from Amfipoli to Kavala you cannot miss this finely sited Byz tower; it must have formed part of the coastal defence and signalling system along the N Aegean. Some 20 m of it is still standing, and there are further minor outworks to E and S. With considerable use of brick, its construction sets it apart from the prevailing type of med tower in Greece: two bands of four courses, and then good dressed stone quoins (see p. 46). It is a reason for taking this road to Kavala rather than through Eleutheropolis.

LYGOURIO   Λυγουριό   Argolida
Three churches *. Easy access by car/bus.

The three churches in Lygourio provide a good range of Byz building: an interesting earlier example of church architecture, a complete fresco scheme and the attractive surroundings of the remoter church, while all of them exhibit the enthusiasm for the classical spolia available locally in massive quantities.

The earliest church here is that of **Ag Ioannis Eléimon** beside the road as it leaves the village on the E. It can be dated to *c*. 1080 and its design is of interest in that it represents a tendency to merge the spaces of the naos and bema by combining the two E supports of the cupola with the piers of the bema; the interior space (except for the narthex, which may be later) is thus so unified that it is not a true inscribed cross plan. The exterior is remarkable for the quantity of large-scale spolia that has been used – much of it quarried from the nearby site of Epidauros; on one piece in the N wall (clearly a marble door threshold, set vertically) you can even find that the builder has left a rough inscription, giving his name: Theophylact from the island of Chios. The masonry is otherwise simple, only giving way to cloisonné in the upper areas, and with only a small amount of dog-tooth ornament visible. The interior would have had frescos, but only a few traces of them now remain.

You will find the **church of the Koimisis tis Theotokou** up the steep hill to the N, towards the edge of the village. It is a modest inscribed cross, domed, single apse church of the late 13th or early 14th C. Externally, the church is unsophisticated but striking, as it is largely built from huge slabs of plain cut marble and stone (even the odd column), all again presumably excavated from the classical buildings of Epidauros, nearby. Its construction is picturesque, rather than skilled; originally its windows were quite small, but some are now enlarged. This may have been to allow the very complete and quite striking wall paintings inside to be more easily seen; they are probably later than the church itself, but still of the Byz period, and are in generally good state. They are an effective example of such a fresco scheme, with the Pantocrator, angels and prophets in the cupola and drum, evangelists in the squinches, Passion scenes and a fine Anastasis in the N and s vaults, with many standing saints lower down and a memorable Last Judgement on the w wall.

The **church of Ag Marina** lies outside the village to the w, at the foot of Mavrovouni; it is reached down a rough track. It is probably of the 14th c, and is quite a modest building, with the common plan of an inscribed cross, dome and three apses; the narthex may well be a later addition. Inside, there are some quite good paintings on the templon, but the chief interest is provided by the four columns supporting the cupola, each with quite a fine reused classical cap.

MAINA, GREAT MAINA CASTLE
See **Mani**

MANI Μάνη Messinia/Lakonia
Churches with frescos and ruins of three castles; collectively ***.

This entry deals with the whole area of the middle of the three tongues of rocky land that form the s tip of the Peloponnese, and which is known as the Mani. Among modern Greek travellers there is a group for whom the unique qualities of this region – particularly the s – have a permanent fascination. The border between Messinia and Lakonia meets the coast at a point just N of Areopoli where it could be said that (approximately) the N Mani ends and the s Mani (also called lower, or deep, Mani) begins. The N Mani can be thought of as the relatively narrow coastal strip where the huge, desolate mountain range of the Taygetos descends to the sea, while the saddle that divides this from the lower Mani and the Sangias has been used for the main road from Areopoli to Gythio. There is effectively only one road down the whole of this w coast from just s of Kalamata to Gerolimenas, so for ease of reference the whole area between *Stavropigi* and *Ano Boulari* will be treated as a journey from N to s, with entries given in this geographical, rather than

alphabetical, sequence. As elsewhere, remote sites are denoted by
the name of the nearest village(s).

The Mani, due to position and different historical conditions,
always retained a degree of independence. It seems certain that the
Slavs who invaded the Peloponnese during the early med period
eventually collected here, and so became a constant problem to
whatever power was trying to control the rest of the country. (Even
the Turks, after their occupation of the rest of Greece, appear to
have given up trying to impose some order on the Maniotes in the
same way as they did the other indigenous Greeks.) The name first
appeared in written form in the mid-10th c, when the Emperor
Constantine VII Porphyrogenitos, in his treatise on government *De
administrando imperio*, wrote of 'the fortress of Maina' where the
inhabitants were specifically not Slavs, but Hellenes (see *Great
Maina castle*).

The architectural interest of the whole region is overwhelmingly
that of its churches, and it has long been recognized that those of the
Mani, particularly the s, have some characteristics that make them
of special concern in the field of Byz church building. The area was
evangelized in the 10th c by Osios (the Holy) Nikon, and the first
major phase of church building on the peninsula seems to run from
the late 10th c to the later 12th c. The overwhelming majority of
these churches are very modest in size, and given the barren and
inhospitable terrain it is often surprising to find them, many of them
quite accomplished in construction, rising in unexpected locations;
decorative brick patterns abound, and all except the humblest are
domed. Particularly you will find considerable care has been
lavished on the decorative carving of the marble members of lintels,
templa, caps and transoms.

There are scores of churches in the Mani, but many are ruined
and many more are post-med, so only a selection is given here; for
example, although the church of Ag Prokopios, near Kitta, may
have the earliest surviving fresco decoration in the Mani, it is so
fragmentary and the church is so ruined that it seemed best to omit
it. Mani enthusiasts will know of it from more specialized literature.
All the sites mentioned here are of interest, as is so much of the
Mani, but if suggestions for priority are needed, emphasis could be
given (for varying reasons) to the churches at Kharouda, Episkopi,
Vamvaka and Ano Boulari, and to the site of Great Maina castle on
Tigani.

Stavropigi (Σταυροπηγή) is the modern name for **Zarnata** where the remains of a **fortress** * still survive, dominating the town of Kampos in the valley below. Access is from the s, up an easy foot track, which is now very overgrown. The area enclosed is a rough quadrilateral with one corner extended to an acute angle, and is some 150 m across. The origins of this castle are obscure, but it was still in use and garisonned by Greeks under Dimitrios Palaiologos when the Turks arrived in 1459. Its design is a normal one of a keep with a surrounding enceinte; no part of the site is particularly precipitous. Considerable lengths of the wall survive with their crenellation in a rather battered state, and the masonry suggests that this was mainly a Byz construction; the remains of a cistern can also be seen. You will see quite easily that the keep, now cracked and damaged and used as a shelter for farm animals, is a hybrid construction; earlier parts must be Byz, but most of it is known to have been built by a Turkish general, Ahmed Kiuprili, in 1670, and the later Turkish detail is evident.

Kardamyli (Καρδαμύλη), in common with other villages along this coast, had its own **castle**, although only a little of it now survives. Medievalists may be intrigued by a detail of the exterior marble framing of the window of a Venetian 18th-c church built inside the castle grounds. Here it can be seen that the bottom section is a piece of reused med carving, and it is interesting to see how this was respected by the 18th-c sculptor, who adapted his design to integrate with it. (The 18th c was the first period of economic revival in the Mani since the Turkish conquest, and a number of quite large churches, such as here and at Areopoli, were built then.)

In **Proastio** (Προάστιο) (just E of the coast road) there is a quarry still producing a fine limestone; this has been used for centuries locally, and must have affected local building habits. It was used in the main church in the village, which is dedicated to **Ag Nikolaos**, although partly plastered over now. This is slightly larger than most Maniote churches, but the plan is usual for its 11th/12th c date – an inscribed cross, with three externally faceted apses, although no separate narthex; the two original supports of the dome have been replaced by modern concrete. The good cloisonné of the exterior (where it can be seen) is relieved by dog-tooth brick courses. Inside there are extensive frescos, although later and in poor state. This church is very accessible and would seem to be a good case for careful restoration.

If you have half an hour to spare, you will find about 1 km further on above the village, turning right off the road past the quarry and less accessible, the small ruined church of **Ag Nikolaos** *. (Leave the car by the tractor track and walk up through the olive terraces.) It is the 11th-c katholikon of a small monastery and is now in a ruinous state, although you can still find some fragments of fresco; its dome is still standing, and some areas of criss-cross brick pattern still survive in the lower walls. It must have been replaced by the nearby later church of Ag Theodoroi (kept locked) but you will find the monastic well still intact; the rural site has great atmosphere.

Stoupa (Στούπα) is the modern name of the coastal village where in *c*. 1250 Guillaume de Villehardouin built the **castle of Beaufort** * – '. . . entre Clamate et ıa Grant Maigne, lequel s'apelle en françoys Beaufort et en grec s'apelle Leftro' (*Chronicle*) – for the purpose of establishing some control over the Slavs in the Taygetos. The summit of the outcrop of rock a short distance from the sea on which Villehardouin built his castle is some 70 m high and is not large, forming an approximate oval of about 60 by 30 m running NE–SW. The outer defences have disappeared without trace, so the approach through bushes and undergrowth is steep, though not difficult. You will be rewarded by some modest remains at the highest point of what must have been the keep; this is at the end of the oval nearest to the sea, about 1 km away. The destruction of the castle has been so nearly complete that it must have been deliberate, either by Greeks using it as a quarry, or Turks not wishing to leave it as a temptation for an occupied people.

Prominently close to the road at **Platsa** (Πλάτσα) is the quite substantial **church of Ag Nikolaos Kampinari**. It is an 11th/12th-c domed, inscribed cross, three-apse plan, with no narthex, and is one of the largest Maniote churches, but is at present closed and under restoration.

Also at Platsa is the smaller **church of Ag Ioannis Prodromos** *; with a single apse and cruder masonry than most 12th-c churches, the main interest here are the frescos. They are of several periods from the 12th to 18th c, and although not in good condition are worth visiting; note the fine Virgin Platytera in the apse, the signs of the Zodiac in the vault of the naos and scenes from the Akathyst hymn in the bema.

In **Nomitsis** (Νομιτσής) the domed **church of Ag Anargyroi** is beside the road. It might be said to be interesting rather than attractive, with cloisonné masonry used for the drum of the dome, which is quite tall for its cupola, and some criss-cross brick patterns showing in later masonry over the door. Inside, the dome can be seen to be carried only on vaults, with just the springing of squinches visible, and no columns; there is no apse. It is as if there was a change of plan during the building, with the original being almost encased in a slightly later design in which squinches played no part; it is probably 12th/13th c. The interior, including the templon, is covered with 14th-c frescos; they are in a poor state, but very extensive and in an individual style.

In **Thalames** (Θαλάμες) there are two churches which are quite easy to visit. The first that you will meet coming from Nomitsi is the **church of the Metamorphosis** *, about 50 m from the Ag Anargyroi; it is beside the road, and is used as a cemetery church. Although modest in size, it has signs of being a more ambitious building than its size would suggest. It dates from the 11th or 12th c and is built on an inscribed cross, three-apse plan, but has four columns, and the brick patterning round windows and apses is unusually elaborate. Inside, the 14th-c frescos are in poor state, but there is some quite interesting carving on all four of the caps and on the templon. Further on, in the village of Thalames, but just off the main road, is the tiny 12th/13th c **church of Ag Basilios**; it is so small that it needs no columns to support its dome, although the drum is quite high; the cloisonné masonry is of surprisingly good quality, but is not continued in the later narthex. Inside there are remains of 14th/15th-c frescos, which are undistinguished.

In the village of **Langada** (Λαγκάδα) the **church of Ag Sotiros** * beside the road in the village is medium-sized and relatively sophisticated; it is not very well known as its rather fine masonry and brick patterns were only revealed in 1985 when plaster rendering was removed. It must be an 11th-c building, with fairly standard features of inscribed cross, two-column design; the central of the three apses may have been enlarged. Inside, the iconostasis is modern, but in several places thick plaster has been removed from walls and vaults to reveal that the interior is probably covered with 11th/12th-c paintings. When these become visible this will be one of the larger and more striking churches of the Mani, which suggests that this is a foundation of greater prestige than most in the area.

At **Kharouda** (Χαρούδα) the 11th/12th-c **church of the Taxiarch** * is of surprising scale and quality considering its remote position. It is a domed, inscribed cross, three-apse, four-column plan, with a narthex that seems contemporary. There are still some glazed ceramic bowls in the apses and the drum of the cupola (which has a later modification rounding the octagon into a cylinder), and the lintel and threshold are both of reused, finely carved marble (perhaps too fine to have been made locally?). Inside, the relatively lavish use of carved marble continues with transoms common in the Mani. Quite extensive frescos remain, of the 14th c and later: the Virgin Platytera in the apse, Pantocrator and prophets in the cupola (poor condition), scenes from the Dodecaorton in N and s bays, and scenes of martyrdoms lower down, with St Barbara meeting a particularly gruesome end. A 14th-c inscription in the narthex shows that painting continued in later phases. Of the many Maniote churches this is among the better preserved, larger in scale, and easier of access.

At **Gardenitsa** (Γαρδενίτσα) the small 11th-c **church of Ag Sotiras** is of domed, inscribed cross, two-column design; it also has a substantial domed porch with dog-tooth brick courses, probably 12th c. The cupola has an impressively broad drum, with the eight small arches neatly rounded in brick. Of interest here for its relatively early date is the use of brick, with some large limestone spolia reused, and the simple, rather rustic carving in the porch and on the masonry templon.

In **Vamvaka** (Βάμβακα) the **church of Ag Theodoros **** is close to the main road and in the village. It owes its modest importance not so much to its architecture (it is of fairly standard domed, inscribed cross, two-column, triple-apse Maniote design, although the cloisonné masonry, now crumbling, must once have been impressive) but rather to the fact that it contains some marble carving to which the sculptor added an inscription giving his name and (almost uniquely) the date. The exterior has the treatment (quite common from the mid-11th c) of rougher masonry in the lower courses, with cloisonné above, and the dome has retained some of its glazed pottery bowls; on the lintel and jambs of the entrance door there is an inscription and some attractive carving depicting doves and other motifs. Inside, the only real interest is provided by the four carved marble transoms; although the quality of carving, with its simple repeated patterns, is unremarkable, if you look up at the underside of the w transom you will see the inscription carved by 'Nikitas the marble-worker' (Νικήτας μαρμαράς) and dated 1075. This inscription has allowed the identification, and therefore the dating, of several other later 11th-c churches in the Mani with marble carving by Nikitas; these include the churches of Ag Giorgios and Ag Triada at nearby Briki. Nikitas, who elsewhere calls himself 'the servant of Christ', is one of the few such figures from this period known by name; it is just a pity that his extremely modest gifts (there is no evidence that he even carved the more attractive reliefs over the outside of the doorway here) do not permit any further comparison with Gislebertus, the brilliant 12th-c sculptor who left his name in the Burgundian cathedral of Autun.

The 12th-c **church of Ag Varvara *** at **Erimos** (Ερημος) is quite remotely sited in fields, but can be reached down a rough track. Its design is quite standard, being a domed, inscribed cross, triple-apse plan, but the quality of its cloisonné masonry is surprisingly high and there are some finely inventive brick and ceramic patterns, particularly on the exterior of the main apse. Its only unique feature is some unusually good relief marble carving; in the windows of all three apses, in both N and S gables, as well as over the door and window in the S side, you will find surprisingly accomplished areas of decorative marble sculpture.

Between **Mezapos** and **Ag Giorgios** is the small and remote church of the **Vlakerna ***. Having reached Ag Giorgios (nr Stavri) by car, access is quite slow through overgrown terraces and goat tracks, but the site is magnificent, looking across the bay sw to Tigani and *Great Maina castle*. The church is an 11th-c building of standard inscribed cross design, with a narthex and one apse; it is unusual, however, in being built largely without the use of brick, except for the dome. It is worth pointing this out as it can be seen inside that the two columns which supported the dome have broken, and the pieces are stacked on one side; the four marble transoms are also broken, but still in place, as is the dome itself – surely a tribute to the building skills of the masons. The frescos, where they survive, are of quite good quality; note the painted figure of John the Baptist on the masonry templon, and the Raising of Lazarus in the N vault. These add some modest distinction to the atmosphere and surroundings of this fine site.

Only about 400 m due S of Vlakerna is the **church of Episkopi **** (take same rough footpath, but veer left after some 250 m). This is certainly one of the most sophisticated churches of the Mani, and has one of the more complete fresco schemes; its name implies that it may have been the seat of a bishop. It is built on a standard 12th-c inscribed cross, triple-apse, two-column plan, but the masonry shows a more wholesale attempt at cloisonné, and the rain-spouts on the cupola are carved animal heads.

Inside, the columns carry two classical Ionic caps, there is a good masonry templon and all four transoms are still in place. The frescos are mainly 12th c (just a few are from the 18th c), and are by a considerable artist, giving an idea of the riches that are now lost from so many Maniote churches. The narthex (contemporary with the naos) shows part of a Last Judgement and there is a developed cycle of St George in the s of the naos; less usual are the paintings of the Mandylion and Keramion (from the Abgar legend) on the w-facing arch of the bema, and the scene of the Ascension in the vault of the bema has figures with a real sense of movement and variety of gesture.

The church and its frescos have been restored, and although not of exceptional interest, their setting and condition means that they must count as one of the treasures of the Mani.

On **Tigani promontory**, between **Stavri** and **Mezapos** are the extensive ruins of a castle and a large Byz church. Access is best by car to Stavri, then on foot by a track which peters out among sharp rocks. Allow half a day for this spectacular site, and take strong shoes.

At least four sites for the **castle of Great** (or **Grand**) **Maina** ** have been proposed, but this one seems to fit the facts best. (Other candidates include Porto Kagio, a small fishing village on the SE coast of the peninsula, Kelefa to N and Kastro tis Orias to the S.) Of the two passages in the *Chronicle of the Morea* that relate to it, one (Ch. 205) says how (in the 1250s) Guillaume '. . . fit encore construire dans le Magne, sur un rocher terrible au-dessus d'un promontoire, une autre forteresse qu'il appela Maïna (le Grand-Magne)'. Later (Ch. 762) a deception by Florent of Hainault, who arrived by sea in 1291/2, is described: '. . . il vint droit a la pointe ou est le chastel de la Grant Maigne. Et ancoys que il preist port, se fit lever les banières de Saint Marc . . . semblant que il estoient marcheant de Venise . . . pour decevoir celle gent'. The remains which correspond best to a castle built on a rock, but which were arrived at by sea, are on the tip of this magnificent but harshly exposed, jaggedly rocky promontory, some 16 km NW of Tenaro. The site here is such that it is one of the very few castles which could be approached and serviced from the sea; communication on land is so slow and rocky that mules could only manage it with great difficulty, and there is a small cove beside the rocky neck of land attaching the headland to the Mani peninsula that must have been

used as a harbour. (*Tigani* means 'frying pan' and the causeway is
therefore a broad 'panhandle'.)

The castle would have been built with a single enceinte fortified
with towers; Villehardouin probably built on to the minimal remains of some ancient structure, but of his castle only ruins now
survive. You can see the remains of a curtain wall running sw from
the castle to a bluff overlooking the sea; was this the harbour where
Florent of Hainault arrived? In spite of the ruinous state of the
defences you can still only enter the area through the old gateway in
the SE corner, where the rock-cut stairs are worn smooth (again,
impossible for horses). The lower parts of some of the towers
survive, some walling and seaward facing fortifications to the NE
looking out from the sheer cliffs, and many cisterns and ruined
buildings along the w sector. The remains of a chapel with a curved
apse and part of a conch survive in the sw corner of the site.

What the *Chronicle* does not relate is that Villehardouin would
have found the site occupied by the ruins of a substantial **church**,
and it is these excavated ruins which, with the location, create with
the castle such a unique site. In plan the church is a three-aisle,
three-apse basilica, with a narthex, and an overall length of some 24
m; even in a ruined state it is an impressive structure, and no other
Maniote medieval church is of this size. A 9th-c date has been
suggested for this, and the remaining masonry, with fragmentary
remains of fresco in the narthex and bema, could confirm this.
Parapet fragments suggest that it was galleried.

What also makes Great Maina of such interest is that it was the
first name in the entire peninsula to receive a mention in Byz
writing. In the treatise on government called *De administrando
imperio* by the Emperor Constantine VII Porphyrogenitos *c.* 1050,
he wrote (Ch. 50): 'Those who live in the fortress of Maina (Κάστρου
Μαίνης) are not of the race of the Slavs, but of the more ancient
Romans (παλαιοτέρων Ρωμαίων), and are even to this day called
Hellenes by the local inhabitants . . . In the time of the great Basil
they were baptised Christians . . .' It is clear that this had been an
exceptional outpost of Byz culture, and there is some evidence such
as reused carved marble screen slabs in the threshold which (with
other features) show that some EC or early Byz material of 5th to 7th
c was imported here. You will see that there are dressed limestone
blocks in the lower walls, with local stone and mortar above,
suggesting successive phases of building. A second unique feature is
that the area of the nave and s aisle is occupied by numerous graves;
this would confirm the special and isolated character of the site and

suggests a local cult. It also seems that the floor of the whole of the N aisle covered what looks like a large cistern (the supports of the floor over it are still visible); this may also be 9th C, or have been created by Villehardouin when he built the castle in the mid-13th C. Further cisterns to the immediate SW of the church and by the seaward ramparts all point to there having been, despite the windy and barren desolation of the site today, a sizeable Byz population here.

The destruction of Great Maina castle (like *Beaufort*) is so advanced that it cannot have been just the work of the elements; the Turks may have further dismantled it when they occupied the area and built Kelefa to the N. In spite of this, you will find that the desolate site provides a truly memorable visit.

The **church of Ag Sergios and Bakkhos *** near **Kitta**, and easily seen from the road some 80 m to the E (use the oblique dirt road to it) has a local name of Tourloti ('the domed one'). It is a small, 12th-C inscribed cross design, with four columns supporting the dome. The exterior is unusual for the large vertical stone blocks incorporated into the cloisonné, bands of tile and plentiful use of brick round windows in the three gables. You may find this exterior somewhat over-restored, but the general setting is attractive. Inside there is the predictable interest in carved marble, with transoms and caps all decorated. The frescos have mostly gone, but, uncommonly, there is a dedication inscribed over the W door by the founder, 'George the Marasiate'.

At **Ano Boulari** (Ανω Μπουλάρι), inland from Gerolimenas, the small **church of the Ag Stratigos *** is on the NE edge of the village. It is an early 11th-C domed design, with an inscribed cross, two-column, triple-apse plan; a substantial porch has been added to an existing narthex – perhaps used as the village schoolroom at one time. The cloisonné of the exterior is relieved by some sound (if modest) decorative brickwork. Inside, the masonry iconostasis has some of its original paintings, and, as so often in the Mani, it was on the decorative marble of the interior that considerable care was also spent. Here all four carved transoms are still in place and some marble templon members are stacked in the S bay; while the quality of the carving is unexceptional, when all was in place it would have been a major feature of the interior.

This church is most notable, however, for retaining (though with some damage) one of the most complete fresco schemes in the Mani. That occupying the narthex, naos and bema is late 11th to 12th C and keeps largely to conventional distribution but with an emphasis on healing miracles with lively presentation; note the fine St Michael adjacent to the templon, and the Virgin Platytera in the apse. The frescos of the exonarthex are later (?13th or 14th c) and of less interest.

While at Ano Boulari leave time to visit also the **church of Ag Panteleimon** * in olive groves to the NW, reputedly late 10th c. (Start from the modern church lower down the village, cross the concrete bridge there and walk some 600 m along an overgrown mule-track; you will see the flat stones of its roof to your left.) It is the simplest of barrel-vaulted halls (no dome), of which the w end has collapsed, but the real surprise is to find that the E end forms two equal apses – unique in the Mani. There are frescos remaining of several different periods; the most accomplished is a superb figure of St Kyriaki on the s wall which could be 11th c or even 10th, but the conches of the apses contain the most unusual subjects: portraits of St Panteleimon in the N one and a bearded saint in the s who has lost his inscription. These are of the same phase of painting as the Ascension in the vault of the bema and the bishops in the lower part of the apses, and although more primitive in character than the female saint, may be of the same date. There is random repainting evident in other frescos here, such as the Nativity and Baptism, where in both the head of Christ is quite recently painted. Of all the contrasts that you will encounter in the Mani, this half-buried, half-ruined chamber with its powerful frescos must be one of the more extreme.

MEGARA Μέγαρα   Attika
Conventual buildings *. About 6 km NW of Megara. Easy access by car.

The **convent of the Panagia tis Kypariotissa and of Ag Hierotheos** provides a good opportunity to experience a middle Byz monastic complex, comparable with *Sagmata* in Viotia. The surrounding buildings are largely later, but the katholikon is a modest, 12th-c cross-in-square building, with a later parekklision built on to the N. It has some 13th-c frescos which are reasonably well preserved; their subject-matter and distribution is largely standard, with an enthroned Christ in the cupola and adoring archangels below as can be found in other schemes of this date, evangelists in the squinches, and part of the Dodecaorton in adjacent areas. The more unusual features here are the Etoimasia and Virgin in the E and w of the drum, and particularly the presence of the Lamentation and

Resurrection in the soffit of the w arch; the latter, even if later, suggests some Western influence; the standard Byz scene for Easter is the Anastasis, and this must be somewhat later than the other frescos. They are in a provincial style consistent with the relatively remote site. As is now common, the convent buildings have been recently restored but have retained an attractive simplicity.

MENDENITSA Μενδενίτσα Fthiotis, nr Thermopylae
Castle *. Easy access by car, then short, steep walk.

Largely through its position close to the pass of Thermopylae, the **castle of Bodonitsa** has had an unusually colourful history, even for med Greece. From 1205 to 1410 it was the seat of the Italian Marquises of Pallavicini, a noble family from near Parma; Boniface of Montferrat had given the fief of Bodonitsa to Guido Pallavicini, the family's ne'er-do-well youngest son who had come to Greece to escape trouble at home. By good fortune and opportunism it was to survive longer than almost all the other Western strongholds; in 1335, long after the Catalan invasion, it was still in the hands of the same family, and the Marquis Giulielmo Pallavicini placed himself under the protection of the Venetians. The marquisate passed in this way to the Venetian family of the Zorzi, who were still in possession in 1410 when the Turkish Sultan, Musa, marched into Thessaly and besieged the strategically vital castle. A traitor assassinated the Marquis Giacomo Zorzi, who was defending the site like Leonidas of old; the Turks took it and carried off his son and heir to Adrianople. Venetian diplomacy saved both him, his title and the castle, but the latter did not survive after 1414, when the Turks could not be prevented even by the might of the Republic from destroying the castle's fortifications and enslaving much of the local population. As an empty title, however, the marquisate still lives on in Venice among the Zorzi of S Giustina.

The site of the castle is a fine one, unencumbered and looking down N to the sea and NW towards Thermopylae. It can be approached either from the sw, involving a steep climb up the hill from the road from Thermopylae, or (less steeply) through a series of modern farm buildings on the E. There are two baileys and the remains of a single outer enceinte, with towers descending on the s almost into the modern village below. The enclosed area of the hill-top is an oval of approx. 100 × 50 m.

It is clear even from the road that there are several phases of building; some of the w wall is constructed of large dressed lime-stone blocks that must be from a classical fortress, but most is of undressed stone with ceramic slip filling in the mortar. Over the doorway into the second bailey there is a passable attempt at copying a Greek dog-tooth course using tiles and thick mortar layers, but it lacks the crispness and skill that you can see in so many churches. The wall dividing the two baileys is surmounted by a tower, the upper parts of which show yet another phase of building – possibly under the Zorzi? The inner bailey shows the remains of a cistern, but there are no signs of a castle chapel. The combination of site, ruins and history conspire to make this a memorable site.

MERBAKA Μέρμπακα Argolida
Church *. Easy access by bus/car.

This village (officially known as Agia Triada) derives its name from Guillaume de Mörbecke, a learned Flemish Dominican who was Bishop of Corinth 1278–86.

The **church of the Panagia**, on the sw edge of town, is built on a cross-in-square, triple-apse plan and is of quite impressive size; the dome, with its octagonal drum, is supported on four columns. The design relates closely to those of the *Ag Moni, Areia* and of the *Panagia, Khonika*, 5 km away. The windows are sizeable and arcaded, with the centre raised. The exterior, apart from the unusually high drum of the dome, with each facet pierced by quite a large window, is notable for the ornamentation which relieves the fine cloisonné masonry. Some of it is in brick and tile, set round windows and in dog-tooth and meander pattern courses, and there is an unusually large assemblage of 11 coloured pottery bowls still in place; these have been used to suggest a date of *c.* 1200 for the building of the church, which must in any case be before 1210 when the Franks captured Nauplio and Argos. In other areas there is extensive use of spolia, both classical and Byz, including carved fragments with vine-scroll and vegetable ornament, fishes, and two fine classical grave slabs. There is also the external feature of large crosses let into the masonry at ground level. There are the remains of supports for porches on both n and s doors, which is unusual; the belfry over the gabled w façade is clearly later.

This is an unusually attractive church, and you may wish to combine a visit here with the *Ag Moni, Areia*, that at *Khonika* and the earlier church of *Ag Ioannis*, *Lygourio*, which form a distinct Argolid group.

METEORA Μετέωρα   Nr Kalabaka, Trikala

Monasteries, collectively ***, but you may not wish to visit all of them. Most easily visited by car, but coach transport available in summer. Crowded in tourist season; clothing regulations are enforced. Allow at least a full day.

It is impossible to remain unimpressed by the extraordinary geological formation of this area, where a succession of isolated craggy masses of eroded grey rock have produced a strange landscape of an almost lunar unreality. These precipitous and towering pinnacles have, since the mid-14th c, been made the site of a number of monasteries and their dependencies; at its period of greatest expansion in the 16th c there were 13 active monasteries here, with over 20 dependencies of varying size and status. As with the monasteries on *Mount Athos* much of the building and art that the modern visitor sees is of quite late or even recent date, but as a spectacular manifestation of Byz monasticism the Meteora monasteries are unrivalled in Greece. A visit to the metropolis in *Kalabaka*, nearby, should be included if at all possible.

Five of the monasteries are discussed here, and they include all the most interesting and rewarding to visit (Ag Triada is of minimal interest); the sequence given here is based mainly on geographical logic, the chronological order being rather different.

The undoubted star of the Meteora group is the **monastery of the Great Meteoron**, dedicated to the Transfiguration, and it makes the best starting-point for a visit. It was founded by Osios Athanasios (1305–83) some time in the mid-14th c, but had as its beginning just a large cave, through part of which you will pass on the modern stairway into the monastery; it was here that Athanasios lived from 1344.

Serbian influence was paramount at this period, and it was the Serbian leader Symeon Uroš who first granted the monastery privileges in 1362. His son, John Uroš Palaiologos, who had reigned as co-emperor with his father at Trikala, became a disciple of Athanasios. He took monastic vows in 1381 as the monk Ioasaph, and on the death of Athanasios was then to become in effect the second founder of the monastery here. At his own expense from 1383 he had built the first katholikon of the Theotokos, and this is

still the first part of the building that you will see; the exterior of the
E end, with its three faceted apses, remains as the memorial of this
unusual royal *ktitor*, who was famed for his piety.

The katholikon was enlarged to the w in 1483, and much of the
painting that you see today was done at this time; again in 1544–55,
by cutting away some rock to the w, the katholikon was further
enlarged, being then given its present grand and lofty appearance.
(It was in 1541 that the authority of the Great Meteoron over all the
other monasteries was confirmed by the metropolitan of Larisa,
and it may have been the acquisition of this new status which
prompted the further expansion.) Once you are inside the very
spacious square narthex, its vaults supported on four columns, it is
difficult to realize that the whole edifice is confined to the summit of
a broad column of rock.

The earliest of the frescos are in the apse, but the most evident are
those in the narthex and naos; these are mainly 16th C, and
surprisingly bear no signature. They are in good (though restored)
condition, the colours perhaps over-bright, and they cover all the
surfaces of the building in great profusion. The subject-matter is
conventionally arranged, although you may be surprised to see a
font in a niche of the narthex with the Baptism of Christ painted
above it.

The other monastic buildings here (all basically late 14th C) are
also some of the most interesting in the whole Meteora group.
Apart from the kitchen with its dome, and even an infirmary, do not
miss a visit to the large trapeza (itself an impressive hall 35 m long,
with a rounded apse behind the high table, still with some of its
16th-C frescos) as there is here the most extensive and interesting
museum of the group – and (except for Athens) in Greece. Items
displayed include many icons, three of them good 14th-C pieces
(two of the *Man of Sorrows*) and a complete 16th-C set of the
Dodecaorton, many illuminated MSS, including an Evangelistary
dated 1297, a 12th-C ivory relief and a steatite, many textiles
including a 14th-C epitaphios, and much later silver.

The **monastery of Ag Nikolaos Anapavsas** was one of the latest
foundations in the group, and the present katholikon only dates
from the early 16th C; its name probably derives from the original
founder, named Anapavsas, and it is now staffed by nuns. The chief
interest here are the frescos in the katholikon by the famous artist
Theophanes from Crete, who later worked on *Mount Athos*. He
completed the work (according to the inscription over the door) in

October 1527; they have now been well restored, and in their way are, with those of *Varlaam*, one of the show-pieces of the Meteora. The katholikon itself is a simple hall plan, and the small narthex is entered on its corner; the paintings here are of standing figures below, with miracle scenes above and a Last Judgement over the door into the naos. Of the impressive paintings which cover the walls of the naos, note particularly the large scene of the death of the Syrian monk St Ephraim, who is shown being buried with an icon on his breast and with other ascetics inhabiting the desert round him.

The founders of the present **monastery of Varlaam** were two brothers from Ioannina, Nektarios and Theophanes Apsaras; although the katholikon that they built was completed on 17 May 1544 (the day of Theophanes' death), there were already the remains of a later 14th-c church built by an earlier monk called Barlaam. The monastic buildings here are, with the trapeza, kitchen and infirmary as well as the famous winding machinery, very complete; the katholikon, dedicated to All Saints, has two tall cupolas over its naos and narthex. It can offer (with *Ag Nikolaos*) the other major show-piece of later Byz art of Meteora. Its 16th-c frescos, although restored in 1780 and again in recent times, make an immediate impact; those in the narthex were painted by Frangos Katellanos and his brother George of Thebes in 1566, and those in the naos a little earlier, in 1544. In the large square narthex, you cannot miss the imposing Last Judgement over the door into the naos, and impressive portraits of Byz hymnographers, with many martyrdom scenes above. In the naos (only just larger than the narthex) the distribution of subjects is conventional, but the artist's personality is strongly evident; the Koimisis on the w wall is typically rich in luxuriant and colourful detail, and there are full-length portraits of the founders, Nektarios and Theophanes, de-noted as *Osioi*. The chapel of the Three Hierarchs is in reality the site of the original 14th-c chapel which pre-existed the 16th-c foundation; the frescos here are 17th c, and include another repre-sentation of the death of the monastic saint, Ephraim. A small museum has been set up here, but its contents are less impressive than in the Great Meteoron or Ag Stefanos; there is an epitaphios of 1609 with other embroidered textiles, a number of later icons, two cases of old printed volumes and a case of later silver.

The **monastery of Roussanou** is not only one of the smallest, but could not be enlarged without advanced engineering: it fits precisely on to the top of its rock, its walls growing sheer from the vertical cliffs below. It is now staffed by nuns. The origin of its name is uncertain, although it may be associated with the Thessalian village of Rousana, but it is known that the buildings now present were founded around 1545 by two brothers who came from Ioannina, called Maximos and Ioasaph; their signed testament and typikon for the monastery still survive.

Its katholikon, of which the forms merge into some of the other monastic buildings, with only a modest cupola protruding, is now dedicated to Ag Varvara. You enter it through a small narthex, and the naos is an almost square space under the tall dome, with two columns and absidioles to N and S. We are fortunate that its frescos still survive, as by 1614 the monastery was already largely derelict and was placed under the Abbot of Barlaam; the paintings are dated 1560 in an inscription over the door, and are all now in good, if restored, condition. Those in the narthex display many martyrdoms, and striking images of the 'Second Coming in a shallow cupola; in the naos the subject-matter is mostly conventional for this period.

The **monastery of Ag Stephanos** is the easiest to visit of the whole group, having just a bridge across a ravine to its main entrance, and it is the only other monastery to be able to trace a continuous history back to the late 14th C. Its founder (like that of the Great Meteoron) had imperial connections; he was called Antonios Kantakuzene, being a grandson of the Emperor John VI, and died in 1404. The date of its foundation is not known, but must have been in the years just before 1400. Now staffed by nuns, this is a less satisfactory monastery to visit, as the original katholikon (a single nave, wooden-roofed basilica) cannot currently be entered. The present main church was built in 1798, and its frescos suffered during the use of the monastery by Communist forces in the 1940s. There is a small museum here with some quite good later embroidered textiles, a 16th-C liturgical scroll and other documents with lead seals, and some good later icons.

METHONI Μεθώνη Messinia. Med Modon
Castle *. Easy approach by car.

This port was of little med importance before 1204; Justinian's general, Belisarius, had used it as a base from which to attack the Vandals in N Africa in the 6th C, but its later use by pirates (encouraged by the Byzantines to attack Venetian shipping) had caused the Venetians to destroy the place in 1125. From 1209 it was exclusively under their control, and they fortified it to serve as one of the ports of call for the lucrative pilgrimage trade to Palestine, of which Venice had built up a virtual monopoly. Its bishop was, from 1210, a suffragan of the archbishop of *Corinth*, and Methoni, with *Koroni* on the other side of the peninsula, was known as 'the eyes of the Serene Republic'.

The **castle** is on a spectacular site, occupying the whole of the peninsula. Although the castle was originally built in the 13th c, when Methoni was allotted to the Venetians, much of what you will now see is of later construction. You enter it through its most recent addition – a gateway built by the French in 1828 – and then through a huge second Venetian gateway of *c.* 1700; you are then in the large expanse of the single main enclosure, where a basic *pavé* road system (presumably French?) still survives.

You will see at once a 14th-c Venetian well-head, its Gothic arcading still visible despite the weathering, and a bit over to your right, set in the wall, a dated 15th-c relief of the lion of St Mark. Turning to other parts of the castle, the well-built tower in the E curtain wall may have survived from Byz occupation before 1125, and there is also a postern gate in this wall, with a fine tower, which must be no later than 13th c. For the rest, the Turkish engineers and builders have done a thorough job of 16th- and 17th-c modernization, even providing a bath-house as well as the much-photographed octagonal Bourzi tower, visited from the sea gate in the s defences. A visit to Methoni is certain to be scenically exciting and memorable, if mildly frustrating for a medievalist.

MOLYVDOSKEPASTOS Μολυβδοσκέπαστος Ioannina.
Med Depalitsa
Monastery and three churches **. w of Mount Smolikas, close to Albanian border; all easily reached by car.

Now a very modest and straggling village, this once had imperial associations; the Emperor Constantine IV Pogonatos (668–85) was a visitor here and his name survives in the nearby village of Pogoniani. He founded the **monastery of the Koimisis tis Theotokou**, and while nothing remains of this building, the existing katholikon is its successor, and its cupola showing above the surrounding wall is the first building you will see on your right as you approach the village.

The circuit wall, gateway and monastic outbuildings are all relatively new, having been replaced after major damage in 1944, but the ensemble still reproduces a conventional med monastic complex. The oldest part of the katholikon must be late 13th/14th C; it is an impressive building on an inscribed cross, triconch plan, with a single E apse, and buttressing apsidal forms on N and S sides; the exterior shows some use of brick over the windows and in the drum of the cupola – quite a high one, comparable to some of the Serbian churches to the N. There is an attractive blind arcade of brick round the main apse, above the window, and a large, later, arcaded exonarthex has been added on the W. There may have been an early reconstruction of the W part of the original building (replacement of a W apsidal form?); certainly the masonry and the form of the present narthex suggest such a change. This feeling is increased when you enter the building, as the arches and vaults which support the cupola and create the interior space (there are no columns) leave an otherwise unexplained area at this point. The frescos are mostly contemporary, but are in a poor state; a fragment now in the Museum at *Ioannina* suggests that they must have been of high quality. As it is, the best preserved of them is an interesting later version of the Second Coming on the E wall of the exonarthex, over a fine carved door-frame (possibly 14th C?).

If you continue up the valley to the village you will find three further church buildings; although two of them are now roofless, they are eloquent evidence of the importance that this small village once had. The only complete church is the medium-sized one of **Ag Apostoloi**, a few yards from the Albanian border; this was the seat of the bishop of Pogoniani. It is a 13th C, inscribed cross plan with four columns supporting a very substantial cupola with a twelve-sided drum. It was restored in the 16th and 17th C, and the exterior is now cement rendered, although some brick can be seen round the windows; the interior with its 17th-C frescos is dark, with the four windows on the S side bricked up.

Overlooking the village is the partly ruined **church of Ag Sozon**, protected by a modern iron-frame shelter. Probably 12th C, it is built almost entirely of local stone; its single large, faceted apse shows limited use of brick in dog-tooth courses and tiny arches over the window. Its size is still impressive: almost 17 m from the W wall of the narthex to the apse; an interesting fragment of fresco survives inside, just below the window in the middle of the apse, showing a well-preserved double-headed eagle – the imperial symbol.

The **church of Ag Dimitrios** is slightly downhill from the main village; it is also roofless, and although slightly smaller, it must have been a more ambitious building. There is quite a lavish use of brick, with double courses used in much of the walling and in the apse; as in the monastery, there is a row of blind niches round the exterior of the apse, and brick arches over the windows. All this suggests a late 13th- to 14th-c date, implying a revival in the fortunes of the area at this time.

MONEMVASIA Μονεμβασία Lakonia. Med Malvoisie, Malvesie, Napoli di Malvasia, Napoli di Romania and Malmsey

Site, two churches and fortress ruins ***. Access by car to lower town and then steep footpaths. At least half a day; try to allow one day.

The extraordinary mass of rock rising abruptly from the sea towards the most SE extremity of the Peloponnese had great strategic importance throughout the med period and beyond. Its name grew from its impregnable position, as the causeway by which the town was reached gave it 'only one entrance' (μόνος and ἔμβασις); it was this feature which meant that time and again it was the last part of the Peloponnese to be occupied by successive invaders. The Normans tried unsuccessfully to capture it in 1147, and it took the determination of the combined forces of the Franks and Venetians, besieging it from 1246 for three years, to wrest it from Byz control, and even then only with special privileges. Then in 1262, with *Geraki*, *Mystra* and *Great Maina*, it returned once again to the Greeks and remained their headquarters in the Peloponnese until *c.* 1280. The town always enjoyed special trading privileges and exemptions, including (as part of the terms for ending the siege) commercial protection; these were continued under Andronikos II and III. Under the former, the town was made the seat of the tenth bishopric of the Byz Empire. Its significance was recognized by the Latins long before they gained actual control of the town, as they had appointed a suffragan bishop of Monemvasia as early as 1210, subject to the metropolitan of Corinth.

In 1460 the immense natural strength of its position meant that even Sultan Mehmed refrained from trying to take it; the governor, Manuel Palaiologos, was respected by the sultan, and he was required merely to give up the mother and daughter of Dimitrios (his brother, the despot of Mystra) who had taken refuge there; they were placed in the sultan's harem in Viotia. The populace had always maintained great independence (even the *Chronicle of the Morea* had said of it 'liquel estoient le plus loyal et li plus fort de tout le pays'). Having thus seen off Mehmed, they first invited a Catalan pirate who happened to be in the area, Lope de Baldaja, to be their leader but he very soon proved to be too autocratic for them, and so they decided to place themselves under the protection of the pope, Pius II. He was happy to maintain any Christian outpost against the Turks, and was for three years their protector until the Venetians took it over; they were then in possession for almost 80 years before yielding to the Turks in 1540. A second period of Venetian rule lasted from 1690 to 1715. The famous (or notorious) sweet Malmsey wine took its name from this town, from where for centuries it was exported to western Europe.

The **lower town** is enclosed by a sea wall and two land walls, which stride up the steepening slope to meet with the rock face of the acropolis. Of the several med churches that must have existed here, all have either disappeared or been rebuilt; the main one is the **church of Christ Elkomenos** (Χρίστος Ελκόμενος). This rare dedication is the title of an episode in the Passion of Christ in which the Saviour, with hands bound, is shown being 'dragged' (ελκόμενος) to the Crucifixion. The earliest surviving occurrence of this iconography is probably now in a fresco in Cyprus and an enamelled Byz reliquary in Esztergom, and it must be fairly certain that reference was being made to an original image in CP, now lost; this church would certainly have contained an image (probably an icon) of the subject of its dedication. There may indeed have been here a short series of large icons of Passion subjects, of which that of the Crucifixion now in the *Byzantine Museum, Athens* is the only survivor; the 13th-c fresco in the *church of the Zöodokhos Pigi, Geraki* may well also reflect the image that could once be found here. Unhappily, the only survivals from the med church would seem to be the relief sculpture over the entrance door and (possibly) the stone seating round the apse – the broken fragment with two peacocks, even in its damaged state, is particularly fine. The date of 1697, below the sculpture, refers to the rebuilding of the present façade.

   Although there are 24 other churches in various stages of repair in the lower town, none retains sufficient of its medieval fabric to be mentioned at all fully here. The period of the second Venetian occupation saw 17 of them either newly built or reconstructed, and many churches from the Byz period must have disappeared at this time. Ag Nikolaos, just above the Elkomenos, was built in 1703 by a patrician named Likinios, and another is the Panagia Kritikia (or Myrtidiotissa), further to the E which is also 18th C; here, just a fine Byz inscription and relief of a double-headed eagle are set incongruously into its rusticated Venetian façade – presumably survivals from an earlier church.

You will have to make the steep ascent on foot to the acropolis (ungated) to visit the undisputed gem of Monemvasia, the **church of Ag Sofia**, which clings precariously to the cliff edge; this must be one of the most spectacular sites for a church anywhere in Greece. (Its present dedication is in fact only a 19th-c one; previously it was dedicated to the Theotokos Hodegetria.) Traditionally founded by the Emperor Andronikos II (1282–1328), the grandeur and scale of its design certainly suggests an imperial connection. The plan, like that of *Ag Theodoroi*, *Mystra* and *the Parigoritissa*, *Arta*, is a close development of that of the katholikon at *Dafni*, with the very short arms of a basic cross-in-square absorbed by the adjacent vaults, giving maximum emphasis to a very large dome. The result is more spectacular here than anywhere else, with the weight of the broad, 16-sided drum carried on an octagon of vaults and squinches. This design produces a sequence of small chambers to either side, and these enhance the feeling of light and space under the broad cupola with its 16 windows. The fine cloisonné masonry of the exterior is relieved by the substantial brick patterns around the arcaded windows; note also the uniquely inventive caps of the two S windows, carved with a costumed female figure and two fantastic animals.

You enter the church through a massive 18th-c Venetian porch, and although most of the frescos have gone from the interior, the scale and lightness are still impressive. In its original state the interior decoration must have been unusually rich; the walls would have been marble-clad (traces at floor level to SW), and of the five doors into the naos, three have retained their carved marble lintels, with further carving round some; the mutilation of these must date from its period as a mosque. The moulding round the base of the dome is unusual in being ceramic, with eight medallions; in the N bay you can see richly carved marble members that once formed the templon beams across two of the apses. Of the few surviving frescos, the medallions of martyrs in the octagon under the dome must have been an unusual theme, as also the Ancient of Days in the vault of the bema; look also for the interesting scene of the Birth of John the

Baptist in the vault of the prothesis. Outside again, you might speculate on the original form of the substantial remains immediately to the s; there may have been an arcade here, as at Mystra, although the evidence suggests something more substantial.

For the rest of the **acropolis**, as in so many of the coastal castles, where the Venetians and Turks were the last to use them, it is their building that is most in evidence. Today most of the very large area that is formed by the acropolis is heavily overgrown, although there are the ruinous remains of hundreds of dwellings; absence of wood on the summit must account for them all being barrel vaulted with the local stone. Many had their own water storage, but a huge barrel-vaulted cistern, some 24 m long, still holds some water. These are a reminder that the citadel once supported life for several thousand inhabitants. The whole magnificent circuit of walls as you see it today, although having Byz origins, cannot for the most part be earlier than the 1460s, with the Venetians (and probably the Turks as well) building on earlier foundations. You can still walk around considerable sections of the s and e ramparts.

A rough track leads up through the gorse and thorn bushes to the highest part of the citadel, which is dominated by the ruin of what has been a fair-sized **fortress**. This must be the chief relic of secular Byz construction, its craggy ruins still visible from the mainland. Already in 1154 Monemvasia was reported to have 'a castle very high above the sea, from which one may look across to Crete'. The masonry is unlike other parts of the fortifications, and has much more in common with 12th-c Byz building technique, but the surviving remains do not justify attempts to differentiate between the earlier and later (after 1262) Byz periods here. Did the Normans reach here before they were finally repulsed in 1147? The Venetians were later using it as a powder magazine when, in 1689, it exploded and the scattered ruins that you see today are no doubt the result of this event.

MOUKHLI Μουχλί Arkadia
Ruins of Byz church and fortified town *. Access by steep goat tracks from road. Allow 1½–2 hours.

Shortly after the road from Argos to Tripolis has crossed into Arkadia you will see a small modern chapel at the roadside on your left; beside it is a sign pointing into the country to the se under Mount Partheni, and inscribed Η ΠΑΝΑΓΙΑ ΜΟΥΧΛΙΟΤΙΣΣΑ.

This is the hill of Palaio-Moukhli which dominates the valley of
Akhladokampos. Following this general direction you will come to
the lonely and desolate ruins of one of the last major fortified towns
that the Byzantines held in the Peloponnese. It was founded in the
late 13th and early 14th c by the Byz governor of Mystra, Andronikos Palaiologos Asan, and after long resistance was finally
surrendered in 1458 and destroyed by the Turks in 1460. One
Aragonese version of the *Chronicle of the Morea* (the only one to
mention it) states that the same Greek *maréchal* also founded
another fortress at Cépiana, the modern Tsipiana.

Most of the area that you will see is dotted with the ruins of the
outer circuit wall and defences, with more of buildings visible right
up to the summit. The most prominent surviving part of Moukhli is
however the **church of the Panagia Moukhliotissa**; it is oriented
NE–SW, with the three apses partly embedded in the hillside, and,
oddly, surmounted by a square tower which formed part of the
defences. The central and N apse still have areas of late 13th-c fresco
adhering, although weeds and weather are fast eroding them; there
is no roofing at all and the walls have largely collapsed. The largest
and best preserved part is what seems to be a bell-tower to the SW,
directly in line with the nave, and some 10 m from the apex of the
central apse. Nearby are fragments of carved marble which must
come from a templon. The remains here are not spectacular, but are
of distinct historical interest; the peaceful site is atmospheric and
quite dramatic, and (except for the occasional goat or tortoise) you
will have the hillside to yourself.

MYLI Μύλοι Argolis. Med Kyviri
Castle ruins *. Unenclosed. Allow 1½ hours.

You will easily see the hill-top **castle of Lerna** from the road beside
the sea; you can reach it either by a tractor track on a curving route
from the N, or by a steep footpath which zig-zags up the hill from just
opposite the large modern church in the village. Most of what
survives is Frankish, but there was ancient and med Greek building
here before, and there are traces of houses to the N of the main site.
You can see that the Frankish keep had a polygonal enceinte
forming an irregular hexagon some 30 m across and rounding off to
the N and NE; there are the remains of seven towers, and two lined
cisterns and other buildings. Although the site is now ruined, the
superb outlook directly across the Gulf of Argos to Nauplio and its
bay are ample reward for your climb here.

MYRTEA Μυρτέα Etolia-Akarnania
Convent and katholikon with frescos *. Easy access by car.

As the road climbs steeply up from the N bank of Lake Trikhonida, the **convent of the Panaghia Theotokos** is signed on your left. On entering the courtyard you first see the single apse and bema of a very modest hall-church that was the original 12th-C katholikon. The domed naos was added to the W in the 15th C, and the narthex some time later still; the surrounding buildings are all late.

The katholikon contains an interesting range of frescos, some in superimposed layers. The earliest is on the N wall of the bema; it is of the *Koimisis* and the central area of the Virgin and some of the apostles must be from the 12th C, with the head of Christ somewhat later. An inscription on the S wall gives both the artist's name (Xenos Dighenis, from the Peloponnese) and the date (1491) of the paintings in the apse of the Virgin Platytera and figures of bishops. Frescos on the piers of the naos of ss Basil and Nicholas date from the 15th C, while other areas of fresco are dated 1539 and 1712, and include a cycle of the Akathyst hymn.

MYSTRA Μυστράς Lakonia. Med Myzithra, Misistra
Site, castle, houses, churches, frescos, museum ***. Access easy by car/bus to gates, then steep footpaths. Museum opening hours; allow at least a day.

For the Byz enthusiast Mystra is the premier site in Greece. Clinging to its formidably rocky spur of Mount Taygetos, the ruined city is not only among the most spectacular of the med sites (sharing honours in this with *Monemvasia* and *Acrocorinth*) but preserves a completely unique wealth of both secular and ecclesiastical building and art.

Its origins, however, are quite late. While most other such sites have a known classical or EC past, the nearby town of Sparta never felt the need to extend out here in earlier centuries. It was not until 1249 that the fourth of the Frankish princes of Akhaia, Guillaume de Villehardouin, in a bid to secure the S Peloponnese against the Slav tribe of the Melings, decided that it was the best point on which to install a defended position and began building a castle here.

He chose a superb position. As you will see when you have climbed up to the summit, sheer cliffs make it unassailable from the S and SW (which was the direction from which attack could be

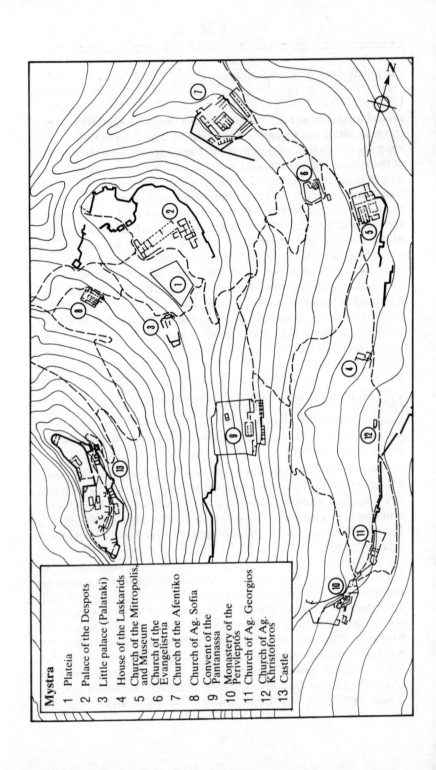

Mystra

1 Plateia
2 Palace of the Despots
3 Little palace (Palataki)
4 House of the Laskarids
5 Church of the Mitropolis,
  and Museum
6 Church of the
  Evangelistria
7 Church of the Afentiko
8 Church of Ag. Sofia
9 Convent of the
  Pantanassa
10 Monastery of the
   Perivleptos
11 Church of Ag. Georgios
12 Church of Ag.
   Khristoforos
13 Castle

expected), and Villehardouin's operations soon made this rocky crest virtually impregnable from the more accessible N and E slopes. He could never have known that it was to be his for such a short time. The castle, its enceinte and perhaps part of a settlement lower down the hill forming part of the surviving palace complex, must have been built for only a short time when, in 1259, he was defeated at the Battle of Pelagonia.

After two years' imprisonment (albeit quite comfortable), Villehardouin, as the asking price for his freedom, had to cede not just the newly built castle of Mystra, but also those of *Monemvasia*, *Geraki* and *Great Maina*, and so they were duly made over to Michael VIII Palaiologos (see pp. 20–23). This was how the history of the later Byzantines' most important outpost began.

From 1348 Mystra became the seat of the despotate of the whole of the Morea. While the Turks pressed ever closer on the capital, Mystra was able to retain considerable freedom of action and outlook. A good example of this independence of spirit occurred in 1400; the Order of the Hospitallers had already bought *Corinth* from the old and sick despot, Theodore, and now offered to buy *Kalavryta* and Mystra as well, to protect them from the infidel Turks (the despot himself would withdraw to Monemvasia). The deal was not completely clarified, however, and when the Knights' delegates arrived to claim Mystra they were almost lynched by an enraged populace; the bishop saved them, and calmed the crowd, but the townspeople still would not allow the despot back into the city until he had repudiated the deal and returned the purchase money.

Nothing could stem the tide of the Turkish armies, however, particularly when they were helped by the internal strife of their enemies, and so it was finally in May 1460 that the last despot, Dimitrios, was forced to leave the city's gates and enter the tent of Mehmed who had encamped outside the walls. There he was given no option but to hand over Mystra, seven years after the fall of the capital.

The position of Mystra, assisted by its enlightened government, and perhaps also helped by its relative newness and absence of ancient traditions, meant that successive despots were able to encourage a stimulating climate of intellectual enquiry that would probably not have been possible in the capital. First under the Kantakuzene despots, Michael, Matthew and Dimitrios, and later the Palaiologue dynasty of successively Theodore I and II, Thomas, Dimitrios and Constantine, Mystra emerged as a major cultural and intellectual centre. It is striking that John VI Kantakuzenos, who had reigned as emperor in CP before abdicating in 1354 and becoming a monk, seems to have so much enjoyed the visits that he made as a monk to Mystra that in 1381 he was glad to leave the troubles and insecurity of the capital, and settled for good in the city, later dying there.

It is perhaps significant that the names of the philosophers and scholars who made this hillside city of Mystra such an agreeable and stimulating intellectual haven do not figure greatly in studies of late med thought; rather it is in histories of the early Renaissance that we meet them. When Gemistos Plethon, immensely learned in both the Aristotelian and Platonist traditions, began to lecture on the latter in CP around 1400, his approach was too radical for the ecclesiastical establishment there; to avoid alienating his clergy the Emperor Manuel II, a personal friend, suggested that Mystra would be a better place for him. From 1407 until his death in 1452, with just a break to attend the Council of Ferrara/Florence in 1438–9, Gemistos lived and taught here. Although his ideas have been identified as tending towards a neo-paganism, eminent clerics came and listened to him. He became the adviser and counsellor of the despot Theodore II, and wrote lengthily to the emperor Manuel in CP advising him on the best policies to adopt towards the whole of the Morea.

One of his most famous pupils was called Bessarion, who came from Trebizond to Mystra in 1431 and stayed for six years; he was later to achieve lasting fame as a cardinal of the Roman church. The isolation of Mystra meant that it was to be mainly through Plethon's pupils that Platonic studies were introduced into the Italian academies; Marsilio Ficino, the Florentine humanist and translator of Plato into Italian, paid Plethon the ultimate honour, calling him 'the second Plato'. So it is as providing a foundation stone of the new learning, rather than as a perpetuator of the old, that Mystra's most famous intellectual is remembered.

A mention should be made of the great French Byzantinist Gabriel Millet (1866–1953), who devoted many years of his life to the restoration and consolidation of the city's buildings and paintings. While his approach to restoration was more radical than is the norm today, the fact that we still have so much to see at all is certainly due in large part to his efforts.

It is standing in the **Plateia** that a modern visitor will perhaps be able to feel most readily the link between the med existence of

Mystra and that of a modern Greek town. It is hard to see anywhere else in the town that would have served as a meeting-place, either formally or informally, for its inhabitants, and one must assume that it was here that much of the communal and secular everyday life of the town was lived.

Was it by chance that this space was developed so close to the **Palace of the despots**? We do not know. This is the name now given to the large structure consisting of two wings which occupies the NE and NW sides of the Plateia, and there can be no doubt that the succession of imperial Byz governors of the city lived and held court in it. It must count as the most substantial secular building to survive from the pre-conquest period, and so, rather piecemeal in its construction, like other buildings in Mystra it can be regarded as

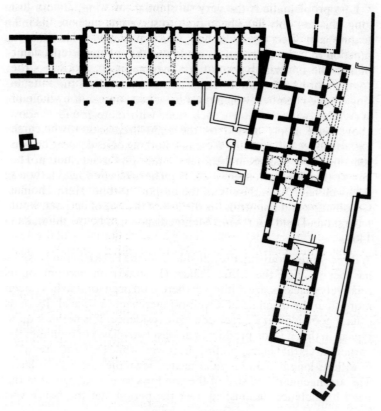

Palace of the despots

offering some indication of comparable buildings in CP that no longer exist. (Entrance is unfortunately not normally allowed.)

The earliest part of the complex is one of the less prominent – the easternmost part of the NE wing – and it is possible that it was in fact built by the Franks during their brief tenure of the castle (1249–62). In the same wing the kitchen building must have been erected shortly after, with water storage cistern and fireplace, and the two other buildings in this range must have both been built at much the same time; one of them – the two-storey structure nearest to the NW wing – has been identified as the residence of the despots. This certainly has all the characteristics of such a building, with an interestingly formed porch on the far side which supports a balcony looking out over the valley towards Sparta. There is also a room on the upper floor here which must have been a chapel.

Less problematic is the very substantial NW wing; almost 40 m long, this can only have been built to serve one purpose: its main feature is in effect one great hall, which must always have had the function of a throne room. It could well have been a reflection of that in the imperial palace at Vlakhernae in CP. A lower storey complex of barrel-vaulted rooms above some cellars supports this single huge chamber, which must have been amply lit by the eight very large windows down each side, with more round windows above, and amply heated by the eight fireplaces, of which the external flues still remain. We know nothing of its decoration – the remains of the plaster on the interior walls give us no clues, nor has any written description survived. A niche half-way down the w wall may well have been the site of the despot's throne. Here Thomas, Constantine and Dimitrios, as the last of the line of despots, would have sat and held court until Mehmed appeared below the walls in 1460.

A three-storey house up the hill-side from the Palace of the Despots has been called the Little Palace (Palataki) on account of its relatively spacious size, although there is no need for it to have been more than the dwelling of a well-off merchant or official. Its ruins offer a good idea of a larger domestic residence. It is perhaps quite typical in that it is the product of at least two phases of building: the earlier part is that incorporating the tower, while the structure to the s, with its long hall and regular niches down the side wall, is later. The arrangement and size of the windows would indicate that the need for defence diminished over the period that the house was built.

The so-called **House of the Laskarids**, down the hill below the Pantanassa, displays its original design clearly, although a later dwelling was built onto it. The slope of the hillside was exploited to give a large vaulted room at ground level, probably used as a stable and above this a second chamber which may have been used for storage. The life of the household was lived on the storey above this, entered by a stone staircase at the side; due to the fall of the land this storey runs back to be almost at ground level at its furthest point from the front. The rooms had large windows, and opened out on to a broad balcony formed by the roof of the storage chamber, and looking out E over the valley. This house must have been of later 14th- or 15th-c construction.

It seems certain that the building called the **church of the Mitropolis** and dedicated to Ag Dimitrios, was from the first intended to serve as the leading church of Mystra, and the seat of its bishop. Two inscriptions, one over the door into the narthex, record that the church was dedicated in 1291/2 by one Nikiforos, Bishop of Lakedaemonia. This relatively late date suggests that there may have been an earlier building used as the Mitropolis, but if so, no trace of it survives, either here or elsewhere. (The orientation is slightly eccentric, being due SE–NW, but for ease of reference here it will be held to be correct.)

Due to a later radical reshaping you will probably find that this is a complex and rather puzzling building to visit. In its original, late 13th-c, form it was apparently not domed, but was of basilical design, with the nave substantially higher than the two side aisles; three columns on each side carried the barrel vaulting of the nave, and separated it from the aisles. All over Greece you will find that a basilica form has been used for churches which have a metropolitan function, for example at *Kalabaka* and *Serres*.

The distinctly heavy-handed reconstruction, which, according to the inscription on the cornice to the W, was due to Matthew, Bishop of Lakedaemonia, was probably carried out as late as the early 15th c. He must have decided that his church should not be the only major one in Mystra without a dome, so he had the roof of the nave removed, a gallery built at the level of the old aisle vaults, screened with carved marble slabs, and a dome erected on four piers supported by the original columns of the aisles.

The result is a spatial conflict between the upper and lower storeys. When you look down on this building from higher up the hillside of Mystra you will see four small domes sited round the main central one, with another one of intermediate size to the NW; these, with four groin vaults, form the roofing of the gallery that Matthew had constructed. This was clearly intended to serve as a *gynaikonitis* which he must have felt had become necessary – possibly in emulation of major new churches in CP; modesty was clearly not one of his traits.

The bell-tower, built on to the SE corner, is probably early 14th C. The best impression of the original external appearance of the mitropolis can be gained now from the apses to the SE; the carefully laid cloisonné masonry, with the dog-tooth brick ornamentation round the windows, is all from the original building.

One result of these alterations is that the interior is actually quite well lit, and this allows a relatively clear view of the painted decoration of the walls. The recent restoration reveals it as being mostly poorly preserved, and indeed you may find it something of a disappointment. Apart from the 17th/18th-c overpainting in the apse, there are certainly at least three phases discernible, and no unified programme of subject-matter is evident.

The earliest phase, and probably contemporary with the original building, is the Virgin and Child Kyriotissa in the conch of the apse. From a slightly later period and painted in a more rustic style are the paintings in the long shallow barrel vaults of both aisles, where there are miracle scenes of both Christ and Ag Dimitrios, the patron saint of the church. You may find the most memorable of the frescos to be the colourful scenes of the Marriage at Caana and the Birth of the Virgin in the s apse, or some of the scenes from the Last Judgement in the narthex, all from the early 14th C. The figures that now appear in the nave paintings (with their heads cut off – a result of the 15th-C reconstruction) must be a third phase, and were very likely a replacement of the original decoration; money ran out before they could be replaced.

The carved decoration is mostly undistinguished, and largely assembled from other sites. This reflects the limited finances available at the period of the original building. Only the two marble icon frames, and the adjoining carving of the templon, have any distinction. The carved relief of the double-headed eagle in the floor in the centre of the nave traditionally commemorates the coronation of Constantine XI on the feast of the Epiphany, 6 January 1449; certainly the ceremony took place in Mystra on that date.

While here, do not omit a visit to the small **Museum**, on two floors leading off from the courtyard; it was initiated by Gabriel Millet, who did so much to restore the buildings of Mystra. Though not housing any major works, it displays a modest assemblage of carved marble fragments and caps, some with interesting monograms, a marble icon carved in relief, part of the iconostasis from Ag Theodoroi with an inscription, some detached fragments of fresco, a few later icons, some coins and other bronze finds that can all fill out our image of the city's medieval past.

Closest to the Mitropolis is the small **church of the Evangelistria**. It is one of the more modest churches surviving, and it is the only one of which there is no information of any kind as to its origins. For centuries after the Turkish occupation it was used as a funerary chapel and this may have been its original function. Its plan is a conventional two-column, inscribed cross, with two columns supporting the w half of the octagonal drum of the single dome. The only feature here that is not found elsewhere in Mystra with the two-column plan is a *gynaikonitis* above the narthex. The masonry is undistinguished, with only the apses retaining the decorative cloisonné masonry.

The interior has lost much of its painted decoration, but what has survived suggests a fairly pedestrian version of late Palaiologue style. The figure of Ag Polykarpos on the facing of the arch leading from the bema to the prothesis may indicate something of the style of the large missing areas. The most interesting aspect of the interior is the ornament of the caps; although not spectacular, their deep relief carving combined with corner bosses in the form of pine cones is interesting and certainly unique to Mystra; it is also apparently original to the church. The usual dating for this church is late 14th to early 15th c, which must be broadly correct.

To the NW of the Evangelistria is the large complex known from the earliest documents as the **Vrontokhion**; it comprises chiefly the two biggest and most impressive churches in Mystra: the **church of Ag Theodoroi** and the **church of the Hodegetria**, usually called the *Afentiko*. They are both more accurately oriented E–W than the Mitropolis. Both buildings were due to the drive and energy of a cleric called Pakhomios, who was active from c. 1290 to c. 1322. He succeeded in raising substantial sums of money and tax-free imperial gifts of land and property which were devoted to their construction. He was rewarded by being made first abbot of Ag Theodoroi and the monastery of the Hodegetria, and later ecclesiastical chancellor of the Morea.

Ag Theodoroi was built during the mid-1290s and must always have been (after the Mitropolis) both one of the oldest, as well as one of the most substantial, churches in Mystra. Its exterior is dominated by the huge dome, and the richness of its bands of cloisonné masonry is emphasized by the alternation with unfinished stone. The apses, in particular, are a brilliant essay in late Byz decorative building technique, with the cut stone forming an undulating screen, pierced by the windows and blind niches, all framed by dog-tooth brick ornament. The drum of the dome, too, with eight tall windows alternating with blind niches, and separated by 16 engaged columns, is a dazzlingly inventive exploitation of standard building materials.

The size of the dome means that there is a spacious central naos; its weight, however, would have been too great for just four piers, so it rests on an octagon formed from four squinches alternating with four barrel vaults. (This system, which by this date was no longer new, must almost certainly have been first developed in CP, but the builders in Mystra may have taken as their model the church of *Ag Sofia*, *Monemvasia*, itself an imperial foundation.)

The sophistication of the design of the building is not matched by the small amount of carved decoration; you can see that the few remaining pieces of the carved moulding running round below the drum of the dome show little of the skill or confidence of the builder of the dome itself. (The dome itself is a modern reconstruction.) When the paintings on the interior wall surfaces were all new, however, the effect must have been quite spectacular. They are now in poor condition, and must date from about a century after the church was built; the figures of the warrior saints on the two w piers are particularly impressive.

In the NW corner of the walls is sited the most innovative of the churches of Mystra – that dedicated to the **Virgin Hodegetria**, now more often known as the **Afentiko**. Taller than Ag Theodoroi, this has always been recognized as being a more completely modern and 'metropolitan' building in its design and appearance than anything else in Mystra, and its restoration allows us to see this clearly. Both the Mitropolis itself, and Ag Theodoroi, must in their own way have been to some extent old-fashioned (the latter less so); with the Afentiko we may have the closest reflection possible of the very latest new building in CP.

It was built between 1310 and 1322, and its height is achieved not just by using successive storeys (as at *Arta*) but by the device of supporting a major central dome, with four smaller domes, over what is essentially the colonnade of a basilical nave; the weight of the main dome is carried by the gallery piers, which are in turn supported by the colonnade. This scheme gives an evident space and lightness to the interior that would be denied a conventional cross-in-square church of this size; in the gallery the absence of marble screening increases the sense of openness. The building was enlarged with a later parekklision to the N, which has frescos in damaged condition, but this is currently closed. The Mystra custom of having an open colonnade on the exterior of the S side was continued here – the carved marble supports are still there. A fifth dome is sited over the gallery, itself above the narthex. The bell-tower has been rebuilt on the basis of surviving evidence.

Inside the Afentiko the wall paintings still give an indication of its original decorative richness; one reconstruction of the interior suggests that there were large areas of marble revetment providing framing for the frescos. You will find several iconographic groupings: scenes from the Dodecaorton predominate in and near the sanctuary, while a superb sequence of 16 bishops dominates the main apse. This theme had been increasing in importance during the 13th C, and the artist has made the most of the opportunity offered by the robes of these figures, with a different pattern of crosses on the vestments of each figure. A cycle of eight feast scenes would have occupied the four barrel vaults below the dome, and pairs of saints can be seen in the gallery and figures of martyrs in the tympana, but only two of the ten saucer domes down each side below the gallery have retained their fresco decoration. In the dome of the *gynaikonitis* a bust of the Virgin with Child occupies the oculus, the centre of the dome. Of the many other areas and scenes, note the vivid paintings of the miracles of Christ in the narthex – a part of the church often used for teaching purposes – with an interesting scene of the young Christ among the elders in the temple.

Before leaving the Afentiko, it is worth visiting the impressive remains of the monastic buildings to the N; you will find the shell of the refectory still standing, lacking only the roof, with adjoining it the domed monastic kitchen. (This is a useful reminder that domes were not just used for ecclesiastical buildings, but served, as here, a completely functional role as a flue.)

Just as the great church of Ag Sofia in CP was officially the palace church of the emperor, so it would be expected that the church in Mystra now known as **Ag Sofia** would be the despot's palace church, although there has in the past been some uncertainty as to which

church served this function. It was built between 1350 and 1365
(with the dedication of Christ Zöodotes, 'Christ the giver of life') by
the despot Manuel; it also served as the katholikon of a monastery.
It is taller in relation to its ground-plan than the other churches of
Mystra, although it has a simple, cross-in-square, domed plan, with
two columns and two piers; the domed narthex is unusually
spacious. You will see remains of what must have been a very fine
floor of *opus sectile*, and note the capital carved with the monogram
of the founder, the despot Manuel Kantakouzenos Palaiologos, and
two imperial double-headed eagles. The external cloisonné
masonry is comparable with that of the Hodegetria; there is a
separate bell-tower (as normal in Mystra), and a small complex
adjoining it, which includes a chapel, may have had a funerary
function.

The wall paintings are generally poorly preserved, but you will
find impressive images of Christ enthroned in the main apse, and the
Ascension in the vault of the bema adjoining. Perhaps the most
interesting of the paintings is in a chapel to the s, added at an early
date to the main building. The subject-matter of the decoration here
is unusual, and an orientation towards women's interests has been
suggested, with a large scene of the Birth of the Virgin and other
subjects just discernible, reminiscent of those in the Kariye Djami
in CP; an association with the wife of the one of the Palaiologue
despots is quite possible.

Another small chapel built on later to the NE still retains some of
its frescos, with large images of the Virgin and Child and of Christ
(both enthroned) facing each other, and of the Anastasis and
Koimisis to N and s with further subjects in the cupola and apse and
in the tiny diaconicon. There must surely have been a tomb here
originally.

The **Convent of the Pantanassa**, built towards the E flank of the
hillside, and oriented NE–SW, must be one of the latest major
buildings in Mystra. It is now used as a convent, and nuns live in the
row of cells adjoining the E side of the complex. It is known to have
been founded by a chief official of the despotate, John Frango-
poulos; his name may be one of the four carved in relief on the
cushion of the capital of the NW column inside the church, and while
his dates have not been established, another inscription (now lost)
gave the dedication as taking place in 1428.

In design the church emulates the Afentiko, with the upper storey
forming a five-domed cross-in-square supported below by the struc-

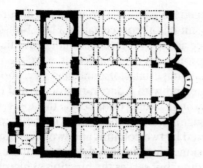

Convent of the Pantanassa

ture of a short basilica, using six columns in all. Once again, a
substantial bell-tower dominates the aspect of the church from
below (its dome must be later), and as in other churches of Mystra
there is a fine exterior arcade looking s across the valley. Be sure to
walk round to the exterior of the apse, where the decoration is both
rich and puzzling: manifestly of strongly Frankish Gothic character,
it is hard to explain why foreign ornament, presumably reminiscent
of a hostile power, should have been built into a completely Byz
church. Could the Italian wife of the despot Theodore II, Kleopa
Malatesta (d. 1433), have been involved in some way?

The paintings on the interior walls vary in period; those of the
lower part of the naos are all slightly later, but in the upper areas and
in the arms of the cross they are contemporary with the building,
and are generally in fair condition and quite well lit. The design of
the naos has formed a gallery, providing eight saucer cupolas, with
four further cupolas and two barrel vaults. In the four saucer
cupolas down each side Old Testament figures give way to those of
the New; note too the fine scenes from the Dodecaorton, where the
Nativity, the Raising of Lazarus and the Entry into Jerusalem
display great richness of detail; these are good examples of later
Palaiologue style, full of invention and movement, and even the
mutilation of many of the faces (presumably under the Turkish
occupation) does not diminish their interest. In the narthex there
are yet more, and still later, frescos, with a fine Tree of Jesse, and a
wall-tomb with a richly clothed portrait figure.

Of the **monastery of the Perivleptos**, built slightly uncomfortably
against a cliff face near the SE corner of the walls, only the
katholikon survives, with one other structure rather uncertainly
called a refectory. It is oriented approximately NE–SW; its history

has to be deduced from its appearance, as no documentation has yet come to light, but it is almost certainly a late 14th-c foundation.

The rock face against which it was built prevented a regular plan, and the most prominent external features are the three apses, built with five facets in the usual cloisonné masonry, and the dome, in the same technique and with a decorative octagonal drum. You enter the building through a small door beside the apses, which opens into a narrow passage, entering the church in the N corner. The dome here is supported by two columns and two piers, and there is quite a long sw extension, which further detracts from the symmetry of this system of building, but serves the function of increasing the interior space.

You will at once find that the most striking feature of the interior are the wall paintings; limited window space meant that large areas were available to the artists, and they have filled them with some of the finest surviving paintings in Mystra. Several themes are developed; the Life of the Virgin, the Dodecaorton (see particularly the Ascension in the vault of the bema), the Passion (note the expressive painting of the Denial of Peter in the prothesis) and a group of scenes with Eucharistic subjects. Striking for their lively content are the paintings of the Birth of the Virgin, the settings of the Baptism of Christ and the Transfiguration, with vivid landscape detail, and the unusual form and figures in the Passion scenes of the Deposition and Denial of Peter. There are also fine standing figures of saints, such as the four military saints on the sw wall, although some have been disfigured by having their eyes gouged out. The style of the paintings suggests a date during the second half of the

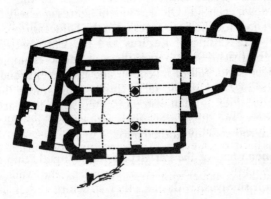

Monastery of the Perivleptos

14th c and has been cited as an example of a 'Mystra style' of painting.

Quite close to here you will find two of the smallest churches in Mystra, **Ag Giorgios** and **Ag Khristoforos**. They were both built without domes, and are representative of quite a numerous class of privately built small churches – almost chapels – of which those that have survived are in a more ruined state; they may have had a funerary function. Ag Giorgios is an attractive double-nave hall-church with a single apse; there are some engaging brick patterns on the exterior walls, and it probably dates from the 13th or early 14th c. Ag Khristoforos is even simpler – a single nave, single apse church, but its masonry templon has some modest paintings still surviving on it.

Due to its position at the summit of the hillside, the **Castle (Kastro)** may be the last of the buildings here that you reach but, begun in 1249, it was the first to be built. The castle, like almost every other in the Peloponnese, has certainly undergone alteration since its construction, but it never underwent a severe siege nor was it dismantled by the Turks. It conforms largely to the Frankish pattern of a keep built on the highest part of the site, with two baileys, and a curtain wall forming an enceinte, strengthened by a number of towers. The keep merges with the enceinte on the sw, where the fall to the huge ravine below is precipitous, but it must date from the original construction of 1249, with only minimal Byz rebuilding.

For much of the rest it is virtually impossible to know quite what you are looking at; the work of the original builders, only effectively in possession for about 12 years, must surely have been overlaid and altered during two centuries of use by the Byzantines and over three and a half by the Turks. The destructive sack of Mystra by Albanian troops in 1770 and Turks in the 19th c would also certainly have been as thorough here as elsewhere.

The first of the gates that you reach has no facility for a portcullis, and is probably a Turkish construction. When entering, you will gain a better idea of the complex by not climbing at once to the second gate, but continuing along to the e end of the enceinte; the rounded tower at this end gives a good view of the surviving parts, which it is hard to achieve from other points. You will find one of the two cisterns here, with the other just above the second gate – a barrel-vaulted chamber with a tower above it. Continuing on above this you will reach the ruins of what must have been the castle chapel, with steps carved in the rock leading down to the w entrance. William's church would not have had a dome, but nearby remains of substantial marble columns suggest that the Byzantines may have improved it in this way, in spite of its modest width – some 4 m. There are other points, too, where it is clear that reconstruction has been carried out to allow for the use of artillery; the round bastion at the sw end of the enceinte is an instance of this, and so must be Turkish.

The climb up to the castle summit is essential for a full grasp of the site of Mystra, and for an appreciation of its dominance of the adjacent Taygetos; you will be richly rewarded by the prospects on all sides once you reach it.

NAUPAKTOS   Ναύπακτος   Etolia-Akarnania. Med Lepanto
Castle *. Easy access by foot/car from town, then paths.

This attractive harbour town was of considerable strategic importance in the med period, and in the early 13th c was the seat of a metropolitan with ten suffragans; its most famous holder was bishop John Apokaukos. Like other towns on the outer areas of the despotate of Epiros it was to change hands several times, and for over 70 years in the following century there was Western rule here (and even a Latin bishop) until the area fell to the Albanians; from 1407 it was Venetian until the Turks occupied the area in 1449.

The road to the **castle** above the town pierces an outer circuit wall; the castle itself occupies quite a large hill-top site, and from the keep you can see across the straits and far into the Panakhaikos range in the N Peloponnese. There are two baileys, but the later occupation of the Turks has made it very hard to distinguish different building periods; the w wall has an earlier (?)Hellenistic base, but the later castellation may well be Venetian. There is considerable Byz masonry in the lower parts of the N wall, with attractive dog-tooth brick patterns round small niches, and the castellation above is again probably Venetian 15th c; a number of buildings in the outer bailey (mostly ruined) have Byz brick features, as does the entry to the second bailey. A substantial cannon-ramp leads up to the keep on the point at the NE end of the site, where the Turks installed massive artillery emplacements reusing earlier building materials. The views from here are almost 360° and, combined with the historic interest of the site, reward you well for the modest climb up.

NAUPLIO Ναύπλιο Argolida
Castle. Easy access by car or foot.

Considering its long and important med history, during much of which it was held by the Venetians as one of their main coastal sites in the Morea, the Byz and med survivals in Nauplio are minimal. Again, it is due to its continuing importance to both Turks and Venetians (and then the modern Greeks), and its consequent prosperity, that it now has so little to offer us from its earlier history. The most prominent feature of Nauplio is the fortress of Palamidi, which is entirely 18th c.

The **citadel of Acronauplia** still retains some Byz elements in the fortress; this was originally ancient Greek, before passing from Byz and then to Venetian control, but successive periods of neglect and rebuilding have left very little of the original plan or fabric. The Xenia hotel is a modern comment on the function of the site.

The Archaeological Museum contains no med material, but you may wish to see the excellent Museum of the Peloponnesian Folklore Foundation, which won a European award in 1981, or pay a visit to *Areia*, a short distance away.

NEA AGKHIALOS Νέα Αγχίαλος Magnisia
Ruins of EC churches **. Easy access.

The road into Volos runs due NE beside the Pagassitik Gulf as it passes through this small seaside town; you will at once see the two main sites that have been excavated to the N of the road, and their scale indicates the considerable importance that this little town must once have had.

The first site that you reach (Basilica B, still under excavation) contains principally the basilica of the Archbishop Peter, and is in reality three superimposed basilicas of the 4th, 5th and 6th c. It has some fine floor mosaics and caps, and the rows of re-erected columns down its nave of over 40 m convey an impression of real grandeur. Adjoining this is a 4th-c baptistry where an almost complete floor of *opus sectile* marble survives.

The second of the two sites here (Basilica A, fenced, but open daily) is even larger; the ground-plan of the basilica dedicated to St Demetrios shows it was over 70 m in overall length, and the plan is quite a complex one; it is of the later 5th c – roughly contemporary with the *Akheiropoietos*, *Thessaloniki*. The basilica itself must have

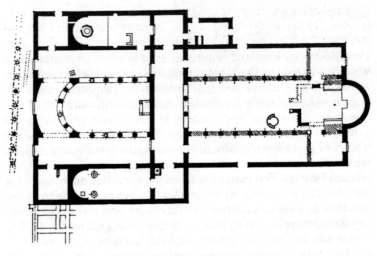

Nea Agkhialos: Basilica A

been very impressive, with side galleries and parapets, but you can easily see that the atrium (forecourt) to the w was truly palatial; three colonnades surrounded the open centre, with the middle one curving to meet the other two across the w end. Two superb double-zone caps from the entrance of the basilica are on view, each with six lions' heads in the upper zone; the N aisle floor has an unusual design of panels of white and red marble with grey stone chippings set in patterns; there is a baths complex further to the w.

Quantities of carved marble building members have been collected, and there is interesting evidence of a marble workshop on the site; there are two unfinished 5th-c sarcophagi, and two 'melon' caps in process of being marked, cut and drilled with designs very comparable to those in the 6th-c Ag Sergios and Bakkhos, CP. It must be from there that the builders and craftsmen came. Although scarcely any walls are standing, the surviving remains here are very impressive, and well repay a leisurely visit.

NEA KERASSOUS　Νέα Κερασσούς　Thesprotia
Ruins of castle **. Unenclosed. 14 km w of Arta. Easy access from road, then overgrown tracks.

The ruined **castle of Rogoi** can be seen to the N of the road between

Arta and Nikopolis; the site of its steep, overgrown hill is surprisingly similar to that of the castle of *Arta*, occupying as it does a bend in the river Louros, but it is more precipitous and (in spite of its overgrown state) better preserved. The two castles were the main strongholds of Epiros, and it was here that in 1340 Alexios Kabasilas defied the Byz Grand Domestic, John Kantakuzene, while the emperor himself was besieging Arta during the restoration of Byz rule.

Immediately evident are the extensive pre-Christian walls and towers all along the s and sw sides, overlooking the broad curve of the river; these were constructed over several phases between the 5th and 1st c BC. The least difficult entry is scrambling up on the w side, but before doing this a walk between the river and the huge fortifications will give you an idea of the site and its locality. Once you have arrived within the main enceinte you will find that it forms a substantial broad polygon of roughly oval shape, some 100 by 60 m. Three baileys were constructed by the med Epirote builders, with substantial gateways still leading from one to the other, and each guarded by the remains of towers; the whole site is heavily overgrown.

At the N end a simple 15th-c hall church has been built on the only flat area, perhaps dating from just before 1429 when the Turks occupied Epiros. It has considerable frescos of that period remaining inside – rather grimy, but they include an imposing row of standing female saints occupying the N wall, and a Koimisis over the w door.

If you felt that the castle of Arta and its surroundings were lacking in period atmosphere, a visit here will certainly correct the balance, and you will have the site to yourself.

NEOPATRAS
See **Ypati**

NIKOPOLIS   Νικόπολι   Preveza
Byz fortifications, two ruined basilicas and museum **.

An important city in the classical world, in the EC period it became the seat of an archbishop due partly to the fact that St Paul had stayed here; his epistle to Titus was written from Nikopolis. It retained some importance well into the Byz period as the capital of a *theme*, and it was here that Senacherim, a relative of Michael Doukas, was governor when he was killed in 1204; Michael married his widow and occupied Arta, so founding what was to become the despotate of Epiros.

The showpiece of the site will be immediately evident as you approach: the hugely impressive range of massive **fortifications** built by Justinian stretches for some 500 m quite close to the road, and is still some 10–12 m high. Nowhere else in Greece (or indeed in Europe) can you see 6th-c military building on this scale. (The fact that in building them Justinian reduced the defended area by about three quarters is an indication of the extent of the classical city.) Huge rounded towers guard the main gateway, and steps up on to the summit of the wall every 100 m or so allow you to assess the scale of the whole site.

The entrance to a small **museum** is near the s extent of the Justinianic ramparts, and on the footpath to this you pass the earlier of two excavated basilicas; known as **Basilica A (of Doumetios)**, it dates from the second quarter of the 6th c – just before Justinian's building. Its plan shows a square atrium leading into a basilica some 40 m long with two aisles and a substantial apse. Most unfortunately the great interest of this basilica cannot now be seen: it has an exceptionally fine floor mosaic, but this has been covered in polythene and gravel to preserve it.

The museum itself displays mainly classical items, but there is an interesting Christian mosaic of a saint's head still attached to the carved cylindrical base of a Roman statue; it had been used as the base of a pulpit in Basilica B.

The phylax (custodian) will conduct you to the site of **Basilica B** some 500 m down the road and on the other side; this is slightly earlier (*c.* 500) and larger, with its main w doorway still standing. The builders used much carved Roman spolia in its construction; its plan shows four side aisles and the plentiful remains include many column bases, templon fragments and the remains of the altar and ciborium. The mosaics here are also covered, but are geometric, and of less interest.

Nikopolis is an easy visit to make from Arta, and if you extend your viewing to the many Roman survivals you will have a full and memorable day.

NOMITSIS
See **Mani**

OMORFOKKLISIA Ομορφοκκλησιά Kastoria
Church with icon in high relief **. Easy access by car/bus.

Of the monastery that once was here only the katholikon remains as the village **church of Ag Giorgios**. It is a 14th-c, medium-sized building on an inscribed-cross plan, with quite a high cupola and an integral bell-tower over the w porch that could well be original. There is attractive use of brick to form tall blind arcades on the drum of the cupola, the n and s gables and on the apse, where they are filled with herring-bone patterns; the large arched spaces on the s side must be remains of previous monastic buildings.

The main interest here is inside the church (ring the bell in the tower and someone with a key should appear). The interior walls are covered in modern soot and the iconostasis is unusually ugly, but in the s bay you will find a unique **icon of St George** carved in high relief in wood, and with traces of polychrome pigment still visible. The figure in its Roman armour and cloak is over lifesize; it is in good, if grimy, condition, and makes an immediate and powerful impression. Lack of comparative material on the same scale makes it hard to date with certainty, but its proportions and general character are close to the standing figure of the same saint carved in steatite now in *Vatopedi, Mount Athos*, which is usually dated to the 11th c; this may well be the period of this icon, which in any case must certainly be pre-Palaiologue.

ORKHOMENOS Ορχομενός Viotia
Church **. Easy access by car/bus.

This is always referred to in reference books as **Skripou**, but as this name does not appear on either road-signs or maps, we will adopt that of the village, which does. The **church of the Koimisis** here (previously the Panagia) is one of the architecturally outstanding buildings in the s part of central Greece. A long inscription round the outside of the apse records that it was built by an important official (called a *protospetharios*) named Leo in 873/4; with its massive and simple forms it is immediately impressive, and it was probably intended to convey the power of the Emperor Basil I in the *theme* of Hellas.

Its exterior is dominated by the high projecting wings of the transepts – as high as the e bay and wider than the rest of the nave altogether. Their great weight does to some extent diminish the

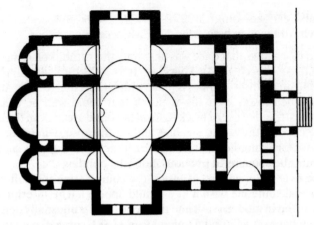

Orkhomenos: Koimisis

effect of the fine cupola, and the three apses (the central one much
larger than those flanking it) seem applied, rather than organic to
the main structure. In only a very few respects does this seem to be
at all the experimental building which its date would suggest. Yet
one of the chief features of the exterior are the sculptured spolia and
inscriptions incorporated into the building, chiefly round the apses,
and on the s walls; it is among these that the foundation date is to be
found, but look too for the reliefs of peacocks, sundial, etc.

Inside, the weight of the walls is again very evident, and the
impression of the exterior is confirmed: this is really a hall-church,
to which cross-arms and a dome have been added, rather than a
cross-in-square of which the arms extend to N and s. It is in this
aspect of its design that its importance lies. It must now be the only
survivor (indeed, it may even have been the only example) from
which the true domed, cross-in-square church plan eventually
developed; when all its numerous successors are counted its
significance becomes evident.

It is interesting to see how the naos (with quite a real longitudinal
emphasis provided by the massive walls enclosing it, and so taking
the place of columns or piers) is nevertheless quite well lit. The
narthex is roofed by a single massive transverse barrel vault, and
this increases the sense of a change of direction on entering the
naos. There are virtually no frescos now, but rich bands of carved
ornament run all round the naos and narthex. It also had a substantial templon of which numerous fragments (carved with the same

designs) can be found around the site, some embedded in the gateway to the courtyard outside.

The lack of any prior ancestry in Greece for this design has caused speculation on where the ideas originated: rather than CP, which is the usual assumption, the court buildings of the rising 9th-c Bulgar power have been suggested as a source. Its immediate, short-term effect is also still quite unclear, due to few surviving earlier 10th-c examples in Greece.

While at Orkhomenos try to allow a further 2 hours to visit the small and remote **church of Ag Nikolaos sta Kambia** * (Αγ Νικολάος στα Κάμπια) (i.e. 'in the fields'). About 5 km NW of the town is the small village of Dionysio, from which a dirt road is signed the 2 km or so through open country to the church. It was a *metokhi* (monastic farm) attached to *Osios Loukas, Stiris*, and the design of this accomplished little church is so like a reduced version of the much larger katholikon that it has been attributed to the same builder, and is certainly of much the same date. Its form is an inscribed cross, two-column, domed design with a single faceted apse; its exterior of finely-cut limestone is a real surprise in this desolate landscape. The interior of the main church, with its two reused early Byz caps, is whitewashed, but the **crypt**, dedicated to Ag Varvara, has some 12th-c frescos. Although rather damaged, you will find the Christ Pantocrator in the apse impressive, and there are figures of bishops in the bema, and roundels of evangelists enclosed in scrolls in the vaulting, not unlike those in the crypt of the mother-church.

OSIOS LOUKAS
See **Stiris**

OSIOS MELETIOS   Οσιος Μελέτιος   Attika, on border with Viotia
Convent and katholikon *.

Built on a terrace of Mount Pastra, and almost mid-way on a direct line between Thebes and Athens, the buildings of Osios Meletios have retained much of their original form. While modernization has (as so often) overtaken the living quarters of the nuns, the disposition of these, with that of the communal buildings, is largely unchanged and the katholikon still has much of its 11th-c fabric and character; the peaceful and rural outlook, too, will hardly have altered.

In plan the core of the katholikon is a standard inscribed cross, four-column design, with the main apse so large as to reduce the other two to niche size; this must represent the scale and intention of the original founder. There have been many additions since, however. A domed parekklision was built on to the s side in the 12th c and (at about the same period or slightly later) a large exonarthex was constructed; this is two bays deep and has two further columns to support its own cupola. With other additions to N and s of this, and then a large porch added to the w, the building almost fills the available courtyard space.

Wooden scaffolding now supports parts of the building, both inside and out, and there is damage to much of the fresco decoration; there never was much carved ornament, with sculptured decoration on only one of the caps in the naos, and some on the

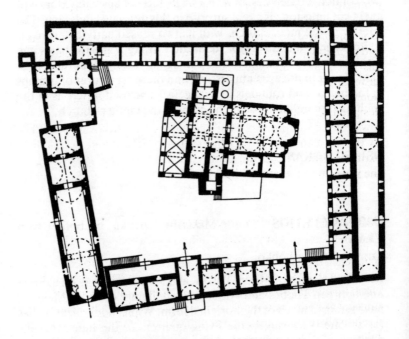

Monastery of Osios Meletios

lintel of the entrance. In its present state the most interesting area is the exonarthex; there is a good *opus sectile* floor and some 14th-c frescos in fair condition: the death of the titular saint is represented over the w door into the naos, and there are other subjects such as Jacob's Ladder and martyrdoms in the upper walls and vaults.

While this route from Athens to Thebes is slower than the new National Road, it is infinitely more attractive, and the presence of Osios Meletios a short distance off it offers an opportunity to visit a Byz monastic complex which, although not in its original state, still has a great deal of its original fabric and layout.

OURANOPOLI Ουρανόπολη Khalkidiki
Tower. Easy access from village or by sea.

For anyone not making the journey on to the Athos peninsula, the massive **tower** here gives a perfectly good idea of the many others of the same type which survive as the main defences of most of the monasteries of the *Agion Oros*; in a number of them the tower is the only surviving element of their med buildings (see p. 46). The function of towers such as this would have been purely defensive, and probably this one dates, like the others, from the 11th/12th c. It has lost a little of its height (some of them on Athos still have castellation and no tiled roof, as here) but its aspect and construction give a vivid impression of the dangers which they were all designed to evade. There is a written record of how in 1307 the tower of the monastery of Ag Panteleimon on Athos was attacked by the Catalans; the monks had retreated into it and were able to extinguish the fire that the raiders had lit against the wall by pouring the wine on to it that they had stored inside.

PANTANASSA Παντάνασσα Lakonia
Church **. sw of Monemvasia; access by car (rough road).

You reach the **church of Ag Athanasios** (formerly of the **Pantanassa**) by a road that traverses the village of Pantanassa and continues to climb further for about 2 km. In completely rural surroundings, it is unusual to find a medium-sized church of this sophistication in such a relatively remote position; the village must have receded down the hill since the med period. It is a 12th-c construction on an inscribed cross, triple-apse plan, but its chief interest lies in its being one of a

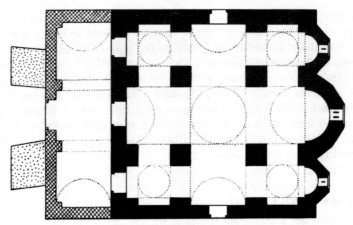

Pantanassa: Ag Athanasios

select group of five-domed Byz churches to be found in Greece; its date means that it anticipates all those of *Mystra*, *Arta*, *Thessaloniki* and *Feres*. Its masonry, with its faceted apses and five cupolas built in good cloisonné, brick arches to all the windows and framing the triple arcade of the main apse window, is much more sophisticated than that of the earlier church of *Peristera*. Only the later narthex, heavily buttressed, is of cruder construction. Its presence here must be due to influential patronage associated perhaps with nearby *Monemvasia*. The interior has almost nothing to offer, there being no frescos or decorative sculpture, but the interest of the building and its attractive surroundings will reward a visit.

PASSAVAS Πασσαβάς Lakonia, SE of Gythion. Med Passavant

Castle **. Easy access by car/bus, then steep goat tracks.

Passavas was one of the smallest of the 12 original baronies of Akhaia, being worth four knights' fees in 1208. The castle here was built by Jean de Neuilly, 'Marshall of the Morea', in 1254, and it traditionally took its name from his family battle cry of 'Passe en avant!'. Marguerite, the daughter of Jean II de Neuilly, had been one of the hostages sent to CP in 1262 as surety for Guillaume de Villehardouin. In 1278 the castle was taken over by the Byzantines based at Mystra, but does not seem to have been held with any great tenacity. There are no indications that it was greatly valued by the

Turks; certainly there is no trace of modernization for artillery as there is at *Acrocorinth*, *Argos*, *Naupaktos* and even *Karystos*; in 1670 it was repaired and garrisonned, but can never have been regarded as of importance.

The site is quite a fine one, with sheer cliffs to N and E. The castle is constructed on the plan of a crude parallelogram, as dictated by the land, with the E and W walls roughly parallel, and these joined by shorter walls to N and S; the original entrance was in the S wall. The area enclosed is considerable, as the longest wall (the E) is almost 200 m long, and the W about 150; the N and S walls are about 110 and 100 m long. The area enclosed is now so densely overgrown that the easiest way to make a tour of the surviving walls is to use the sentry walk along their parapets.

The least difficult approach is from the W, where you will find about 100 m of the wall still standing, and mostly in quite good state;

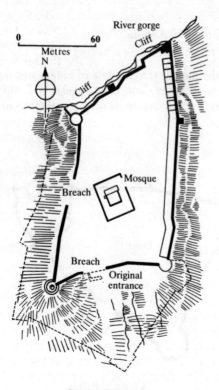

Castle of Passavas

one entrance to the bailey is now on the corner where this wall meets the s wall at an acute angle, but a gateway that was still usable here after the last war is now just a heap of rubble. Further large sections of wall survive to s and E, with substantial plaster rendering. There is no sign of a keep, but the walls of a square structure, with an apse-like recess in the s wall, and the base of a spiral staircase, survive in the middle of the enclosure; this was almost certainly a small mosque, and if so must be 17th c. (It has been suggested that the entire remains are post-medieval, but this does not seem possible in view of the type and state of the surviving masonry and of the total lack of provision for artillery, which would have been essential under full Turkish modernization.)

The lack of major rebuilding at Passavas, combined with its site, make a visit here a rewarding experience, if a somewhat strenuous one.

PATRAS Πάτρα Akhaia
Castle *. Easy access from town by foot/car.

Throughout the med period the fate of Patras was dominated by its commercial importance, and this in turn was due largely to its position and its port; its name recurs several times in Byz historians

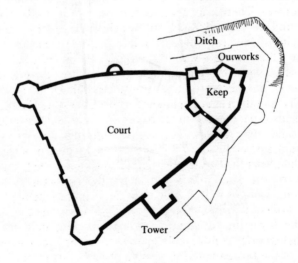

Castle of Patras

in this context, even overshadowing its association with St Andrew the apostle, who preached here. Venice, never slow to seize an opportunity of this kind, acquired special trading privileges there in 1199 from Alexios III. In 1204 they even claimed the city for themselves, but were ejected by the Franks the following year, and in 1208 it was designated as one of the largest and richest of the 12 Frankish baronies. Patras became increasingly important to the Franks, being made the seat of the Latin archbishop of Akhaia; by 1266 the town was being governed by its archbishop, who thereby assumed the status of a baron. Venice did not reappear on the scene here until 1408, when the republic rented Patras from the archbishop for five years, and again in 1417 they called for help to defend it from the Greeks of Mystra. It was not until 1429 that, under the despot Constantine, Patras reverted again to Byz rule, but it was to fall to the Turks finally in 1460.

All these powers have left their mark on the **castle of Patras** (the Frourion), of which substantial parts can still be visited on the spur above the modern town. You receive an early impression of the castle's history at the gateway; besides abundant classical fragments from the ancient acropolis, this has a Byz outer vaulted space, a second Frankish gateway with portcullis channel, and a Turkish inner arch. The interior has a massive keep in the NE corner; the construction of this must be Byz, with liberal tile filling of the rough stone courses. There is an enceinte formed both by walls and a dry ditch round the N, E and S sides, still largely visible. Patras is unusual not just in still having quite substantial areas of Byz construction to be seen – the N curtain wall is good evidence of this, being built partly of classical column-drums and other architectural pieces which must have been to hand from the buildings of the ancient acropolis, and then later heightened, probably by the Franks – but there is also space in the outer bailey for quite extensive lemon, orange and olive groves. The slightly different masonry of the prominent salient tower, with its rectangular design, suggests it might date from the last decades before 1460, when the Palaiologoi were in control. The Turks would have added the parapets to all of the curtain walls, as well as various artillery emplacements.

The castle of Patras, although now not readily seen when viewed from the town on account of the high modern buildings, can nevertheless offer considerable interest to anyone looking for the history of the Morea in the successive phases of its refortification; the atmosphere of the bailey with its fruit and olive groves is also relatively peaceful after the commercial bustle of the city below, and the outlook towards the gulf is spectacular.

PERISTERA Περιστέρα Khalkidiki
Church **. 30 km SE of Thessaloniki; easy access by car/bus.

The exterior of the **church of Ag Andreas** displays some of the contrasts that persist inside this complex and interesting building, with its remarkably early date of 870–1. While its multiple cupolas show that it is one of the quite rare five-dome churches in Greece, its masonry is very unsophisticated, and its crudity contrasts with the decorative qualities of its profile – the octagonal drum of the main dome among the other four circular ones. Its plan has the central dome supported on four columns in a conventional inscribed cross, but surrounding this are four domed areas grouped symmetrically round it, each originally supported by three absidioles; the only asymmetrical features would have been the rather broad chapels of the prothesis and diaconicon either side of the main E apse.

The plan begins to recall much later buildings to the N (Bulgaria, Russia), and it is interesting that its founder was a disciple of St Methodius, one of the 'apostles to the Slavs'. A large later narthex has been built on at the w end, but you can see traces in the flooring of the absidioles that supported the w cupola. Inside, the modesty of building materials continues with very crude columns and the simplest of caps; there are no frescos. The church must have been used as a mosque, as outside a truncated minaret has been turned into a detached bell-tower. You will find this a rewarding church to visit.

PHILIPPI Φιλίπποι Kavala
Ruins of EC basilicas, Byz fort, tower and museum ***. Easy access by car/coach.

Although deserted by early in the 10th C, this town had considerable importance in late antiquity and the early med period, both through its position on the Via Egnatia, and by its association with St Paul. It must rank as one of the principal EC sites in Greece – the area which seems, by the later 5th C, to have rivalled most of the other Aegean centres. Parts are still under excavation.

The most impressive of the surviving remains are now those of the so-called **Basilica B** (or Direkler-Basilica, to the sw of the road to

Drama) but it is advisable to begin a visit here with **Basilica** A to the
NE of the road (try to park on the area below the museum rather
than in the coach park). Basilica A was founded *c.* 500 on a vast
artificial terrace, and although little more than the plan and some of
the N wall can now be seen, the scale that this conveys is huge – more
than 80 m in overall length. You can gain some idea of its original
splendour from the superb sheets of marble flooring still in place in
the vast atrium; the w wall of this had niches and fountains, and you
can see traces of an ambo in the centre of the nave (as still stands at
Kalabaka). There was a transept and large rounded apse, as at *Ag
Dimitrios, Thessaloniki*. A baptistry (the best preserved part of the
complex) opened off the narthex to the N, and has fragments of
fresco still visible, with flooring of various kinds of marble. The
basilica itself had a broad nave and two aisles with galleries, and
there are still parts of a fine *opus sectile* floor to be seen; its original
splendour can be imagined also from the pieces of marble revetment
that are still just showing in places, and must once have covered all
the interior walls.

To reach **Basilica** B you cross the road and the site of the forum,
where the Via Egnatia ran along the N side. This basilica was built
about 540, and seems to have been a more experimental building.
Again a large atrium to the w had steps up to the broad narthex, and
the basilica itself had galleries and barrel vaults over the side aisles;
the innovation here was a dome sited over the crossing, but this
seems to have collapsed at an early point, perhaps even before it was
completed. The rest of the building was used until the 9th c, then the
w end collapsed, leaving only the narthex standing, with a baptistry
leading off it.

The most impressive remains here are the towering wall sections
of the w end, formed from brick bands and marble – some of them
reused classical blocks (see the bits of dog-tooth ornament here and
there). You will find the floor mosaics impressive and plentiful, and
the sculptural decoration must have been outstanding. Besides
pilaster caps still *in situ* on the standing walls there are exceptionally
fine capitals now at ground level; their spiky acanthus forms, deeply
undercut, clearly owe some of their quality to the new style of
Justinian's sculptors who would have just then been completing Ag
Sofia in CP.

At Philippi, too, there is the site of a smaller but rarer church type;
to the SE of Basilica A the plan of an **octagonal church** has recently
been uncovered. A central octagonal area, defined by columns

which must have supported the roof, had an ambulatory of the same shape around it; the whole structure was built inside a square. it dates from *c*. 500, and may reflect the tradition of centrally-planned martyria as it had developed further E; it is still under excavation and cannot yet be visited, although you can see its layout from higher up the hill to the N.

The **Museum** here has a number of superb pieces of 5th/6th C sculpture, including two magnificent double-zone caps from Basilica B, with eagles' and rams' heads. There are also templon plaques, large sections of mosaic flooring from the excavated churches and a collection of Byz coins from Constantine the Great to Justinian.

If you make the ascent of the hill above the site (a track past the museum zig-zags up the mountain side) you will find that the med remains of Philippi are continued on the **acropolis**. According to an inscription of 963 the Emperor Nikiforos Focas renovated the fort here; you can see the ruins of the fortifications and a tower (usually called a keep) which was probably for storage. There are also the remains of two more later towers, and the height here gives you an unmatched view of the whole site with its Greek, Roman and EC survivals and associations.

PLATAMONAS Πλαταμώνας Pieria
Castle **. Easy access from road.

While the impressive **castle** here was never as grandiose as that of *Khlemoutsi*, it does bear comparison with those in the Morea on grounds of completeness; it is this impression that a modern visitor may feel most strongly. The site, on the coast to the SE of Mount Olympus, is a magnificent one, and must have been intended primarily to guard the road as it winds past on the way to the *Vale of Tempe* and into Thessaly; it was no doubt also meant to strengthen the defence of Thessaloniki by dominating the entrance to the Thermaic Gulf. Its position and siting, although on the site of an ancient settlement, could never have made it easy to defend, however, and it is mentioned little in the accounts of med Greece. Its name first appears in 1198 as a Byz fortress, and the Franks would have added to it in the early 13th C; in 1218, however, when just newly fortified, it apparently fell quite easily to Theodore Doukas, the despot of Epiros, on his campaign to take

Thessaloniki. In spite of its size and relatively undamaged state this is actually a rather problematic castle, and a recent opinion on it claims that it is mostly Turkish.

Its freedom from assault means that we can see the castle, whatever its date, in a relatively undamaged state. You will be struck by its spectacular profile from several points on the road as you approach; the long and largely undamaged enceinte is most probably Frankish work, with some later Turkish rebuilding in parts; if it was all 15th and 16th c Turkish there would surely have been some provision for artillery. It encloses a loosely polygonal area of some 200 by 200 m. The entrance certainly has later (probably Turkish) outbuilding. The whole area is dominated by the unique and prominent octagonal keep, and it must be this which is the chief survival of Byz building; certainly the brickwork round the high windows suggests 12th-c Byz workmanship, and the doorway some 3 m off ground level recalls the design of the tower at *Galatista*, with just the ramp up to it being obviously later. The castellation round the top must be quite late Turkish replacement, as there are rifle-slits clearly visible. The keep has its own castellated enceinte which is still virtually complete and with its own sentry-walk all round; it is not possible to tell if this is Byz or later Frankish work, but there is nothing quite like the octagonal keep itself anywhere in Greece, and it confirms the inventive approach of the Byzantines in this field. Excavations current at the N end of the enclosure show considerable earlier buildings with traces of fresco decoration.

If you are taking the main N–S highway, try to allow a good couple of hours here; you will find the time is well spent, and you will also be rewarded with the sight from the battlements of both Olympus and Ossa.

PLATSA
See **Mani**

PORTA PANAGIA   Πόρτα Παναγιά   Trikala
Church, with sculpture and mosaic icons **. Easy access by car from Trikala, 18 km to NE.

The beautiful but puzzling church dedicated to the **Porta Panagia**, or **Virgin of the Great Gates**, is set in rural isolation in the valley where the pass from Arta to Trikala reaches the plain of Thessaly. The problem that it poses is that although it is clearly the work of two different periods, there have been differing views as to which is the earlier. We know that a church was founded here by John I Doukas, *sebastokrator* of Thessaly, in 1283, and there is a chryso-bull of 1331 given to the church by the Emperor Andronikos III Palaiologos, but neither of these facts fully explains what we find here.

The most prominent feature to strike you as you approach is a very substantial cupola, with a tall, wide drum pierced by 16 windows; this is not over the naos, but towers above the narthex. The church itself is a barrel-vaulted basilica with a transept that is higher than the nave, but no dome; going round to the E end you will find that the rougher masonry of the narthex gives way to fine cloisonné, with elaborate and finely set brick patterns focused round the windows. The three apses are faceted, with the central one considerably larger; all have arcaded windows, and another higher window reaches almost to the apex of the w gable. We are clearly dealing with two distinct building periods, and the variety of views on this church has been due to its highly unusual form.

Entering the high, well-lit naos, you will at once be impressed by its chief glory: a superb marble templon with (either side of the main opening) two beautiful mosaics of standing figures of Christ and the Virgin Hodegetria. These figures, in their carved marble shrines, are unique in Greece, and alone will well reward your journey here.

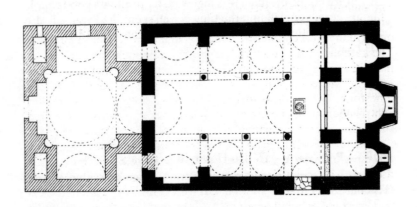

Porta Panagia

The templon has finely carved members and even some coloured inlay; one of its caps displays the imperial double-headed eagle.

The remainder of the interior decoration is less significant, with the frescos of the large narthex, dating from the first half of the 15th c, now in poor condition. The mosaics of the templon can only be just in the Palaiologue era, and so must date from the foundation of John I in the 1280s. The clear division in the history of the building means that while the main body of the church, with the uniquely fine templon, must be late 13th c, the narthex with its exaggerated cupola is probably mid-14th c, and comes from the period of Stefan Dušan (1331–55), when Serbian influence was at its height. Why the basilica was built without a cupola will never be known, but the Serbian emperor must have thought that a church of this scale should be endowed with one.

PROASTIO
See **Mani**

ROGOI
See **Nea Kerassous**

SAGMATA Σάγματα Viotia
Monastic buildings and katholikon *. Easy access by car.

The **monastery of the Metamorfosis** is an early 11th-c foundation; with *Osios Meletios* and the convent at *Megara* it provides an opportunity to see monastic buildings in a relatively original state. The katholikon is a good, although not exceptional, example of an inscribed cross, four-column design; the first part that you see on entering the courtyard are the faceted apses in good cloisonné limestone. The windows form an attractive triple arcade with taller central opening, and there is restrained brick decoration. There is a small dome over the narthex, but the main dome collapsed in 1912.

Note the classical caps reused in the spacious narthex, but easily the most unusual feature here is the fine mosaic and *opus sectile* floor, with a variety of animal and abstract designs; the monks keep most of it covered with matting, but won't mind if you ask to look at it. The iconostasis and paintings are late, but there are relics kept on unusually open display in three 18th-c silver reliquaries.

The site is high in the hills to the NE of Thebes, and the road up to it offers fine views over the Theban plain.

SAMARI
See **Ellinoekklisia**

SANTA MAURA   Σάντα Μαύρα   Etolia-Akarnania
Castle *. Usually open.

Approaching the N tip of Leukas (Lefkas) from the mainland, you cannot miss the **castle of Santa Maura** perched on a steep and rocky outcrop at the foot of Mount Lamia. (The name of Santa Maura was given by the Italians to the whole island of Leukas.) The castle was built by John Orsini *c.* 1330 to look out over the causeway below; although most of what can now be seen is subsequent Venetian and Turkish reconstruction, the S salient survives from the 14th-c structure. It is a compact building with quite a cramped courtyard, but in basically good condition; once the farm animals were cleared out it could be brought back into use in a few days. You gain an excellent view of the unusual surrounding terrain from its battlements.

SERRES   Σέρρες   Macedonia
Two churches and a monastery *. All easy access.

Both of the church buildings here lie on the N side of the town. The earliest foundation must be the **church of Ag Theodoroi** (the old mitropolis), although it underwent drastic restoration in 1725 (inscription in brickwork of exterior of S wall) and again in 1952, when it was reroofed. In form it is an impressively large (about 47 m overall length), three-aisled, wooden-roofed, galleried basilica with three rounded apses, and probably dates from the late 11th C; the central apse may have been enlarged, and has simple star patterns in the exterior brickwork, but those of the diaconicon and prothesis have had later cupolas added with quite high drums; these must be later and look slightly flippant beside the massive simplicity of the form between them. There is quite a substantial exterior baptistry to the SE.

The basilica has not been used for many years, and its interior is now painted in plain colour, with only a few fresco fragments still visible; of the substantial 12th-C apse mosaic of the Communion of the Apostles nothing is now left here – and the part of it in *Ag Giorgios*, *Thessaloniki* cannot be seen either. Round the walls are ranged scores of sculptural fragments, including some quite small caps from the gallery. Remains of the marble synthronon round the apse, as well as throne fragments, demonstrate its use as the seat of a bishop. Outside to the NW is a small, centrally planned, inscribed cross, 14th-C chapel with a tall drum which looks rather impertinent beside the ponderously grand w front of the basilica.

To reach the **church of Ag Nikolaos** you have to take the road for the ascent to the acropolis, and you will find it down a short branching road to the left just below the summit. The plan is quite a standard 12th-C one, with a medium-sized inscribed cross design, narthex and exonarthex, and faceted absidioles to N and S as well as four supporting columns. On this base, however, besides the large central cupola, the radical rebuilding in 1937 gave it a further tiny one over the bema, three more over the narthex (the central one slightly tailer) and yet two further low ones over the exonarthex; with the integral bell-tower these seven domes give the profile of the building a rather busy profile that you may find over-elaborate. The interior has mainly late painting, although a few fragments survive from the 12th C, such as the figure of St Damian.

If you continue up to the summit of the acropolis you will find some impressive fragments of the Byz fortress still visible.

While at Serres, if you have a spare couple of hours, an interesting visit can be made by a drive of some 9 km into the mountains to the NE of the town; here, folded in a high and peaceful mountain valley, is the **Moni tou Timiou Prodromou Serou** *. Originally a monastery founded in 1270, it has since 1986 been staffed by nuns; the layout and general *mise-en-scène* have retained their med character well.

The katholikon dates from 1300–32, the period of the rule of a Bishop Joachim (a nephew of the founder), and is a standard inscribed cross, triple-apse design; it has a notably broad and rather flat cupola with six windows, which is supported on vaulting without any columns. Enlargements have been made to N and S, with an exonarthex being added already in 1333. There are many frescos, although most are from later periods (those in the exonarthex are dated 1630); the earliest are in the narthex and date from the 14th-C foundation, and a pair of good late Palaiologue icons to the N and S of the naos.

This is a foundation of unique interest, however, because it was here that the first patriarch of CP after the Turkish conquest, George Skholarios, otherwise Gennadios II, chose to retire. He had been made patriarch in 1454 by the Sultan Mehmed II, and he established with him the concordat that governed the relations of the Orthodox and Muslim powers into the 20th c. Gennadios first retired in 1456, but was recalled to CP twice more before his death here in 1472; you can be shown his tomb in the floor, carved with a long contemporary inscription.

SERVIA Σέρβια Kozani
Ruined basilica with frescos *. Unenclosed. Easy access by dirt road.

The Byz **kastro** would always have been prominent above the town, but there are only scanty ruins of it now left; you will pass through them as you approach the much more spectacular remains of quite a large, three-aisled 11th-c **basilica** on the highest part of the original enclosure, first dedicated to St Demetrios. A basilica on this scale and on this site could only have been intended as the seat of a bishop.

Its wooden roof and most of the rounded apse have now gone, but the nave (some 22 m long) and narthex are largely intact. The remaining frescos are in two layers: one is 11th-c and contemporary with the building, and the second is later 12th c; they vary in the degree of damage they have sustained. There are few of the earliest phase left, but some can be seen on the s wall where the later layer has fallen away; most interesting (although in poor state) must be an unidentified imperial portrait in the narthex, and there are still some fine 12th-c figures of full-length bishops in the remaining part of the apse; there is a faded sequence of Passion scenes down the s side of the nave, and an impressive, almost undamaged, head of a male saint in the soffit of an arch in the NW corner. This is a fine and atmospheric site, with considerable interest, and should not be hurried.

SIDIROKASTRO Σιδηρόκαστρο Serres. Turkish Demir Hisar
Ruins of Byz fortress. Steep road, but easy access.

The site of this castle, guarding the N–S road as it winds into the broadening valley of the river Strymon N of Serres, must always have been important. The few remains of the Byz fortress lie above the town to the E, where the rocks rise steeply towards the Vrontous range, and are largely out of sight from below. Although it was clearly this which gave the town its name, the remains are now sufficiently modest to be of interest only to the specialist. The w defences are precipitous, and this would seem to be one of the few Byz forts that was built making good use of a naturally sound position.

SKRIPOU
See **Orkhomenos**

SOUNION, CAPE   Σούνιο   Attika
Churches and one tower *.

The cape of Sounion, to the E and SE of Athens, could until recent years offer a genuinely rural atmosphere, with an agricultural landscape serving what were never more than large villages. With the expanding population of Athens so near, its character is now changing rapidly, but it is still possible to find survivals of the area's med past, although often either neglected or engulfed by modern development.

There are over 20 small churches in the area of the cape, although probably only eight were built before the Turkish period. Almost all are quite difficult to locate, and while they all have some features of interest, their artistic status is for the most part not high and so only some are mentioned here. For these reasons the area is being treated in a single entry, and specialists will need more detailed sources.

The only church of medium, rather than small, size is happily also one of the easiest to locate. At the 37th kilometre mark on the coast road that runs beside the Saronic Gulf from Athens to Sounion, take the road inland; within 400 m you will find on your right the **church of Ag Dimitrios Saronikos**. It is an almost centrally-planned, inscribed cross, single apse building of a type known as a 'triconch': two further apsidal forms to N and S support the dome. In fact it is only the N side of the church – apse and wall – which survives from the original 11th- to early 12th-c building; the rest has been rebuilt during the Turkish period. However, this church is of interest in that it is the only one on the Cape to have Kufic ornament: although now whitewashed, you will see the simple tile shapes let into the mortar at the top of the N wall, made otherwise from good cloisonné. This marks the church as having been of distinct importance in the Byz period. The interior is of minimal interest.

The area round Markopoulo offers several more churches, all of very modest size. Two km to the N, off the road in open country, is the **church of the Panagia**, Varaba; it is a domed, centrally planned, single apse church with quite crude masonry; it is probably late 12th or 13th C. You will find that a Byz plate is let into the W wall, the drum from a large column has been built into the S wall, and there are other small spolia visible; the interior has little of interest.

Off the road to Porto Rafti, some 2 km from Markopoulo, you will find on the right the **church of Agia Triada**. Although it dates from the Turkish period, it is of interest in that it is built on a double-nave plan, and there are a number of fragments of good EC sculpture both built into it and in the immediate vicinity. This suggests the earlier presence of an EC church either on the exact site or nearby.

The small **church of the Taxiarch** at Dagla, just outside Markopoulo to the E of the road to Sounion, demonstrates the hazards to which these med buildings are subject. A large cement works has recently opened beside it, and huge lorries frequently grind up the slope past it; the dumping of rubble has also begun close by. Although the small, cruciform, domed church has Byz origins, it has been altered several times and its earliest paintings have now largely gone, but it still deserves better surroundings. This is particularly true in view of the fact that the med **tower** just 100 m away is the only one in the area and is unique in having an original entrance door at ground level, although the upper storeys cannot be entered from it (see p. 46).

About half-way between Markopoulo and Keratea, to the left of the road in an olive grove, is the **church of Ag Giorgios**. It achieved its present form after several alterations, but originated in the early Byz period, and the apse certainly dates from then; classical Ionic caps have been re-used in the interior. The paintings are from various periods, but the earliest may be 13th or 14th C.

Finally, the small **church of Ag Kyriaki** off the road in open country just over 1 km W of Keratea, and of the simplest possible form (it is just a wooden-roofed chamber with a later narthex, some 9 m long) has frescos which, although in poor state, date from various periods from the 12th to 15th C.

STAGIRA   Στάγιρα   Khalkidiki
Ruins of Byz fortress. Unenclosed. Easy access from road.

Just to the s of the road passing Mount Stratoniko you will see an open area which is the site of the Byz **fortress of Sidirokausia**. Only two of its towers still survive, both are quite substantial, still standing some 7 m high; although largely held together by ivy, considerable amounts of Byz military masonry can still be seen, with quite liberal use of brick amongst the local stone. The site (the birthplace of Aristotle) is not mentioned by Prokopios as one of those fortified by Justinian, and in spite of its apparent size, the later historical sources are also silent about it.

STIRIS   Στείρι   Viotia
Monastery: katholikon, crypt and church; sculpture, frescos and mosaics ***. Easy access by car/coach. Open all day. Entrance charge.

Besides the later monastic complex, there are three separate church buildings on the site of the **monastery of Osios Loukas**: the **katholikon** of the monastery, the **church of the Theotokos** and the **crypt of the katholikon**. Although the katholikon was not the first to be built, it is the first building that you will reach on your visit, and is easily the most significant in every way. If you arrive here after visiting a number of other Byz churches in central or s Greece, you will be

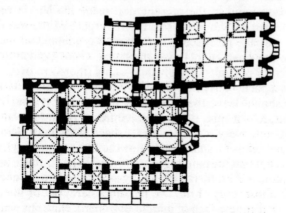

Monastery of Osios Loukas: the Katholikon and Church
of the Theotokos

struck first by its sheer scale, which at once sets it apart from most of what you will have seen: with the great height and size of its dominating cupola, its marble-clad lower walls, and extensive mosaics, it clearly ranks among the major buildings of the empire.

The dedication is to a local hermit, 'The Holy Luke', who died nearby in 953, and the early local tradition that the Emperor Romanos II was the founder of a church here in 961 may be correct. The katholikon was built *c*. 1040, and its design is an impressive refinement of the system in which the dome is supported over an octagon formed by a complex arrangement of vaults; the fame of its mosaics may in fact have acted to obscure the virtuosity of its architecture. The natural comparison is with *Dafni*, but besides the loss of its marble wall revetment, the design there is slightly less complex. Here the introduction of a gallery increases the variety and subtlety of the vaults adjoining the central area under the dome.

The superb mosaics represent a more severe and abstracted style than those of *Dafni*, which are more reminiscent of the Hellenistic element in Byz art. Enter the building through the narthex, and you can then see the mosaics of the Crucifixion and Anastasis there before proceeding on into the naos; the other feast scenes inside are much further from the eye. These are in fine condition, and exemplify the austere style of Osios Loukas well. The cupola would have contained the Pantocrator and archangels, now seen in later fresco, but the mosaics of the squinches are still present, and show well the inventive use made by the mosaicists of the concave surfaces on which they worked: the river Jordan 'encloses' Christ at his baptism, and in the presentation scene the Virgin passes the infant Christ to Simeon across the real space of the squinch. In a similar way the rarer scene of Pentecost is adapted with complete logic to the small cupola over the bema. Osios Loukas is particularly rich in portraits of individual saints (there are over 130) and there is a particularly fine one of the titular holy man in the N bay.

You should leave the katholikon by the door leading off the N bay, but do not miss the impressive fresco of Joshua on the wall here. Its discovery in 1965, when a sheet of the marble revetment was removed, set a small cat among the Byz pigeons, as its placing there meant that the painting must have been in existence before the katholikon was built. It dictated a basic rethinking of not just the relative chronology of the two buildings here, but of the development of a distinct range of middle Byz architecture. Its significance is due to the fact that it must have been painted on the façade of the church of the Theotokos, which until then had been assumed to be later than the katholikon. A further point of interest is that among the prophecies of the Holy Luke was one that Crete would be reconquered from the Arabs; this actually took place in 960, shortly after his death, and the inscription beside this warrior figure may refer to this event.

Opinions as to when the **church of the Theotokos** may have been built vary from the mid-10th c to some time after 960, and it may be a foundation of the Emperor Romanos II (959–63); the relative richness of its ornament can be explained both by political motives and stylistic developments, and must represent a phase which gave way to the greater severity of the katholikon. You enter its open exonarthex from the N bay, close to the Joshua fresco.

Its design is certainly simpler than the katholikon, being a relatively common form of inscribed cross, only with an extended E bay, and a much more spacious narthex which needs two columns to support its width; both these features may be due to its particular function and location, although the slight parallelogram of its plan is unexplained. But while the chief glory of the katholikon is the mosaic decoration, with the Theotokos it is undoubtedly the sculpture and other surface decoration. The caps, some even retaining their polychrome embellishment, and the carving of the templa, are in superb condition and are brilliant examples of this class of work.

Before visiting the crypt you might wish to climb the terrace at the E end of the complex, from where you can see both the buildings at once. The emphasis on surface decoration in the Theotokos is still much in evidence here, with not just the successive rows of dogtooth, with some areas of Kufic ornament, giving an added element of relief, but from here you can see how the drum of the cupola has richly carved vertical members as well as small carved heads projecting from the corner posts. Even with its two storeys of arcaded windows, the adjacent katholikon shows us a more sober face.

The **crypt** below the katholikon is entered from the S side; logically it should be dated to the same period as the katholikon above, the construction of which it must have anticipated. It partly covers the same area, and retains an inscribed cross plan, with shallow groin vaults forming most of the roof, but providing a surprisingly open effect. There are three tombs located here, that in the N wall, on your right as you enter, being the burial place of the Holy Luke. There are frescos over the greater part of the roof area and much of the walls, and the cleaning of these in the 1960s means that they can be easily viewed. The groin vaults are all divided into four panels, each enclosing a roundel portrait; there is a total of some 40 of these, carefully arranged in three sequences of apostles, martyrs and holy men – the latter being the largest group. The walls beside the tombs have impressive Passion scenes of the Entry into Jerusalem, the Crucifixion, Deposition, Entombment and the Touch of Thomas, closely related in style to the mosaics in the church above.

For the *metokhi* (monastic farm) belonging to Osios Loukas of Ag Nikolaos sta Kambia, see *Orkhomenos*.

STOUPA
See **Mani**

TEMPE, VALE OF   Τέμπη   Larissa. Med Lykostoma
Ruins of castle.

The towering and dramatic cliffs which here form the valley, with the river Peneios running along its floor, always gave Tempe tactical importance as the easiest way to enter the plain of Thessaly from the NE. Heavy traffic and modern tourism have not yet quite succeeded in ruining this famous and beautiful gorge, but any expectations of tranquil enjoyment should be abandoned in advance.

There are said to have been six castles at various periods watching over this narrow and rocky defile, but only one med one still has remains that can be seen from beside the road. Try to travel down the gorge from NE to SW, as there are more stopping points on the side of the road next to the river. Looking up and to the N from either of the two parking lay-bys between the Spring of Venus (Aphrodite) and Ag Paraskevi, some strikingly dramatic remains of the 12th/13th c **Kastro tis Orias** can be seen; the light is likely to be better in the morning.

THALAMES
See **Mani**

THEBES   Θήβα   Viotia. Med Estives
Tower and museum *.

The med history of Thebes was always closely identified with the Duchy of Athens; of the castle of the Cadmea little more remains now than the **Santameri tower** (i.e. of the Saint Omer family) to remind us that this straggling township was once 'le plus beau et riche manoir de toute Romanie' where, it was said, only Paris could provide a higher expression of the ideals of med French chivalry or spoken French of greater purity.

The tower is built almost entirely of fragments and cut marble blocks taken from classical buildings – occasionally a Greek inscription can be seen. (It is worth noting that, to judge from early photographs, the tower on the acropolis of Athens looked very similar to this one.) Of the many works that must have been lost to later periods, there are known to have been some fine paintings in the castle showing the conquest of Syrian forces by the Franks. This reference – the only one that we have to secular painting in med Greece – occurs only in the Greek version of the *Chronicle of the Morea*.

The **museum** is a modern building on land adjacent to the Santameri tower. Of a small amount of EC material easily the most prominent is part of an attractive 4th/5th-c floor mosaic with personifications of the months. It is displayed quite high on an external wall, and was discovered locally in a basilica excavated in 1964; an adjoining inscription named its designer as Demetrios and the mosaicist as Epifanes, while a priest called Paul commissioned it. All the Byz holdings are in the form of sculpture, and are all outside the museum itself. The most striking pieces are some 9th/10th-c templon slabs carved in relief with peacocks, eagles, fish, etc.; there are also relief fragments of Christ and saints, and a sundial. To the N of the tower there is a large collection of 10th- to 12th-c caps, screen fragments and other architectural pieces of various kinds laid out on the ground. You can even sit in a shady part of the garden on a bench seat made from the epistyle (cross member) of a templon with 12th-c relief ornament.

THESSALONIKI Θεσσαλονίκη Thessaloniki/Makedonia

Fortified walls, churches, mosaics, frescos, bath, museum (sites starred individually).

Throughout the Middle Ages Thessaloniki enjoyed a status and significance that, from the 6th c, caused it to be known as the 'second city' of the Byz Empire. This is richly reflected in its buildings and their decoration: the visitor here will find a more complete record of the successive phases of EC and Byz architecture and monumental art than anywhere else in Europe – including

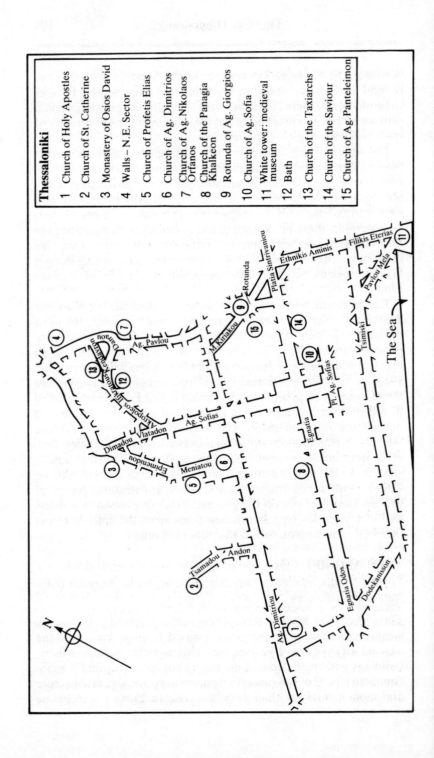

Thessaloniki

1 Church of Holy Apostles
2 Church of St. Catherine
3 Monastery of Osios David
4 Walls – N.E. Sector
5 Church of Profetis Elias
6 Church of Ag. Dimitrios
7 Church of Ag. Nikolaos Orfanos
8 Church of the Panagia Khalkeon
9 Rotunda of Ag. Giorgios
10 Church of Ag. Sofia
11 White tower: medieval museum
12 Bath
13 Church of the Taxiarchs
14 Church of the Saviour
15 Church of Ag. Panteleimon

Istanbul. Yet while the modern world has allowed *Mystra* to retain its med character, Thessaloniki, with its roaring traffic and busy commercial life, has grown with the centuries to become a major 20th-c metropolis; the price to be paid for retaining its treasures has been a high one in the scarce currency of peace and repose.

The city had already become a centre of substantial importance in later antiquity; good evidence of this is the Arch of Galerius (AD 297), which still survives as part of a large and impressive complex. One of the great highways of the empire, the Via Egnatia, which joined CP to the Adriatic, ran through the city, ensuring its continued importance for the whole med period. Thessaloniki had varied fortunes up to the 9th c, being attacked by Alaric at the end of the 4th c, and by invading Slavs and Avars in 597. There were several other significant reverses in its history; one had been in 390 when the Emperor Theodosius, enraged by a revolt of the population against the oppressions of a body of Germanic soldiers quartered there, ordered a dreadful massacre of many of the citizens – men, women and children; another was to occur after an invasion by the Saracens in 904, when a huge part of the population was sold into slavery; there was also the more famous siege and sack of the city in 1185 by the forces of the Norman King of Sicily William II, under Tancred, which was followed by further massacres and destruction.

In spite of these disasters the underlying strength of the city was such that it always recovered, and in 1204 it was the chief prize after the city of CP itself. The title of 'King of Thessaloniki', with ownership of much of E and S mainland Greece, was claimed by Boniface, the Marquis of Montferrat. The strategic importance of the city had always been realized, and this was soon demonstrated again by the ambitious Lord of Epiros, Theodore Doukas, who captured Thessaloniki in 1224 as part of his plan for the reconquest of CP, and proclaimed himself emperor. As the Byz Empire could not be controlled without dominance here, possession of the city was now always sought by later claimants, including the Serbs to the N. In 1246 it was regained and held for the Byzantines by John III Vatatzes; it was besieged again by the Catalan Company in 1308, and in 1387 was taken for the first time by the Turks. They remained in control until the city was ceded back to the Byzantines in 1403, who then gave it to Venice in 1423. In 1430 it was successfully attacked by the Turks under Murad II, thus becoming the first major Greek city to fall permanently under Turkish rule. (For further discussion of the med Kingdom of Thessaloniki see pp. 25–33).

A severe earthquake in June 1978 inflicted damage on a number
of the city's buildings, and in some cases this is still being made
good. Where buildings were still closed for restoration in 1989 this
has been noted, but all should eventually be reopened. There being
no clear route within the city from one monument to another, the
entries below will deal first with the walls and museum, and then
with each of the churches in approximately chronological sequence.

The position and importance of the city has meant that there is here
a series of continuously restored and up-graded **fortified walls** ***
that are second only to those of CP, and are certainly matched by no
other city in modern Greece. Although considerable stretches have
now disappeared, there are still long sections which survive
(amounting to over half of the original length of some 8 km) to
convey a powerful impression of the defences needed by a major
Byz city; they were almost certainly in existence by the mid-3rd c,
and were further consolidated and extended under both Theodosius
(379–95) and Justinian (527–65), but have certainly undergone
much subsequent reconstruction. Besides isolated monograms to
be seen at various points in the walls, there are eight inscriptions
(although not all of them are still in place) which record different
phases of rebuilding from the 7th c through to the later 14th c.
    One of the most substantial surviving sections runs from about
half-way up the E sector and across the N part of the city to the NW;
this provides a good impression of the qualities of the system. You
will see that most of the construction is from undressed stone with
courses of three or four rows of brick laid at intervals; the towers are
mostly square in section, but not sited at regular intervals. There
would have been a ditch and further outworks but there is now
scarcely any trace of these. This sector contains two of the inscriptions which survive as evidence of the continuous reconstruction
which must have gone on: although it is quite easy to miss, you can
see one on your left as you enter the city through the Gate of Anna
Palaiologina. She was the wife of Andronikos III Palaiologos and
this unusually explicit inscription tells us that she built the gateway
in 1355. Another, of Manuel II Palaiologos, is in brick and dates
from 1369–73 when he was despot of the city; you can see it on the
outer face of a tower to the immediate w of this gate, almost in the
centre of the N sector.
    The walls form a continuous enclosure round the acropolis,
projecting to the NE of the city; enclosed within them is the
Heptapirgion ('fortress of seven towers') with its own self-contained

defensive system. A variation on the predominant building system of the walls can be seen in a sector to the sw, quite close to the church of Ag Apostoloi, where brick is used much more extensively and forms a series of arches in the structure of the wall; this was a device to give continued support to walls even when they were undermined by sapping. Although now fragmentary, the walls of the city should be experienced to gain some understanding of the course of its long and varied history.

With the Archaeological Museum now dominated by the superb finds from Vergina, an excellent conversion of the **White Tower** on the sea-front – itself a survival of the city's Venetian or Turkish defences – has provided the city with a fine and self-contained **Medieval Museum ****. Each of its four floors has been arranged to provide a display illustrating a different aspect of the city's med existence. Starting with a glimpse of its urban organization and economic life on the ground floor, the 1st floor is devoted to some features of EC life in Thessaloniki; there are fragments of wall mosaic from Ag Dimitrios, as well as drawings of the lost 7th-c wall mosaics (see below). The 2nd floor display is of finds from Christian cemeteries, with some fine jewellery, coins and glass burial offerings, and a 4th-c painted tomb chamber. You may well find that it is the 3rd floor, with its exhibition of historical and artistic treasures, that is in some ways the most rewarding; among the most outstanding items are two good 14th/15th-c icons, some fine sculptural fragments, a hoard of 12th- and 13th-c coins, some Byz pottery and above all a treasure of 10th-c gold jewellery; this includes a unique pair of gold and enamel Byz armlets, and these brilliant pieces are certainly in a class of their own in this field. There seems to be a shortage of publicity for this museum, but anyone interested in the city's med past should be sure to visit it.

The huge **Rotunda of Ag Giorgios ***** and its mosaics suffered some of the most severe damage during the earthquake of 1978, and in 1989 it was still closed for restoration. Originally a pagan building of late antiquity, it was being built from *c*. 300, and may have been intended originally to serve as a mausoleum for the Emperor Galerius (305–11, caesar from 293), although it was never used in this way. It formed part of a large and impressive complex including a triumphal arch (partly still standing), covered colonnades, a palace and a circus. Its form is essentially that of a huge cylindrical building capped by quite a shallow cupola; early in its life – perhaps late in the 4th c or during the 5th – it was adopted as a place of

Christian worship and an apse was constructed on its E side, using an existing exedra. There were also other med additions built on to the s and w areas of the rotunda, as well as a massive circular wall constructed to form a circular aisle from which the main body of the building could be entered through the newly opened bays. It did not then carry its present dedication, but was probably known as the church of the Archangels, or of the Asomatoi.

Still immensely impressive today, its appearance during the early centuries of its life must have been magnificent. Its interior walls were sheathed in polychrome marble revetment right up to the cupola, and articulated by pilasters; this was a relatively common late antique practice for important buildings but must have been of exceptional grandeur here. New for that period, and unique today, are the large areas of brilliant mosaic decoration that were installed at its conversion to Christian use.

Although partly lost even before the 1978 damage, the surviving mosaics fall into two distinct groups. One, which is decorative and non-figural, is formed by the mosaics of the seven barrel vaults that are built into the thickness of the wall and the lunettes round the base of the dome. The other is an elaborate and brilliantly inventive design that occupied the outer area of the cupola; it is formed from a sequence of 15 full-length figures of saints and martyrs standing in front of and below a design of architectural façades based on Roman stage scenery – the *scenae frontis*. A figure of Christ (now lost) provided the focus for the whole concept. Besides being a brilliantly successful solution to the relatively new problem faced by EC mosaicists of devising new ways of decorating domed church buildings, the mosaics of Ag Giorgios document a stage in the process that would reach its most complete expression in the mosaic schemes of the middle Byz period, such as those at *Dafni* and *Osios Loukas*. A fresco of the Ascension was installed in the sanctuary in the 11th/12th C, but it was severely damaged when it was plastered over by the Turks, who turned the building into a mosque in 1591.

In its original state, and with its richly carved ambo (now in the museum of Istanbul) this building must have been one of the show-pieces of the Greek world: even CP, with its later foundation and development, had nothing quite to compare with it.

The magnificent **basilica of the Akheiropoietos **** ('made without hands'), originally dedicated to the Theotokos, was built in the years following 447, and still conveys brilliantly the grandeur and scale of the great public buildings of late antiquity and the EC period.

It is a broad, three-aisled, galleried structure, and unlike those of Rome which survive, it has escaped the attentions of later architects and builders to a remarkable extent. Earthquakes in the 7th c entailed some reconstruction, and early in the Turkish period the w gallery was dismantled; otherwise in much of its spatial organization we can today experience the same effects as the worshippers of some 1500 years ago.

You will enter first a broad narthex (an exonarthex has disappeared) from which the central nave can be seen through an opening divided by two huge green marble columns – a *tribelon*. There are also broad openings into the wide side aisles, and it is thought that this arrangement was a response to the liturgical needs applying in the E church at this period: the clergy for the most part used the nave and sanctuary, with the congregation confined to the aisles and galleries – suitably broad and spacious. (The *tribelon* would have had textile hangings in its openings.) The 13 bays of the nave are formed by a superb set of pale marble columns with original, deeply cut acanthus caps still in place; the absence of any transept emphasizes the grand simplicity of this design. The apse and chancel arch would almost certainly have had mosaic decoration, but although this has long gone, there are still richly coloured decorative mosaics in the soffits of many of the arches in both the nave and the galleries. The plentiful lighting still shows these up well. Although a commoner type than Ag Giorgios, this must still rank as one of the great European buildings of its period, and it is interesting that it was the first of the city's churches to be used as a mosque, being converted immediately after the city's fall in 1430.

The immense and impressive **basilica of Ag Dimitrios ***** also dates from the later 5th c. It suffered damage first in a fire (*c.* 630), but much more disastrously in the great fire of 1917; it still retains great grandeur, although most of what you see today is in fact rebuilding after this catastrophe, albeit on the same plan and using much of the original materials. This huge, five-aisled, galleried basilica (it is over 60 m in length) must for much of its life have been regarded as the foremost church of the city, as it housed the relics of the patronal saint who was martyred under Diocletian in the early 4th c; his cult early on became synonymous with the city's life, and this church became one of the great *martyria* of the Middle Ages. If the city could be said to have an emotional centre, it was here.

The plan is considerably more complex than that of the Akheiropoietos, as besides the extra aisles it has a broad transept with

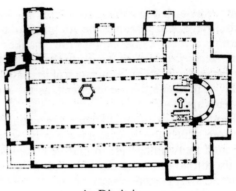

Ag Dimitrios

flanking enclosures on either side of the sanctuary. The exterior view from the E gives a clearer idea than you may receive from the inside of the varying heights of the nave, transept, apse and adjoining masses. The shrine of St Dimitrios was located in the centre of the transept, and from the 10th c was a silver-clad aedicule (shrine) with lamps burning over the saint's tomb.

The decoration and embellishment of such a significant building was naturally of importance, and was in some measure a continuous process. Extensive use was made in the original building of material, particularly in the columns and caps, from earlier periods; the caps of both the columns and the pilasters (when not modern copies) are either Roman, or reused from the 5th-c building, and in both cases you can see that they are carefully balanced in pairs. There was some mosaic decoration which dated from before the 7th-c fire, and this survived in the N inner aisle until early this century, when an English architect fortunately made accurate copies before the fire of 1917. As it is, the votive mosaics which do survive on some of the inner aisles of the nave and the chancel piers date from various periods, and so provide a small indicator of changing styles. The earliest are thought to be from the 5th c, and include the small scene in the inner s aisle showing a child being brought to St Dimitrios – probably an act of dedication. That on the pier on the s of the chancel showing the youthful saint between two bearded figures of a bishop and an *eparch* (secular official) in a golden robe must be from the 7th c, after the fire of 620, as the inscription denotes the figures as founders; on the same pier the mosaic of St Sergios is probably also of this period. There are three more mosaics on the pier to the N, one of them showing the saint with a deacon who was involved with the rebuilding of the basilica in the 7th c. The great interest of these mosaics is that they are some of the rare examples of Byz figurative style from just before the period of iconoclasm.

The **Parekklision of Ag Euthymios**, built in the 10th c adjoining the SE of the basilica, itself has the form of a miniature three-aisled basilica. An inscription in its N aisle gives the date of the restoration of the building, which included its painted decoration, as 1303, and the patrons of the work to be a successful general, given here the title of Protostrator, whose name was Michael Doukas Glavas Tarkhaniotes, and his wife Maria. The significance of this small structure lies mainly in its frescos, as they offer a clearly dated example of the kind of style prevailing in the area at the time of the earliest major fresco schemes in the *Protaton, Mount Athos*. They are unfortunately not in good condition, but some scenes of the saint's life can be made out; you can see the saint being entrusted at the age of three to a bishop, his ordination, his baptism of a convert and his death.

Do not omit to visit the excellent small **museum** which has been installed in the crypt under the transept of the main basilica, where you will find the results of excavation from the Roman and EC periods, with some sculpture, caps, pottery, coins and a reconstruction of the aedicule of the saint's shrine, as well as some photographs of the church taken just after the fire of 1917. In its complexity and enormous scale Ag Dimitrios may have been a more influential building for the Aegean area than the Akheiropoietos, and its prestige in the med period was virtually without parallel; it is only more recent history that has treated it less kindly.

The small church now known as **Hosios David ∗∗** (in Odos Timotheou in the Old Town), was dedicated to Christ the Saviour; it was originally the katholikon of a monastery known as the **Latomus** – the name you will find most commonly on signs. The building is certainly not later than the early 6th c, and may well be 5th c. You enter it from the s arm of what was originally a Greek cross plan, the w section being now destroyed. Its principal interest is overwhelmingly that of its richly colourful apse mosaic, which was only rediscovered in 1921 when the Turkish plastering of *c*. 1430 was removed.

It is contemporary with the church building itself, and its subject, which is unique in this medium, is the Vision of Ezekiel. A youthful, beardless Christ Emmanuel is shown seated on the arc of heaven in a circular glory, and with the four rivers of paradise below; the symbols of the four evangelists emerge from behind the glory. The prophet Ezekiel is on the left, beside the river Chebar, near which he wrote that he received his vision, and ruined buildings behind are probably of the city of Jerusalem, whose destruction he foretold; his gesture is probably intended to be covering his eyes against the brightness of the vision. The identity of the figure seated on the right, holding a book with a dedicatory inscription, has been guessed as either Habakkuk, Isaiah or Zacharias; the absence of any other comparative versions of this theme has prevented certainty here. Besides the beauty of the mosaic, with its richly dark and glowing colours, it is of great interest in that it pre-dates the much better known Justinianic mosaics at Ravenna and Sinai.

For the development of Byz architecture the **church of Ag Sofia** *** is arguably the most significant church building in Greece. This is in part due to the fact that in its design, its construction and in its mosaic decoration it must have always been seen as showing that the second city of the empire could match the glories of CP and the 'Great Church' of Ag Sofia there. Its importance is further increased by the chance that, since 1922 (when the church of the Koimisis in Nicaea – modern Iznik – was destroyed) it has been the only surviving representative of a small but highly influential group

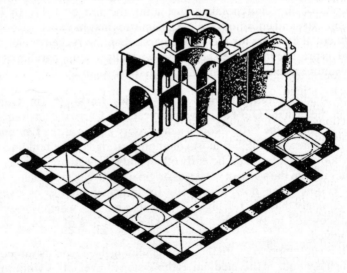

Ag Sofia

of church designs which stand at the beginning of the true 'cross-domed' type which developed in due course into the very common 'inscribed cross' form. It was in use as a mosque from 1524, was heavily restored after a fire in 1890, and returned to Christian use in 1912; it suffered some further damage in the earthquake of 1978.

The date of its foundation is still not finally decided, and restoration work after the 1978 earthquake has confirmed that it may have been built to replace a large earlier basilica, possibly destroyed in an earthquake of 618. Previously a 9th-c date had been favoured by some, but now the 8th may have more support; there were certainly several subsequent building phases, alterations or repairs in the 10th and 11th/12th c, particularly in the galleries, besides further work during its centuries as a mosque. Enigmatic inscriptions in the later mosaics, as well as imperfections in part of the cupola construction, have all contributed to the debate.

Its exterior does not suggest a building of any great subtlety, being rather squat and four-square, but when you enter the broad and spacious narthex, in spite of its rather gloomy painted plaster you are already aware of being in an important building. At either end there are wide entrances to long aisle-like spaces to either side of the naos which end in small enclosed chapels, but your appreciation of the interior space is given more impact by using the centre door, which opens straight into the impressively broad, high naos. This marvellous space is achieved by the exploitation of the large dome and its supporting piers, which are made more effective by the use of a gallery and by the arcade that separates this space from the lateral aisles. The central space is also extended by barrel vaults on all four sides of the cupola, but that on the w is deepest, while that to the E is joined to another, lower one before meeting the conch of the apse; you will see that the cupola has the effect of slightly 'flattened' sections where the vaults abut it. (It is this feature, causing slight distortion of the pendentives, which has given rise to the suggestion that this represents an experimental phase in this kind of construction.)

Ignore, if you can, the rather dour painted plaster that covers most of the interior walls (the result of refurbishment early this century after a fire in 1890, when it was still a mosque), because the surviving decoration is otherwise unusually rich. You will see fine caps of the 'wind-blown' acanthus type in the N arcade of the naos – they are probably 5th c and must in any case be reused. But the most exceptional feature here is the mosaics, and we shall start with the earliest, in the barrel vault adjoining the conch of the apse.

You will see that the only motif here is the large and uncompromising cross, and that above the cornice at either end of the vault there are some monograms; these are of the Emperor Constantine VI (780–97) and of his mother, the Empress Irene (790–97 and 797–802), and there is an inscription referring to Theophilos, a contemporary bishop of Thessaloniki. These must mean (as there are no apparent joins in the mosaic surface) that this mosaic was installed between 790 and 797.

Now turn to the impressive mosaic of the enthroned Virgin in the conch of the apse (the text on the narrow strip joining the two areas is from Psalm 65); if you look closely you will see that this image must have replaced an earlier design, consisting of another large cross – the outline of the disturbed tesserae round the cross arms is most easily seen adjacent to the Virgin's shoulders. The assumption must be that the original decoration of both parts of the apse was installed at the same time, and with two versions of the cross as the main decorative motif; at some later date the mosaic of the Virgin replaced that in the conch of the apse. During the period of Iconoclasm the cross became the single most common decorative motif (indeed, virtually the only one), but in 787 the Iconoclast edicts were rescinded and Iconoclasm became a heresy until 814, when they were re-imposed. (The bishop Theophilos, just mentioned, actually signed the edicts of the Council of 787.) At some point the cross, already installed in the apse, was hacked out, and the present image of the Virgin set in its place; this was probably after the second phase of Iconoclasm ended in 843, but how long after is uncertain – it could even be two centuries later. In any case, there is here the surprising feature of an Iconoclast scheme apparently being installed during the one brief period when it would have been expected that figural mosaics would have been *de rigueur*.

Even more powerful in their impact are the beautiful mosaics of the cupola; again there is controversy over their date, in spite of the presence of two inscriptions (or one inscription in two parts) round the base, which even refer to the date of execution; however, although the terms of the inscription(s) are too imprecise to be conclusive, a majority opinion at present accepts the mosaics as of the later 9th c. It is the only major cupola mosaic which has the Ascension as its subject, and this alone would suggest that it is a work of transition; by the 11th c the Pantocrator is almost universal. In 1989 there was still scaffolding obscuring this mosaic, but its restoration will eventually be completed.

Spend as long as you can here; the buildings and its mosaics will repay as many visits as you can make.

The original dedication of the **church of the Panagia Khalkeon ** ** is not known; its present name, meaning 'Our Lady of the Coppersmiths' is only a translation of the building's title when it was used as a mosque during the centuries of Turkish occupation, and must have referred to the tradesmen nearby. It is the earliest of the city's middle Byz churches to survive in such a complete state; a long and explicit inscription over the w door tells us that it was founded in 1028 by a court official and his family. Enter by this door if you can. The church is domed, with a four-column, inscribed cross design. with three projecting apses, the central one faceted; the narthex gallery has two smaller domes over each end. Built entirely of brick, there was clearly a real attempt to create an interesting and varied exterior; the deep arches on the w front contrast with the triangular gables to N and S, and the three domes have varied profiles. The builders used the recessed brick technique (setting alternate courses of brick slightly back from the main profile, and filling the space left with mortar to give the effect of the mortar courses being as thick as the bricks themselves); you can see this clearly in the exterior of the s apse where some of the filling mortar has fallen away. It is scarcely ever found outside CP.

The interior has a spacious quality given it by the wide dome and four quite slender columns, and there is ample light from the large windows; the four caps are certainly a set which must represent 11th-c practice. The original fresco decoration of the interior was commissioned by the founder and his wife, as an inscription on the w barrel vault shows, but there are now only fragments of fresco surviving from several periods; the best preserved are in the apse and sanctuary, and include the communion of the apostles. As an accurately dated building in quite good condition, this church has considerable importance as the first middle Byz monument in the city.

With the small **church of Ag Katerina *** , quite near the NW sector of the city walls, and dating from the late 13th or early 14th c, we are at the beginning of a remarkable period of church building in Thessaloniki; it has been claimed that during the 14th c the city was the leading centre in the empire for original and prolific architectural experiment. The plan here is one that is found, with variations, increasingly often in Macedonia from now on: it is a compact design, with quite a high dome raised over an almost square central space and supported on four columns. What is new is that the prothesis and diaconicon are reduced to tiny niches, and great emphasis is given to a large, wide gallery – more than an extended narthex, and almost an ambulatory – that encloses the N, W and S sides of the central space with a form of arcade.

On the exterior you will find that brick ornament has been used plentifully and in a very light-hearted way with small blind arcades enclosing areas of varied brick patterns (triangles, lozenges, crosses, etc.), engaged brick colonettes, dog-tooth courses, etc. The ambulatory is emphasized by four further smaller cupolas, one over each corner of the church, and each with a richly profiled faceted drum; the E exterior has a prominent rounded central apse, but only tiny faceted projections at either end of the ambulatory. One also gets the feeling that now the church is much more *open*, with the ambulatory being largely arcaded, and with only low marble screens to knee height. Inside, there is less interest in decorative detail – no particular care has been taken over the caps – but there are fragments of good 14th-c frescos.

The same kind of plan is used on a larger and more serious scale (although less radically) in the **church of Ag Apostoloi ****; dated 1310–14, this is the premier building of the later Byz period in Thessaloniki, and one of the chief monuments of its age. Originally the katholikon of a monastery (remains of the monastic buildings are close by) its date is securely fixed by two sets of monograms and an inscription which give the name of the founder as the patriarch Niphon I. The inscription is on the marble lintel over the W entrance, and the monograms are on the W façade: one set of three monograms is in brick (these are hard to read) and the other on the dosserets of three marble caps.

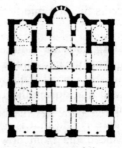

Ag Apostoloi

Before entering, make a tour of the exterior, as it is easy to see all round; you will be struck by the richness and invention of the brickwork, which achieves real virtuosity on the E façade in the area of the large faceted central apse, with successive bands of different designs. The windows here are a tall triple arcade, and even the two lateral chapels have double-arcaded windows, although much narrower. Nowhere else in Greece will you find brickwork of this dazzling richness. Again, you will see that the central cupola with its tall drum is surrounded by four more smaller ones, although the two w ones are sited over the ends of the narthex, not over the w façade itself. There seems again to have been an intention to open out the outer walls, with the ambulatory originally having extensive arcades; were even the low marble screening slabs between the columns added later?

The plan involves a central bay which is here a real inscribed cross, with the E arm extended towards the bema; four columns support the cupola and the lateral chapels have broad openings into the N and S arms. With its narthex, the naos could almost have been a self-sufficient 12th-c structure, but here it has the large ambulatory forming three galleries to N, W and S; the effect that this produces is to extend the high interior space outwards into the lateral vaulted areas of the ambulatory, and with the light from the eight tall windows in the drum there is abundant, airy space.

A further indication that this was intended to be an important building is its interior decoration. While the caps of the four interior columns are reused work of the 5th/6th c, conspicuous consumption was intended here from the start, as it was furnished with an extensive and contemporary scheme of mosaics; although here combined with frescos, by the 14th c this was a sure sign of the availability of lavish funds. It is the only church of this prolific building period in the city to be so enriched, and in all Greece can only be matched in the Epirote capital of *Arta*.

The mosaics are unfortunately not easy to read from the ground; the Turks removed the gold mosaic tesserae when they were plastered over, and the familiar hammer-pecks needed to make a further layer of plaster adhere have spoilt some of the frescos. Even the areas that remain, however, indicate the work of a leading group of mosaicists, possibly even associated with those who worked in the almost contemporary church of the Khora (the Kariye Djami) in CP. There are areas remaining from nine of the Dodecaorton – see particularly the Nativity in the S vault, and the Transfiguration and Entry into Jerusalem in the w vault, Evangelists in the squinches and the Pantocrator in the cupola; the best preserved of the frescos are in the smaller NE cupola. In its original state the interior would certainly have compared in its splendour with anything that could be seen of this date in CP.

On a very different scale is the modest but delightful **church of Ag Nikolaos Orfanos** * – no one has yet satisfactorily explained its dedication. It would not have been an expensive church to build, the core of the building being a small, wooden-roofed basilica, to which has been added a spacious narthex with ambulatory to N and S; for once we have a contemporary (14th-c) templon, and you can see that the reused EC caps still bear traces of colouring. Most of the wall surfaces are left plain, but there are tiny internal apses either side of the main, externally faceted apse of the naos, as well as further apses in both the arms of the narthex as it reaches round.

This arrangement has given immense scope to a highly gifted painter, who between c. 1310 and 1320 covered the available surfaces with a sequence of brilliantly individual frescos: it is these which provide the main attraction of the church. Facing you as you enter is a colourful sequence of scenes from the life of St Nikolaos, and if you move round to the S arm of the ambulatory you will find striking paintings of some of Christ's miracles, with some further (perhaps slightly later) scenes of St Jerome; in the N arm there are two superb standing figures of female saints in royal robes: ss Catherine and Irene. Moving into the enclosure of the naos there is a sequence of scenes from the Passion which include many interesting details – note for example the throne of Pilate as he washes his hands. On the w wall is a fine Koimisis, with the Transfiguration above. A striking series of bishops in their patterned robes lines the apse, and in the conch is a noble figure of the Virgin Platytera. The paintings are throughout in unusually good condition, and the insertion of modern windows in the roof has ensured that they all should be easy to see. You may find that in its modest way this unusual church, set in its small garden and decorated with an exceptionally brilliant and complete range of paintings, is one of the most memorable in the city.

Even more complex and imposing in its scale and the multiplicity of its cupolas than the Ag Apostoloi is the **church of Profetis Elias** *, dating probably from just after the middle of the 14th c. Nothing is known of its origins, and this is certainly not its original dedication. You approach the w end through a large open arcade, or peristyle; at the end of each arm of the arcade as they reach E is a small,

self-contained, pumpkin-domed chapel; these have separate dedications (to Ag Nektarios and Ag Dimitrios) and in ways such as
this the building may indicate some affinities with nearby katholika
on *Mount Athos*. Throughout, the external masonry keeps up its
decorative intention, with alternating bands of brick and stone, and
extensive arcading round the E end.

The narthex is unusually large, and is square, with four columns
supporting a system of seven barrel vaults; the two outer bays on the
W carry quite sizeable cupolas. There is a gallery above part of the
narthex, reached by a staircase in the s wall. All the elaborate w
development here is of a piece and formed part of the original
design. In the naos the major emphasis has been on creating the
widest possible uninterrupted space; the four columns supporting
the large, high central dome have been pushed right back until
embedded in the adjacent piers, and large absidioles to N and s open
the area even further, with the barrel vaults reduced to broad
arches. The modern iconostasis prevents the flow of space into the
large apse, while tiny chambers either side of this open into two
almost self-contained, domed chapels – the latter also an Athonite
feature. No frescos survive in the naos, leaving rather starkly clean,
new plaster, and only a few 14th/15th-c fragments in the narthex and
in the lateral chapels.

While this church is certainly a substantial and inventive one, you
may find that, for all the virtuosity of its builders (it is rare to find a
seven-domed church at any period) it does not fully sustain an initial
enthusiasm.

A number of less important buildings all repay a visit if you have the
time. If you decide to see the **church of the Taxiarchs** (the
archangels Michael and Gabriel) on Odos Theotokopoulou, you
will find a medium-sized church that was originally 14th c, and built
on the plan found elsewhere in the city of a single, wooden-roofed
nave, with ambulatory running round three sides. The main apse
and that on the N have attractive arcading and some cheerful brick
patterns, with varied brick and stone masonry in the side walls.
There has been a major late extension to the w, and the interior is
now a long, three-aisled basilica; the sole interest inside is provided
by three Byz columns in the s aisle and some unreadable fresco
fragments in the E and w pediments of the original structure.

On the way there, you will pass on your left as you go up Odos
Theotokopoulou to the Old Town a decrepit but unique survival of
the city's med life: a **Byz bath** *. The date of its building is uncertain

(13th or 14th c is suggested), and it has undergone many alterations. Although only of modest size, the different areas of the bath can all be identified – the *zeston* (*caldarium*) with a dome above and a hypocaust below, two rooms for the *khliaropsykhrion* (*tepidarium*) with two more for the *psykhrolysion* (*frigidarium*); the water was heated in a furnace on the N side and ran through clay piping. It was apparently still in use as late as 1940, and there is a very Victorian-looking marble, brass-tapped bath-tub still in place. The size of the complex is too small for it to have served as a public bath, but it may have been established as a monastic bath which could also be used by others at certain times; its double rooms suggest it was not for private use. Although difficult of access (the site is enclosed and it is under restoration) you will find this repays a viewing, not least because it shows how dependent the design of the 'Turkish bath' must have been upon its Byz forerunner.

Finally, two more churches survive in the vicinity of the arch of Galerius. One, now dedicated to **Ag Panteleimon**, and originally the katholikon of a monastery, was damaged in the 1978 earthquake and is now closed. It was probably roughly contemporary with Ag Apostoloi, and in its prime it must have been quite a spectacular building. Built on the same kind of plan as Ag Apostoloi, with an ambulatory running round the N, W and S sides, there were not just four cupolas over this, but one over the inner narthex as well as the main, central cupola, making six in all. The ambulatory was destroyed earlier this century, and, now clad in its scaffolding, it is a sad relic of what must have been an impressive building.

Just to the SW of the arch of Galerius the dome of the small, mid-14th-c **church of the Saviour** is dwarfed by multi-storey apartment blocks around it. Originally dedicated to the Virgin, it was apparently a funerary chapel. In its original form it was externally almost a cube, with a slightly projecting apse; inside, the dome was supported by four equal absidioles; no columns were used, and no vaults or arches extended the central space. A later extension built on to the W side has more than doubled the available space. There are some 14th-c frescos in the dome, but they are hard to see; perhaps the most unusual feature here is the original altar – surprisingly rare.

TRIKALA Τρίκαλα Trikala/Thessaly
Remains of Byz fortress.

Although the position of this town, close to where the Pindos range rises from the plain of Thessaly, always gave it strategic importance, there is now little material evidence of its med status. The **fortress** (already incorporating Hellenistic building) is said by Prokopios to have been restored by Justinian, and it was later held either by the despots of Epiros when they were in the ascendant, or by the emperor when he was regaining control of Thessaly. In fact the surviving remains are rather disappointing; although they are quite massive the continuing importance of Trikala in the Turkish period means that most of what can be seen now is Turkish, with only possible Byz sections visible in the SE sector.

Much more rewarding is the nearby Byz fortress of *Fanari*, and the beautiful church at *Porta Panagia*.

VAMVAKA
See **Mani**

VEROIA Βέροια Imathia
Numerous churches *.

Sited on one of the main routes linking Epiros with Thessaloniki (only some 75 km away to the E), Veroia inevitably became involved with the upheavals of Greek med history; it suffered invasion by the Bulgars in the 10th c, and in the Serbian expansion of the 1340s it was for some time occupied by their forces.

Its period of greatest prosperity is reflected in the extraordinary number of small churches which survive in the town, numbering about 40, and dating from the 12th to the mid-14th c. They share many common features of design, one being a complete absence of domes; characteristically they are of very modest size and have broadly sloping wooden roofs; their masonry is for the most part undistinguished, and you can see inset wooden beams in the walls of many of them. As at *Kastoria* the impression is of a large number of private patrons, rather than of major institutions.

Only one of them is maintained as a museum – the **church of Christ** on Odos Mitropoleos, near the junction with Odos Venizelou, and so this is the obvious starting point. In form it is reminiscent of *Ag Nikolaos Orfanos, Thessaloniki*, with a raised central naos and lower surrounding narthex and aisle spaces; there is an arcade to the W and N. Two inscriptions inside provide the information that it was founded in 1315 at the expense of Xenos Psalidas and his wife Eufrosyne, and that it was the katholikon of a monastery. There are tombs with very damaged frescos in the w and s walls. The frescos of the interior are contemporary with the building, and are mostly in good condition; particularly impressive are the Koimisis on the w wall and the Anastasis and Crucifixion in opposing shallow niches in the bema; further paintings on the exterior date from the Turkish period.

The feeling that the church of Christ exemplifies a modest and provincial reflection of lesser churches in Thessaloniki is increased if you seek out a few more examples. Unless you can persuade the local Ephorate to open them for you they will remain locked, but only a few paces to the sw of the church of Christ you will find that the 14th-c **church of Ag Kirikos and Ioulitta** can offer three faceted apses with attractive brick patterns reminiscent of e.g. *Ag Katerina, Thessaloniki*; frescos inside are 16th c, and the masonry templon has carved Byz members. Some simpler designs dispense entirely with the raised nave, and e.g. the 12th-c **church of St John Theologos**, facing on to Odos Venizelou, and that of **Ag Patapios the Wonderworker** at the end of Odos Kap. Agra, off Odos Venizelou, have broad, low pitched roofs with small dormer windows, as if in an Alpine area; the former has some 13th-c frescos. Ag Vlasios on Odos Perdika is a more substantial 14th-c construction with a higher masonry wall to the s, and some impressive 14th-c frescos with life-size figures.

Although it is locked and partly derelict, you should try to see the **Old Mitropolis** before leaving the town, as much can be observed without entering. To the N of Odos Mitropoleos, it is a fine 12th-c basilica built on a substantial scale, and is worthy of its dedication to St Paul, who preached in Veroia with Silas. The whole building is some 45 m long, and the *tribelon* is formed from two massive columns with classical Ionic caps; you can see from outside that the nave has nine bays formed from three piers and five columns. During its time as a mosque (the minaret in the NE corner is now occupied by a stork's nest) the N side was largely filled in and the N aisle has now vanished; there are extensive excavations in progress in this area. Its single rounded apse has the most ambitious masonry in the city, making use of thin bricks and dressed stone.

It is to be hoped that the new local prosperity will encourage further conservation of this interesting heritage of churches.

VONITSA   Βόνιτσα   Etolia-Akarnania
Castle *. Unenclosed. Easy access, then steep paths.

The castle above the town here had some of the same functions for the despotate of Epiros as that of *Rogoi*, acting as one of the several points of outer defence in the area round Arta. It has a fine position overlooking the Gulf of Ambrakia from the s, and the importance that this gave it is reflected in the number of times that the castle changed hands; it was, for example, part of the dowry of Thamar, the daughter of the despot Nikiforos I, when she married Philip of Taranto in 1294. It continued to be modernized by both Turks and Venetians after 1460.

There are no classical remains here, and the earliest surviving building must be 13th c. You enter the castle from the SE by a steep, winding road, and the single massive gateway here, the centrepiece of the outer curtain wall, is the main survival of the original castle. The dog-tooth brick ornament round an inner doorway of the superstructure indicates Epirote builders. There are altogether three baileys, all of different periods, and the substantial polygonal keep which occupies the highest point is certainly Turkish. Although the many periods represented in the fabric here give a confused impression, the outlook over the Gulf is fine, and underlines the importance of the site.

VOULGARELLI
See **Drosopigi**

YPATI   Υπάτη   Fthiotida. Med Neopatras, La Patria, Le Patre
Ruins of castle; two churches. Some 20 km sw of Lamia. Easy access by bus/car.

It takes a considerable effort of the imagination to realize that this quiet village in s Thessaly was for a time, mainly through its adoption by the Catalans, a place with a claim to European fame. In 1204 Neopatras was assigned in the deed of partition to Boniface, the Marquis of Montferrat, and he had occupied the area quite early. Its importance increased when John I, the bastard son of the despot Michael II of Epiros, made this his base and built a castle here. Through misunderstanding his family name of Doukas, the Franks called him the Duke of Neopatras, and the emperor, in an attempt to make him an ally, gave him the title of *sebastokrator*. But it was under the Catalans that it attained its greatest fame, with its promotion to an archbishopric and, as half of the 'Duchy of Athens and Neopatras', was from 1318 the second capital of the whole Catalan dynasty.

The minimal and battered remains of the **castle** (difficult, steep access) can still be seen at the summit of the steep hill overlooking the village, but more interesting artistically are the four good 5th/6th c caps in the later **church of Ag Nikolaos**, indicating the existence of an EC basilica here. The small **church of Ag Sofia** has a quantity of sculptural spolia built into its external walls dating from EC to 11th c – the latter being the likely date of the building. Fragments of classical buildings are also to be seen in the area. This is perhaps a place that is more rewarding to visit for its historical associations than for its present appeal.

ZARAKA Ζαράκα Korinthia. Med Saracez
Ruins of Cistercian monastery **. Just outside village of Stymfalia. Easy access by car.

In 1225 Guillaume de Champlitte was in correspondence with the Chapter General of the Cistercian Order, asking if Cistercian monks could be sent from Hautecombes (diocese of Geneva) to settle in Akhaia. This is one of the two Cistercian houses that are known to have existed in the Peloponnese, and it is probable that its origins lie in this request.

The substantial ruined walls of this simply planned basilica, probably built some time in the 1230s, show that it had a nave of four bays, a square chancel and no transept, the overall length being about 40 m. The only part of the ensemble retaining a roof is the barrel-vaulted gatehouse, some 30 m to the sw. The site is in general overgrown, but the quite extensive ruins show that the walls were built from large limestone blocks (perhaps reused?), with some brick and tile set in the interstices, and with a core of rubble and mortar filling. It has the appearance of being the work of Western monks, but with some help from local Greek masons. Some simple monumental carving can be seen, some engaged caps still in place being comparable with those at *Andravida*, although here at least the Cistercian rule forbade any major display. The nave floor is full of fallen masonry, caps, arch members and some heavy tracery from the windows.

The peaceful valley setting here can hardly have changed since the 13th c, and these unusual and interesting ruins will fully reward your journey.

ZARNATA CASTLE
See **Mani, Stavropigi**

Glossary

Absidiole: architectural form comparable to an *apse*, but smaller and not at the E end of a church.

Acropolis: area of high ground near a city used as citadel.

Akathyst Hymn: liturgical hymn with 24 stanzas, each starting with a different letter of the Greek alphabet; it formed the basis of an illustrative cycle of scenes.

Ambo: pulpit, often entered from two sides.

Ambulatory: curved or U-shaped aisle system.

Anastasis: Greek title for the Resurrection, although the Byz feast scene for Easter invariably shows the apocryphal event of the Descent of Christ into Hades (or 'the Harrowing of Hell'). It is one of the *Dodecaorton*.

Apse: large recess at the E end of a church; it is rounded on the interior, but its exterior is frequently faceted.

Archon: title of a local Greek ruler, comparable with 'lord'.

Bailey: walled enclosure or courtyard of a castle.

Batter: slope of a wall or tower from the perpendicular.

Bema: sanctuary of a Byz church.

Christ, types: Ancient of Days, an Old Testament designation of Jehovah as an antetype of Christ, shown with white hair and beard; Pantocrator, the 'all-powerful' in which Christ holds a Gospel book in his left hand and makes the act of benediction with his right; Emmanuel, deriving from Old Testament prophecies in which Christ is shown as a beardless youth.

Chrysobull: document issued by a Byz emperor to which his gold seal was attached.

Clerestory: upper zone of a basilical church with its own windows.

Cloisonné masonry: decorative building technique in which rectangular blocks of cut stone are separated (or 'framed') by ceramic tiles or thin bricks.

Conch: curved semi-dome that surmounts an *apse*.

Despot: title usually taken by the son or brother of a reigning Byz emperor, and coming immediately after him in precedence; it was comparable with the title of 'governor', hence the designation of Despotate.

Diaconicon: chamber 'pertaining to the deacon' that is normally located to the s of the main apse of a Byz church; it balances the *prothesis*, developed its own programme of decoration and often shows a smaller *apse* on the exterior.

Dodecaorton: collective title for the 12 major feasts of the Greek church, viz: the Annunciation, Nativity, Presentation in the Temple, Baptism, Transfiguration, Raising of Lazarus, Entry into Jerusalem, Crucifixion, *Anastasis*, Ascension, Pentecost and *Koimisis*.

Drum: cylindrical or faceted form that supports a cupola.

Enceinte: fortified perimeter wall of a castle.

Epitaphios: large piece of cloth embroidered with an image of the dead Christ; because it was only used once a year in the Good Friday church rituals, it is often in much better condition than other textiles.

Etoimasia: iconographic theme symbolic of the preparation for the Second Coming; it takes the form of a throne covered by a veil, on which rests a volume of the Gospels.

Exonarthex: second or outer chamber adjacent to the *narthex* of a Byz church.

Fresco: strictly, this term should only be used of painting on a wall, where the pigment has been applied while the plaster is still wet ('*fresco*', as opposed to '*secco*', dry); in order to avoid making this distinction on each occasion, the word fresco is used here to mean any painting that was made directly on to a wall surface, even though in some cases it may be inaccurate.

Gynaikonitis: area in a Byz church, usually a gallery, that was reserved for women.

Hodegetria: see *Panagia*

Hospitallers: members of the Order of the Knights of the Hospital of

St John of Jerusalem; a military order originally dedicated to the care and protection of pilgrims in the Holy Land.

Icon: literally, 'image'; the word is used here when referring to painted wooden panels that are usually portable, to isolated areas of mosaic, and to imagery in relief.

Iconostasis: high wooden screen separating the sanctuary of a Byz church from the *naos*; it came into use from the 17th c, has *icons* fixed to it, and is usually heavily decorated.

Katholikon: church used exclusively by a monastery or a convent.

Keramion: see *Mandylion*.

Koimisis: 'falling asleep', or Dormition – a term invariably used for the death of the Virgin, or for depictions of it; the subject derives from the apocryphal *Discourse of St John Divine on the Falling Asleep of the Mother of God*, and is one of the *Dodecaorton*.

Ktitor: Greek name for the founder of a building or institution.

Kufic ornament: form of external wall ornamentation formed from tiles and thin bricks; it is said to derive from the Arabic city of Kufa.

Mandylion: legendary veil with Christ's image imprinted on it which was sent to Abgar, King of Edessa; it was concealed for a time in a wall, during which the image became transferred to a tile, or *Keramion*.

Naos: central area of a Byz church, corresponding to the nave in a Western basilical design.

Narthex: chamber or space normally occupying the width of the w end of a Byz church.

Opus sectile: literally 'cut work'; imagery or patterns, usually on a floor, formed by pieces of marble cut to particular shapes, and so different from mosaic *tesserae*.

Osios: Greek title for a 'holy man', as distinct from a saint ('agios'), e.g. Osios Loukas.

Panagia (the Virgin) types: Hodegetria, 'showing the way' – a type in which the Virgin points at the infant Christ with her right hand; Platytera (*tou ouranou*), 'the wide wings of heaven' – a type in which the Virgin is shown with outstretched arms, with the infant Christ in a medallion on her breast; Zöodokhos Pigi, 'the Life-giving Fountain' – a type deriving from a miraculous spring in CP, in which the Virgin is shown above a fountain.

Parekklision: chapel attached to a Greek church.

Pendentive: building form presenting a concave surface that derives from a section of a sphere; in Byz building technique four are used to support a cupola over a square space.

Prodromos: 'Fore-runner'; the Byz title for St John the Baptist.

Prothesis: chamber to the N of the main apse of a Byz church, that was usually used for preparing the eucharistic gifts; it is of greater sanctity than the *diaconicon*, on the S side of the apse, and developed its own decorative programme.

Protostrator: high military rank corresponding roughly to 'general'.

Sebastocrator: highest title after those of emperor and despot; it was only available to members of the imperial family.

Soffit: inner face of an arch.

Spolia: building elements (often decorated) that have been reused from an earlier period.

Squinch: concave building form used to span the corner of a square bay.

Steatite: soft mineral, often dark green or grey in colour, which was used for small-scale carving, usually in relief.

Synthronon: superimposed rows of semicircular seating round the apse of a Byz church.

Taxiarch: archangel; a title often used of Michael.

Templon: screen in a Byz church separating the sanctuary from the *naos*; up to the 10th/12th c it was of marble or masonry, and had open areas, but with time it became more solid, and was often of wood and highly decorated; in this form it is normally called an *iconostasis*.

Tesserae: cubes, usually of marble or coloured glass, from which mosaics are made.

Theme: administrative area.

Trapeza: refectory of a Byz monastery or convent.

Tympanum: semicircular space located over a door.

Typikon: charter written for a monastery or convent by its *ktitor*, and containing the rules by which it was to be governed.

Tables of Rulers

Two dynasties of Byzantine Emperors in Constantinople

Komnene dynasty

Alexios I 1081–1118
John II 1118–43
Manuel I 1143–80
Alexios II 1180–3
Andronikos I 1183–5

Palaiologue dynasty

Michael VIII 1261–82
Andronikos II 1282–1328
Andronikos III 1328–41
John V 1341, 1354–91
John VI Kantakuzene (usurper) 1347–54
Andronikos IV 1376–9
John VII 1390
Manuel II 1391–1425
John VIII 1425–48
Constantine XI 1449–53

Byzantine Emperors in Nicaea

Theodore I Laskaris 1204–22
John III Vatatzes 1222–54
Theodore II Laskaris 1254–8
Michael VIII Palaiologos 1259–61

Latin Emperors of Constantinople

Baldwin of Flanders 1204–5
Henry of Hainault 1206–16
Peter of Courtenay 1217
Jolande (Empress) 1217–19
Robert II of Courtenay 1221–28
Baldwin II 1228–61

Greek Emperors of Thessaloniki

Theodore Doukas 1227–30
Manuel Doukas 1230–7
John Doukas 1237–44
Dimitrios Doukas 1244–6
(with title of Despot)

Despots in Epiros

(The title of Despot only used after 1231)

Michael I Komnenos Doukas 1204–15
Theodore Komnenos Doukas 1215–30
Manuel Angelus 1230–37
Michael II Angelus 1230–67
Nikiforos I Doukas 1267–96
Thomas Doukas *c.* 1296–1318
Nicholas Orsini 1318–23
John II Orsini 1323–36
Nikiforos II 1356–59
Symeon Uros Palaiologos 1348–56
Nikiforos II (again) 1356–59
Esau Buondelmonti 1385–1411
(Despot in Ioannina)
Muriki Spata 1399–1414
(Lord of Arta)

Byzantine Despots in the Morea

(Normally based in Mystra)

Manuel Kantakuzene Palaiologos 1348–80
Matthew Kantakuzene 1380–3
Dimitrios Kantakuzene 1383–4
Theodore I Palaiologos 1384–1407
Theodore II Palaiologos 1407–28
with Constantine and Thomas 1428–43
Constantine, Thomas and Dimitrios Palaiologos 1443–60
(In 1449 Constantine became Emperor)

Duchy of Athens

(*'Lords' until c. 1280, thereafter Dukes*)

Frankish

Othon de la Roche 1205–25
Guy I de la Roche 1225–63
Jean de la Roche 1263–80
Guillaume de la Roche 1280–7
Guy II de la Roche 1287–1308
Walter I de Brienne 1309–11

Catalan and Aragonese

Roger Deslaur 1311–12
Manfred 1312–17
Alfonso IV of Aragon 1327–36
Frederick III of Sicily 1355–77
King Pedro IV of Aragon-
    Catalonia 1377–87
John I of Aragon 1387–8

Florentine

Nerio Acciaiuoli 1387–94
(*also Lord of Corinth 1371–94*)
Antonio I Acciaiuoli 1403–35
Nerio II Acciaiuoli 1435–9
Antonio II Acciaiuoli 1439–41
Nerio II Acciaiuoli 1441–51 (*again*)
Francesco I Acciaiuoli 1451–4
Franco I Acciaiuoli 1454–5

Princes of Akhaia

Guillaume de Champlitte 1205–08
Geoffrey I de Villehardouin 1208–28
Geoffrey II de Villehardouin 1228–46
Guillaume de Villehardouin 1246–78
Charles I of Anjou 1278–85
Charles II of Anjou 1285–9
Florent of Hainault 1289–97 ⎱ (both married to Isabella, daughter
Philip of Savoy 1301–07   ⎰ of Guillaume de Villehardouin, 1289–1307)
Philip I of Taranto 1307–13
John of Gravina 1322–33
Robert of Taranto 1333–64
Philip II of Taranto 1364–73
Jacques de Baux 1373–83
(The Knights of St John [Hospitallers] 1377–81)

Main events in the history of medieval Greece

defeated and captured Guillaume de Villehardouin.

1261 CP recaptured by Michael VIII; restoration of the Empire.

1262 Guillaume de Villehardouin freed in exchange for the castles of Geraki, Mystra, Monemvasia and Great Maina.

1308 Thessaloniki besieged by the Catalan Company.

1311 Battle of Halmyros/Kephissos, where the Frankish barons were defeated by the Catalan Company, who then took over the Duchy of Athens and Neopatras; they were to stay there until 1385.

1342–49 Zealot commune in Thessaloniki. Black Death.

1381 Navarrese Company enters the Peloponnese.

1385 Catalans ejected from Athens by the Florentine, Nerio Acciaiuoli, who assumed the Duchy of Athens.

1387 Thessaloniki falls to the Ottoman Turks.

1388 Venice buys Argos and Nauplio from the Franks.

1395 Northern Greece invaded by the Turks under Bayezid I. *Baiazid*

1400 Hospitallers occupy Acrocorinth and Kalavryta for four years.

1403 Thessaloniki restored to Byz rule.

1423 Thessaloniki given to the Venetians.

1427 Khlemoutsi captured by Constantine Palaiologos, despot of Mystra.

1429 Patras captured by Constantine Palaiologos.

1430 Thessaloniki sacked and occupied by the Turkish Sultan Murad II.

1446 Murad II invades s Greece.

1449 Coronation of Constantine XI Palaiologos in Mystra and his departure for CP; Arta falls to the Turks.

1453 Capture, sack and occupation of CP by the Turks under Mehmed II; death of the last emperor, Constantine XI Palaiologos.

1460 Turkish conquest of Greece largely completed.

Further Reading

Greek medieval history

The Cambridge Medieval History, Vol. IV, Part 1: Byzantium and its Neighbours (Cambridge: CUP 1966). The standard work, particularly Chapters 7–9.

Cheetham, Nicholas, *Medieval Greece* (London: Yale University Press 1981).

G. Finlay, *History of Greece, B.C. 146 to A.D. 1864*, 7 vols (Oxford 1877, repr. 1970). Vols III and IV concern medieval Greece.

William Miller, *The Latins in the Levant; A History of Frankish Greece (1204–1566)* (London: John Murray 1908). Still very useful although written over 80 years ago.

Donald M. Nicol, *The Last Centuries of Byzantium 1261–1453* (London: Hart-Davis 1972). Much material relevant to mainland Greece.

——*The Despotate of Epiros 1267–1479. A contribution to the history of Greece in the middle ages* (Cambridge: CUP 1984).

Steven Runciman, *Mistra; Byzantine Capital of the Peloponnese* (London: Thames & Hudson 1980).

Kenneth M. Setton, *Catalan Domination of Athens, 1311–1388* (Cambridge, Mass. 1948).

——*The Papacy and the Levant (1204–1571)*, 2 vols (Philadelphia: American Philosophical Society 1976–8). Much of Vol. I concerns medieval Greece.

The following three books are recent collections of studies; all have some material relevant to the history of mainland Greece:

Benjamin Arbel, Bernard Hamilton and David Jacoby (eds), *Latins and Greeks in the Eastern Mediterranean After 1204* (London: Cass 1989).

Donald M. Nicol, *Byzantium: its ecclesiastical history and relations with the western world. Collected Studies* (London: Variorum 1972).

Kenneth M. Setton, *Europe and the Levant in the Middle Ages and the Renaissance* (London: Variorum 1974). Includes the author's chapter in the *Cambridge Medieval History*, above.

Architecture and art in medieval Greece

Richard Krautheimer: *Early Christian and Byzantine Architecture*, Pelican History of Art (Harmondsworth: Penguin, 4th revised edn, 1986). Substantial sections on church architecture in mainland Greece.

Gabriel Millet: *L'Ecole grecque dans l'architecture byzantine* (Paris 1916, repr. London: Variorum 1974). Although written more than 70 years ago this still has much valid material.

Kevin Andrews, *Castles of the Morea* (Princeton 1953).

Antoine Bon, *La Morée franque*, 2 vols (Paris 1969). This is the definitive study on this area, dealing with all kinds of building and with a full historical treatment.

Char. Bouras, A. Kaloyeropoulou and R. Andreadi, *Churches of Attica* (Athens 1970). The only book to deal with the minor churches of Attica.

Otto Demus, *Byzantine Mosaic Decoration. Aspects of Monumental Art in Byzantium* (London: Routledge & Kegan Paul 1948 and later edns). The standard study in this field.

Ernst Diez and Otto Demus, *Byzantine Mosaics in Greece: Hosios Lucas and Daphni* (Cambridge, Mass. 1931).

Emmanuel Amand de Mendieta, *L'Art au Mont-Athos* (Thessaloniki 1977).

Beata K. Panagopoulos, *Cistercian and Mendicant Monasteries in Medieval Greece* (Chicago/London 1979). Includes full discussion of the surviving remains on the Greek mainland.

Karin M. Skawran, *The Development of Middle Byzantine Fresco Painting in Greece* (Pretoria 1982).

Index of personal names